COMMUNISM, FASCISM, AND DEMOCRACY

The Origins and Development of Three Ideologies

DAVID E. INGERSOLL

University of Delaware

WITHDRAWN

Charles E. Merrill Publishing Company
A Bell & Howell Company
Columbus, Ohio

Merrill Political Science Series

Under the Editorship of

John C. Wahlke

Department of Political Science

SUNY at Stony Brook

ISBN: 0-675-09186-1 paperbound
        0-675-09187-X clothbound

Library of Congress Catalog Card Number: 75-161871

1   2   3   4   5   6   7   8   9   —   76   75   74   73   72   71

Printed in the United States of America

PREFACE

This book is designed as an overview for persons who have little or no knowledge of political ideologies. As such I have constantly been in the frustrating position of over-simplifying, ignoring interesting side issues, and avoiding topics which in a longer work would surely be essential. What follows makes no claim to be original scholarship although the emphases and some interpretations are dependent on my own background and interests. I will be happy if I have provided a partial synthesis of the work of other scholars in these areas. In trying to accomplish this, I am acutely conscious of at times seeming to "parrot" the scholarship of others—if this occurs too often I am sincerely apologetic. Along the same lines it is difficult to sort out in my own mind those interpretations which are mine and those which resulted from the hard labor of others. I have benefited tremendously from the writings of scholars in these areas—many of whom I have never met. My simple hope is that I have assisted in their endeavors by presenting these idea systems in a form whereby they can more easily be digested by beginning students. My fondest hope is that this work will provide a stimulus such that those who read it will go on to explore these ideas systems in all of their complexity.

A final explanatory note concerning the use of footnotes and bibliography seems in order. I have used footnotes only where it seemed absolutely necessary, and have appended an annotated bibliography to each chapter. This is in keeping with the nature of the work which purports to provide an overview of an extremely complex subject matter and to stimulate the student to further exploration on his own. To that end it seemed desirable to avoid copious footnoting while leading the student directly to other more detailed works in the field. I am sure there are many excellent books which are absent from that bibliography, either because of my lack of knowledge or because of space limitations. Hopefully, the ones that are included will be sufficient to assist the student in his pursuit of further knowledge.

Many persons have assisted directly in this endeavor. In particular, thanks to my colleagues Paul Dolan and Y. C. Chang for reading portions of the manuscript. Thanks also to Mrs. Cindy Hartshorn, Mrs. Lois King, and Mrs. Pat Mann for typing the numerous drafts of the manuscript. Special appreciation to Mrs. John Looby who saved me from many errors of grammar and punctuation. Finally, my wife has struggled through every word of the manuscript with a patience and encouragement that know no bounds—it would have been impossible without her. In spite of this direct help, and the indirect assistance provided by many inspiring teachers and colleagues over the years, the errors in what follows are my responsibility alone.

CONTENTS

Chapter 1   INTRODUCTION   1

Chapter 2   MARXISM   17

Chapter 3   MARXISM AND LENINISM   41

Chapter 4   SOVIET MARXISM   61

Chapter 5   THE POLITICAL THOUGHT OF
             MAO TSE-TUNG   77

Chapter 6   FASCISM   91

Chapter 7   NATIONAL SOCIALISM   109

Chapter 8   THE DEMOCRATIC TRADITION   125

Chapter 9   DEMOCRACY IN AMERICA   139

Chapter 10   DEMOCRACY IN THE
             TWENTIETH CENTURY   157

Chapter 11   SOME CONCLUDING COMMENTS   179

             INDEX   187

Chapter 1

INTRODUCTION

Anyone who attempts to write a brief survey of three major modern ideologies will probably be greeted by great cries of laughter from a whole host of sincere students and colleagues. The complexity of the subject matter is such that one is open to all sorts of possible criticism. The expert on the development of Marxian thought will immediately declare the task impossible, students of Nazi Germany will deem it superficial, committed democrats will assert that it is unneeded, and the pragmatist will cry that it is worthless, for ideas have little effect in the real world of action. While all of these criticisms may be in part correct, and some finally just, the fact remains that a general knowledge of a subject matter is better than no knowledge at all. What follows is an attempt to provide that general knowledge of three major systems of ideas of modern times; communism, fascism, and democracy. What is desired is a presentation which is simple but not simplistic, and which makes no claims to be comprehensive, yet satisfactorily explains central themes. Such a purpose is easily stated, but even a superficial examination of the existing literature will indicate how difficult it is to achieve. There are, for example, almost as many ways of approaching the thought of Karl Marx as there are Marxian scholars. Many people feel that fascism is best seen as a phenomenon peculiar to the period between World Wars I and II and is hardly contemporary, or that it is impossible to speak, in general, of democratic thought because it is such a diverse and changing tradition. A further complication is the common identification of these systems of ideas with particular nation-states.

When the average American speaks of communism his referent is normally the present-day Soviet Union, while fascism brings forth dark images of Nazi Germany. Yet it is quite appropriate to see these nation-states as highly imperfect attempts to realize sets of ideals which transcend the political systems that invoke them. That is, these states attempt to apply the ideas advanced in the ideology, but the ideology itself exists independently of them. One of the underlying assumptions of this book is that the three idea systems are capable of being profitably studied as systems of ideas—regardless of their applications in the real world. Obviously, when a major contributor to the development of an ideology is also the head of a political system, as in the case of a Lenin or, in a certain sense, a Madison, the ideological contributions may have a quite direct effect in political action. Even so, Lenin's contributions to Marxism may be studied as an effort to keep Marx's thought and vision relevant in a new historical context. In the same light, Madison the politician may be separated from Madison the theoretician and his contributions in each area judged separately, even while we realize that they were very much interrelated in his personal life.

While the complex question of the relationship of ideas to action is beyond the scope of this book, a few tentative remarks on that subject are in order. It is extremely difficult if not impossible to prove a cause and effect relationship between ideas and action. When a person declares he acted in a particular way because the principles of Marxism-Leninism commanded it, how are we to respond? Obviously, he could be simply lying, using the ideological argument as rationalization to disguise the real reasons for his action. Again, he could be deluding himself, being unaware of the actual motivation for his action—an SS officer exterminating Jews for the good of the fatherland while actually giving vent to his own latent anti-Semitism. Most often, the real reasons for any action are so complex that it is impossible to single out any particular factor which caused that action. Having said all this, it still seems obvious that idea systems do affect human behavior in some way, even if the exact relationship cannot be conclusively proven. The persistence of the Soviet Union in retaining the obviously incorrect genetical theories of Lysenko for many years because they supported the ideological goal of producing a new proletarian generation; the absurd tenacity of Hitler in following minute details written in *Mein Kampf*; the democrat's enduring belief in the essential goodness of the common man in spite of much evidence to the contrary are but simple examples of the effect of ideology. When we recognize the tremendous impact particular cultures and values have upon individual development we cannot doubt the importance of ideas in influencing action. This, then, is an initial reason for studying ideologies—they seem to have a good deal to do with influencing human behavior and perhaps a knowledge of the ideology will assist us in predicting and explaining that behavior. There are, however, other reasons for exploring idea systems which must be mentioned briefly.

As indicated earlier it is worthwhile studying systems of ideas irrespective of their effect in producing action in the real world. The three groups of ideas here under discussion are all attempts to say meaningful things about man and his environment. Thus, we may judge the accuracy of their descriptions. Is man, as Karl Marx believed, inevitably in a condition of alienation under a capitalist system? Does the fragmentation and depersonalization of modern liberal democratic society produce human beings who are stunted in their growth, unable to be truly human, as Mussolini would have us believe? Are these accurate portrayals of reality? Does the democrat's belief in man's capacity for self-governance ring true in light of the discoveries of modern psychology and sociology? Whatever the ultimate answers to these questions may be, their descriptions of man and his condition may be examined and evaluated on the basis of factual information. The ideas advanced may be subjected to tests of their validity and found sufficient or wanting. This is but another way of saying that these bodies of ideas may be examined with the tools of traditional political philosophy, much as the ideas of a Plato or a Machiavelli. Yet the thing which distinguishes "communism, fascism, and democracy" from Plato's idea of a perfect republic is that all of the former, to a greater or lesser extent, demand change in the existing environment. They not only advance a *theory* by describing man and his condition, but they generate an *ideology* by finding deficiencies and demanding solutions. We shall explore this distinction between a theory and an ideology more fully at a later point but for present purposes it indicates another reason for the study of this material. All three ideologies not only attempt to describe reality, they seek to convince other people that their description and their vision is *the* correct one. They seek converts.

The final reason that can be advanced for this type of study is that two of the three systems under consideration (and perhaps the third) are in present day competition for, as is said, the hearts and minds of men. Whether stated in terms of the "free world" versus "atheistic communism" or "fraternal socialist states" against "imperialistic capitalism" the war for converts has waxed and waned ever since the turn of the century. This makes the task of the student of ideologies extremely difficult. While his ultimate objective must be the understanding of ideologies he is, in all probability, either disposed toward or committed to one of them. The classical problem that social science faces in separating personal value judgments from impartial (or "value free") investigation is thus particularly difficult in the study of idea systems. Can a person who believes that one particular ideology is better than another temporarily free himself of that bias to attempt to understand another? This book tries to do precisely that. Ultimately, of course, it will fail in this attempt, for impartial investigation is seldom achieved and in this area seems an impossible ideal. Yet the attempt must be made for the reflexive anticommunist and the unthinking anticapitalist both do a disservice to human intelligence by making no attempt whatsoever to understand the phenomena they are trying to combat. Indeed, they weaken their own cause by knowing little of their enemy. Even the most committed democrat must admit that some sort of vaguely defined communism has been attractive to many people during the past century, just as an avowed communist must realize that men continue to flock to and die under the banner of democracy. The intelligent response to such facts is to ask why; to attempt to understand what it is in both of these idea systems (and fascism as well) that accounts for their continuing viability. The end product of such an attempt at understanding may well be a renewed dedication to fight the enemy, but the combat will be more effective with a knowledge of the opponents' strengths and weaknesses. It is for this reason that this book devotes a larger amount of space to the presentation of communist thought than to fascism or democracy. It will be read primarily by persons who believe that democratic ideas are, if not absolutely correct, at least the best possible in an imperfect world. It is this person who must attempt to understand the appeal of communism, must evaluate its view of man and his environment, and must decide whether its criticisms of democratic capitalism are just. Why then, one might ask, include democratic ideology, or for that matter fascism, at all? Primarily because it is only by contrasting these different pictures of reality that one can come to an understanding of each. As the following discussion will show, they are related in many ways. Finally, we have a vague suspicion that our "committed democrat" is not as fully aware of the strengths and weaknesses of democratic ideology as he might be, and knows little of the phenomena of fascism and its relationship to democracy.

Here then, are some reasons for studying these ideologies as well as an initial indication of some of the difficulties to be encountered. Finally, by way of introduction, one must justify the discussion of only communism, fascism, and democracy and the exclusion of numerous other modern systems of ideas. In addition we must point out some further difficulties in identifying these three ideologies. One of the most widely used textbooks in this field treats four "isms" as relevant in today's world (communism, fascism, capitalism, and socialism).[1] To

---

[1]William Ebenstein, *Today's Isms,* 6th ed. (Englewood Cliffs, N.J.: Prentice-Hall, Inc., 1970).

these one might add conservatism, liberalism, individualism, classical liberalism, and even African socialism. Granted that these labels are somewhat vague and many of the ideas overlap, it should be possible to come up with some relatively concrete definitions of these phenomena. Surely they are relevant in today's world if only in the sense that men habitually describe themselves as liberal or conservative. What distinguishes the three idea systems here under consideration from these numerous other isms? Initially our three isms seem more inclusive; one may be described as a liberal democrat or a conservative communist. More important, communism, fascism and democracy constitute relatively systematic attempts to describe man and his nature, and to set forth goals for him to achieve. Even in the case of democratic thought— perhaps the most ill-defined of the three systems—there have been and presumably will be continued attempts to integrate core democratic ideas into a coherent system of thought. Thus, they may be studied as comprehensive attempts to develop political philosophy and may be subjected to the traditional tests of that discipline. In the end, perhaps it is only a question of how one categorizes various idea systems. One can, for example, make a good case for setting forth a general category of socialist thought, then conceive of communism as the left wing or most radical brand of socialism. Similarly fascism could be seen as a radical modern manifestation of traditional organic political philosophy and treated as merely a part, albeit important, of a long tradition. Disregarding limitations of space and time, perhaps the major justification for speaking only of communism, fascism, and democracy is that they seem to the author to be the most important idea systems of the twentieth century and form a theoretical base for many other ideologies. If this is, as many persons have contended, the age of ideology, surely these are the three most important, if only by a count of worshipping bodies. The difficulty one finds in justifying a discussion of these three ideologies is somewhat a result of the trouble encountered in defining terms. In a sense, the entire book is an attempt at definition, but some initial discussion of these difficulties is in order.

Marxian communism attempts a description of man, his present environment, history and future, showing the centrality of economic factors in his development. As such it can be superficially seen as an economic analysis which, at the appropriate time, provides political remedies. Political institutions for Marx are but reflections of the class relationships which exist at any period of time—indeed it is not inappropriate to describe Marx's pure communist society as an attempt to abolish politics as a relevant factor in human experience. Later interpretors of Marxism, notably Lenin, add a more political dimension to the Marxian presentation in devising institutions which will speed the development of a pure communist state. Marxism-Leninism is thus a political philosophy which, while stressing the extreme importance of economic factors in human development, nevertheless finds it necessary to speak, at least temporarily, of political institutions. Some of the other varieties of socialism, e.g. democratic socialism, retain the essentials of the Marxian picture of the ideal state of pure communism but prescribe different political means for achieving it.

Democratic thought, while containing numerous assumptions about human nature and the innate worth of the individual, is largely a political philosophy. It is concerned with devising appropriate methods of political decision making whereby individuals may satisfy their own self-interest and at the same time contribute to the growth and stability of the polity. Therefore it is quite possible to speak, as we have done earlier, of democratic socialism or democratic capitalism, the word "democratic" signifying merely the method used to develop goals for the system. Yet there is historical precedent for contending that the inherent individualism of democratic political theory makes it more amenable to an individualistic economic theory—i.e., some form of capitalism. We shall discuss this at greater length in the section on democracy and for present purposes it need only be noted that democracy as a method of making decisions need not be associated with any particular economic theory.

Fascism is an effort to maximize the strength and power of the nation-state and, correspondingly, the individuals who comprise the body politic. As such, it is appropriately seen as a political theory. It does, however, possess a definite affinity for socialistic solutions within the borders of the nation-state. Fascism is, its advocates declare, rationalized socialism or national socialism. Yet it may be fair to say that fascist theory will opt for any economic system which will enhance the stature of the nation. Hitler's alliance with highly conservative businessmen in Germany is an excellent example of this pragmatic nationalism.

It can be readily seen from the above discussion that it is difficult to find categories which can be used to compare these three systems of ideas at the same level of abstraction. Democracy is both a method of decision making and a theory of human nature, Marxism-Leninism, an economic analysis of the human condition with political implications, fascism, a pragmatic combination of politics and economics. To the Marxist, democratic decision-making procedures are a sham if they operate in a society based on a class system. To a democrat, Marxist-Leninist talk of "peoples democracy" is ridiculous if it does not include mechanisms for determining the actual preferences of the people. Perhaps the only way of resolving these difficulties of definition and categorization is to examine each of the idea systems and to determine whether its view of the essential factors in human development is correct. The intention thus far is only to give the reader an idea of the complexity of the problems under discussion and to warn him against easy characterization of any of these ideologies.

We have discussed some of the reasons why a study of this subject matter is both important and difficult. Before moving to a presentation of the three ideologies we must make several further conceptual distinctions and must attempt a brief summary of the phenomenon of mass movements and the individuals who join them.

Theory and Ideology

Students of modern idea systems have been unable to agree on a common definition of the term ideology. Some see an ideology as a rather loosely organized folk philosophy encompassing the totality of ideals and aspirations of a people, while others describe it as a weapon to be used in a battle, a club designed to flatten opponents.[2] As in the case of Marxism there are perhaps as many definitions of the phenomenon as there are definers. The following discussion is offered with little hope of clearing up the confusion surrounding this term (desirable as that clarification may be), but to indicate what seem to be the salient differences between ideologies and other types of idea systems. Initially, some distinctions between classical political philosophy, modern theoretical analysis, and ideology are in order.

Classical political philosophy and more modern efforts to develop meaningful political theory share the conviction that it is the task of theory to make correct statements about the existing environment. Their initial endeavor is to use whatever means available (in modernity, of course, scientific method) to establish a body of statements which provide accurate descriptions and predictions of human behavior. These statements may then be tested by reference to the observed facts of human behavior and judged to be more or less accurate. The ideal of modern political theory and surely a major goal of classical political philosophy is the development of an entire system of propositions which, taken together, would provide a complete description of political man and his activity. To use the traditional terminology, the propositions in such a system must correspond to the known facts of existence and the system as a whole must cohere, i.e., one proposition must not contradict another. The prime difference between classical thought and modern analysis is that the classicist felt compelled to go beyond mere

---

[2]Note the definition of ideology in Lee C. McDonald, *Western Political Theory: The Modern Age* (New York: Harcourt, Brace & World, Inc., 1962), p. 495. Another type of definitional structure is used in Karl Mannheim, *Ideology and Utopia* (New York: Harcourt, Brace & World, Inc., 1936).

description, to propose remedies for perceived insufficiencies in the environment. Thus a Plato, while developing a theory of human nature and social interaction based upon his observation and insight, felt it necessary to set forth an ideal society wherein human beings would achieve their ultimate potential. As he saw it, his task was both descriptive (empirical) and prescriptive (normative); he sought both to explain and to reform existing conditions.

In many respects an ideology has more in common with classical theories than it does with modern political thought. An ideology attempts a meaningful analysis of the existing environment so as to discover real truths concerning man. While its analysis is more often far less rigorous and systematic than either classical or modern thought, this is not necessarily so. Marxism-Leninism, for example, is certainly systematic and some would consider it quite rigorous. Whatever the case, the major distinguishing trait of an ideology is its desire for *massive changes* in the existing environment. Based upon its picture of man as he should be, the ideology finds fault with the existing conditions and demands change in the immediate future. An ideology is, then, by definition, anti-status quo; it provides a picture of a better life for man (*goal culture*) once the existing structure is altered. Ideologies share with most of classical political philosophy the desire to significantly alter the world to conform to their conception of a goal culture, whereas modern political theory does not concern itself with this prescriptive dimension, i.e., what ought to be. Despite this common desire for change and a concern with the human situation as it ought to be, ideology is rather easily distinguished from classical political philosophy. Indeed, it can be argued that the age of ideology came about as a reaction to classical thought and its lack of concern with the processes by which change could be affected. Karl Marx put it quite nicely: "The philosophers have only *interpreted* the world, the point is to *change* it."[3] A focal point for the ideologue is the realm of action, whereas classical political theorists tended to spell out utopian ideals and tried to rationally convince other men of the truthfulness of their vision. The ideologue is a revolutionary, dedicated to the overthrow of the existing system and concerned above all with the means by which this can be accomplished. If one can imagine Plato, determined to see his ideal republic become a reality, as the leader and organizer of a mass movement of Athenians bent on revolution, one might have initial grounds for calling him an ideologue.

The reasons for this extreme *action orientation* of modern ideologies

---

[3]Karl Marx, "Theses on Feuerbach," included in Lloyd D. Easton and Kurt H. Guddat, eds., *Writings of the Young Marx on Philosophy and Society* (Garden City, N.Y.: Doubleday & Company, Inc., 1967), p. 402.

are, no doubt, many. Ideological movements may be viewed as similar to the religious crusades of the Middle Ages although they are avowedly secular, believing their ideal state to be possible, indeed sometimes inevitable, on earth rather than in some heavenly kingdom. They may be seen as political outgrowths of the tremendous optimism generated by the Industrial Revolution, an optimism which believed man for the first time in history capable of truly controlling his environment. Undoubtedly, ideologies are part of the rise of masses of men to political consciousness and participation, which is essentially a twentieth-century phenomenon. Whatever the reasons for this revolutionary orientation of modern ideologies there is little doubt that we are dealing with a phenomenon which is quite different from the political theory of the classicists. Some of the preconditions for an ideological movement will be discussed later in this chapter but first it is necessary to explore some other general characteristics of ideologies.

Because of their desire to enlist mass support, ideologies in general are less concerned with logical niceties than either type of theory. We earlier listed logical coherence and a reliance on human rationality as two major characteristics of a theory. Ideology relies greatly on faith and belief; it is much less bothered by logical inconsistencies within the system of ideas. Indeed, it can be argued that for purposes of attracting dedicated followers, inconsistency is desirable, in that it requires total belief. If a man cannot rationally understand a system of ideas and nevertheless chooses to become a member of a revolutionary movement, he can accept additional, even contradictory, changes in the idea system. Total belief in the validity of an ideology, however contradictory it may seem to another man, can produce a person who will carry out any action that seems necessary to insure success. In order to attract followers the ideology must possess a picture of a new society wherein the perceived wrongs of the existing environment will be totally eliminated. Further, unlike classical political theory, this goal culture must be seen as possible in the near future. While men are surely capable of devoting themselves to working toward a new society for their sons and daughters, the revolutionary fervor necessary in ideological movements seems more easily obtained if men believe utopia is attainable within their own lifetime. While it is possible to have an ideology which advocates gradual change in pursuit of the goal culture (democratic socialism, for instance), ideologies generally declare the existing human condition to be so repugnant that a truly revolutionary change is necessary. There is a tendency to see some "fatal flaw" in the present society, so massive that no amount of minor alteration will make it viable. The fascist picture of democracies' individualism and resulting social conflict precludes the possibility of great change within the existing system as does the communist view of the inevitable class nature of democratic capitalism. For a Hitler, the Jews become an element within the state which cannot be tolerated or reformed; they, much as capitalists in the Marxist view, must simply be eliminated. Since these groups ("Jews," "capitalists") have great control of existing affairs, surely one cannot expect them to support societal changes which will result in their own demise. The flaw is fatal, revolution is the only answer.

Although there undoubtedly are other characteristics of ideologies which might be mentioned, e.g., a priesthood which controls the content of the ideology, we now have a sufficient basis for distinguishing an ideology from a theory. As one abstracts from the real world there is, of course, a tendency to build up an analytically pure model of the phenomenon under discussion. It is undoubtedly true that many existing ideologies do not possess all of the characteristics herein outlined, just as no existing political theory completely fulfills our criteria for good theory. Rather, we are outlining two ideal types by which existing systems of ideas may be judged. Indeed, it is more appropriate to think of two *perspectives* which may be brought to bear on any system of ideas. The same body of ideas may be judged from either or both perspectives and evaluated in terms of each. For example, given our definition of ideology, it may be quite appropriate to speak of Marxism-Leninism as poor theory (i.e., its description of existing affairs does not adequately explain them) and as excellent ideology (i.e., it has been quite successful in developing revolutionary movements). By the same token one might judge democratic thought good theory and bad ideology; the criteria of success are simply different. From the ideological perspective, a body of ideas is successful only if it is able to mount an attack on the existing society and eventually implement its goal culture. From the theoretical perspective an idea system is good if it provides an accurate description and explanation of what is. This is but an elaborate way of saying that the function of a theory is largely to explain, whereas the function of an ideology is primarily to change.

This discussion must be ended with the explanation that these definitions are advanced only in the hope that they will prove useful in understanding differing goals of idea systems. Many persons would legitimately argue with a definition of ideology which makes change its central characteristic. Indeed, there are further complications with this definitional structure. If, for example, an ideology is successful in changing the environment to conform to its picture of the ideal society, does it then become theory? Further, as we shall see, a Marxian would deny the validity of arbitrarily separating explanation and activity—the "unity of theory and practice" is an important part of Marxism. Despite these difficulties it seems helpful to look at idea systems in terms of the functions they are designed to fulfill. Throughout the following discussion an attempt will be made to make these two aspects distinct. However, before moving to a presentation of communist ideas from the theoretical perspective we must briefly discuss some of the factors which permit us to call this the age of ideology.

Mass Movements

If, as has been argued, ideologies are distinctive in their demand for and ability to bring about change in the existing state of affairs they must develop a vehicle for effecting that change. While a discussion of the highly complex phenomena of revolutionary change is not possible within these brief confines, the enlisting of mass numbers of men in pursuit of a new society is such a central part of the age of ideology that it cannot be overlooked.

There have been numerous attempts to define the conditions which are conducive to the development of revolutionary movements. Classical Marxism contends that the major factor in revolutionary development is an ever-increasing discrepancy in the amount of wealth in any society— the rich get richer and fewer, the poor poorer and more numerous, and the latter eventually revolt. Others theories contend that the inability of political leaders to respond to demands arising in the society results in a decline in support for the regime and provides the preconditions for revolution. Still others assert that the inability of a society to fulfill the ideals of its culture produces a tension between those ideals and actual practice, leading to growing dissatisfaction with the existing conditions. We know that the revolution of rising expectations, whereby the lot of once poverty-stricken groups in society is significantly improved, does not produce contentment but can lead to demands for further and greather improvement. Whatever theory or combination of theories is correct, most students of the phenomenon would agree that a vital element in producing revolutionary change is the development of an ideology which coordinates the various dissident elements in the unstable society, gives direction to their frustrations, and provides leadership.

Why do people become members of a revolutionary movement? Is there a particular type of individual who is attracted by a mass movement? Does the content of the ideology really matter or is the relief that a person apparently feels in joining a mass movement of prime importance? These are but some of the important questions that the student of mass movements must ask; the answers, unfortunately, do not come as easily. There does seem to be agreement that a convert to an ideology experiences a great feeling of exhilaration, a discovery of a new, more important identity when he enters the ranks. There is evidence that persons who see their status in the present society declining are prime recruits. The *petit bourgeoisie,* the shopkeepers and small merchants in Nazi Germany whose status was severely shaken by the depression of the 1930s, provided one of the important groups for the Nazi movement. Others have theorized that persons who are unable to succeed in the existing society are a major source of potential revolutionaries. Because of this inability to succeed, they experience great feelings of personal guilt which can be relieved only by attacking the society; if it is the existing society and its values that are wrong, the unsuccessful person need feel no guilt. In joining a revolutionary movement the person renounces his old self and all the failures attached to it to become a member of a group and attain a new identity. Most observers agree that this "giving up of self" is a prime characteristic of revolutionary man and that the selflessness produced by membership is a truly remarkable phenomenon. Hannah Arendt in her classic study *The Origins of Totalitarianism* puts it this way:

> The disturbing factor in the success of totalitarianism is rather the true selflessness of its adherents: it may be understandable that a Nazi or a Bolshevik will not be shaken in his conviction by crimes against people who do not belong to the movement or are even hostile to it; but the amazing fact is that neither is he likely to waver when the monster begins to devour its own children and not even if he becomes a victim of persecution himself, if he is framed and condemned, if he is purged from the party and sent to a forced-labor or a concentration camp. On the contrary, to the wonder of the whole civilized world, he may be willing to help in his own prosecution and frame his own death sentence if only his status as a member of the movement is not touched.[4]

If this is the case, if it is the emotional catharsis which accompanies group membership that is most important, one must ask whether the content of the ideology really matters at all. Would, for example, our "true believer" be as eager to join a revolutionary communist group as he would a fascist movement? We know that some of the world's most committed anticommunists are former party members whose God failed. Further, Hitler at one time asserted that communists were the easiest persons to win over to the doctrines of fascism, implying that the tendency to believe was more important than the actual goals of the movement. While there may be some truth to these assertions, in all

---

[4]Hannah Arendt, *The Origins of Totalitarianism* (New York: Meridian Books, 1958), p. 307.

probability the content of the ideology establishes certain limits for the potential revolutionary. It is a bit difficult, for example, to conceive of a well-established capitalist joining a movement which vows to destroy him, or a Jew embracing the Nazi doctrine of anti-Semitism, although such things have occurred. A person's culture and the values he holds dear probably should not be antithetical to the goals of the revolutionary movement. Of course, it may be easier to convert a true believer to another ideology once he has developed the capacity for total belief in any set of ideas. Whatever the case, this discussion is not meant to support the notion that all men committed to ideological goals are somehow demented or sick—surely men's idealism is a prime motivating force in the development of a revolutionary movement. Even if we can support the concept of a true believer who gives up everything in his life to be a member of a revolutionary group, there are important men present in ideological movements who, while totally dedicated to the cause, are also quite aware of more pragmatic goals. As mentioned earlier, most ideologies seem to have a priesthood or a small circle of leaders who can manipulate the ideology to conform to environmental changes as well as formulate revolutionary strategy. While the truly modern element of contemporary ideological movements is their ability to enlist masses of people in the cause, the leadership role of a small group of people is nevertheless quite essential. Lenin's concept of the role of the Communist Party in fomenting and carrying out a revolution is probably the best example of the relationship between leaders and masses. While Lenin did not believe it would be possible to have a *coup d'état* staged by a small group of dedicated Bolsheviks, and insisted that mass support was a prerequisite for successful revolution, his manipulation of Marxist ideology to give it great appeal to the Russian peasant clearly showed that the followers were being used by the leadership elite. Further, the tendency of revolutionary movements to develop one individual as the personification of the movement (Hitler, Mussolini, Peron, Lenin, etc.) generally gives that man great latitude in interpreting the ideology. Perhaps the safest summary of ideological movements is to say they are essentially modern phenomena, involving masses of dedicated people, and they seem to be an essential element in producing revolutionary change. While the content of the ideology seems to be important in eliciting mass support we are not, from the ideological perspective, quite sure just how much it matters.

Here, then, are some indications of the problems involved in the study of idea systems, as well as some reasons which show why such a study is worthwhile. The phenomena of the revolutionary personality and the general subject of the role of mass movements, while they are very important aspects of the investigation of idea systems, are subjects which are somewhat tangential to our main concern. Let us then, without further commentary, move to an examination of the first of our idea systems.

BIBLIOGRAPHY

Arendt, Hannah. *The Origins of Totalitarianism.* New York: Meridian Books, Inc., 1958. A classic study of nationalism, racism and totalitarianism. It is particularly useful for its attempt to describe the dynamics of mass movements.

Bell, Daniel. *The End of Ideology: On the Exhaustion of Political Ideas in the Fifties.* New York: Collier Books, 1962. The definitive statement of the "end of ideology" thesis (to be discussed in Chapter 9) as well as a sophisticated study of the role of ideology in modern life.

Friederich, Carl J., ed. *Totalitarianism.* New York: The Universal Library, 1964. A useful collection of essays on the general subject of totalitarianism, particularly concerned with its effect on various aspects of the total human experience.

Hoffer, Eric. *The True Believer.* New York: The New American Library, 1958. A well-written, nonacademic account, which attempts to give insights into the dynamics of mass movements and those persons who participate in them.

Johnson, Chalmers. *Revolutionary Change.* Boston: Little, Brown and Company, 1966. A short attempt to spell out the prerequisites for revolutionary changes in societies. Despite a somewhat excessive use of sociological jargon it is an excellent summary of a most complex subject.

LaPalombara, Joseph. "Decline of Ideology: A Dissent and an Interpretation," *American Political Science Review* 60 (1966): 5.

Lipset, Seymour Martin. "Some Further Comments on 'The End of Ideology'," *American Political Science Review* 60 (1966): 17. LaPalombara and Lipset engaged in a debate which generated a good deal of heat and some light on the question of ideology in contemporary affairs. If nothing else, this exchange illustrates the difficulty inherent in defining ideology.

Mannheim, Karl. *Ideology and Utopia.* New York: Harcourt, Brace & World, Inc., 1936. The classical study of the relationship of different types of idea systems to action, including a definitional structure quite different than that used in the present work.

Moore, Wilbert E. *Social Change.* Englewood Cliffs, N.J.: Prentice-Hall, Inc., 1963. One of the best short introductions to the overall subject of social change, including some excellent comments on the subject of modernization.

Wallace, Anthony F. C. *Culture and Personality.* New York: Random House, 1968. An anthropologist investigates the relationship between the individual and his culture. Notable is his interesting chapter on "The Psychology of Cultural Change."

Chapter 2

MARXISM

Karl Marx was a revolutionary—it is said he even looked like one! His mature life was spent in never-ending attempts to destroy the capitalist system which he abhorred. History is filled with figures who rebelled against existing societies and failed, their careers being relegated to mere footnotes in scholarly works. Karl Marx and his ideas comprise no footnote in history books. If we were to speak of the number of people who have been influenced by his vision, to say nothing of those who have felt it necessary to condemn him, we would have a vast army indeed. On this scale Karl Marx would rank among the great religious leaders of antiquity with his collected writings constituting some sort of bible for the worshipping multitudes. Herein lies one of the major problems in speaking of Marx. As Robert Heilbroner has put it, Marx the symbol has come to obscure Marx the man, and Marx the revolutionary disguises Marx the thinker.[1] It may be impossible to discover the real man or to set forth a true picture of his ideas—getting inside another's skin is a formidable task. Yet we can attempt to separate the man from the myth, Marx from his interpreters. To begin on relatively safe ground, there is little controversy about his life.

Karl Marx was born in 1818 in Trier, in the German Rhineland, the eldest son of a rather prosperous Jewish lawyer. While appropriately described as bourgeois and secure, the Marx family was subjected to

---

[1]Robert L. Heilbroner, *The Worldly Philosophers* (New York: Simon and Schuster, 1964), p. 115.

abuse from the periodic waves of anti-Semitism which swept most of Europe. Shortly after Karl was born his father converted to Christianity and, despite the elder Marx's somewhat liberal ideas, the family enjoyed a rather safe and comfortable existence.

Karl was a very intelligent, somewhat precocious student, entering the University of Bonn in 1835 at the age of 17 to pursue legal studies. With apparent enthusiasm he entered into the life of a German university student, engaging in his share of boisterous behavior. After transferring from Bonn to the University of Berlin in 1836 he began a more intensive study of law, jurisprudence and, eventually, philosophy. It was at Berlin that the young Marx was exposed to two major influences of his early life, Hegelianism and materialism—ideas we shall explore at greater length in the following discussion. In pursuit of an academic career Marx completed his doctorate in philosophy at Jena in 1841. However, the academic career never materialized. Marx took a job as a reporter and later editor for the newspaper, *Rheinische Zeitung.* Here, perhaps, is an early indication of Marx's desire for action and change, a bent that throughout his life was to make him contemptuous of "armchair" philosophers and academicians. At any rate his early newspaper career ended abruptly in 1843 when the Prussian government suppressed the paper for being too radical (although thoroughly capitalist). Unrepentant, Marx moved to Paris to edit a newspaper for Prussian *emigrés,* only to be expelled at the request of the Prussian government in 1845. His years in Paris did prove extremely important for it was here he met a fellow Rhinelander, Friedrich Engels, who was to be his life-long collaborator and friend. Engels brought to the relationship a first-hand knowledge of the barbarities of capitalism, garnered from his study of the conditions of the British working class, as well as wit, charm, and a writing style much superior to that of Marx. Their collaboration was so close that for most people Marxism has since come to mean the writings of both Marx and Engels; Marx himself referred to his work as "our theory." Expelled from Paris, Marx and Engels moved to Brussels where they attempted to organize workers and became associated with a group of radicals in an organization called the Communist League. It was for this group, in the fateful year of 1848, that they wrote what has become the creed of Marxism, *The Manifesto of the Communist Party.*[2]

The year 1848 saw revolution sweeping Europe; uprisings occurred in Berlin, Paris, Rome, Vienna, and many other cities throughout the Continent. While the publication of the *Communist Manifesto* certainly did not cause these revolutions, it did reflect the generally radical spirit

---

[2]Karl Marx and Friedrich Engels, *The Communist Manifesto,* intro. by A.J.P. Taylor (Baltimore: Penguin Books, 1967).

of the times. Here, many people felt, was the long predicted great workers' revolution and, while he played at best a small role in these activities, Marx was somewhat optimistic about the prospects. Without delving deeply into history, let us merely say that the great revolution substantially failed. Alfred Meyer has stated it nicely: "Altogether, few revolutions had been expected so openly and failed so miserably as that of 1848. The Marxist image of the proletariat had turned out to be a phantom."[3] Marx returned to Cologne late in 1848 and began publishing a revised version of his old newspaper only to have it suppressed once again and be himself expelled from Prussia in July, 1849. Not welcome in Paris, the safest place seemed to be England and, although only intending to remain a short time, he spent the rest of his life there. Depending largely on Engels's money, Marx and his family were never far from the edge of poverty, particularly during the early years in London. He spent his days laboring at the British Museum to produce the long awaited definitive explanation of capitalism's downfall. Only one volume of his magnum opus, *Das Kapital*, appeared in print before his death in 1883, the remaining volumes being published posthumously. Engels outlived Marx by some twelve years, interpreting and refining the basic Marxist ideas as well as engaging in numerous international communist activities.

Even before his death, Marx's ideas were subject to a good deal of interpretation and alteration. After his death (particularly after Engels's demise in 1895) an entire band of followers sought to update, correct, or reinterpret Marxian teachings. This trend has, of course, continued to this day with *revisionists* and *orthodox Marxists*, to name but two schools, vying for the title of true interpreters. Thus we encounter another difficulty in trying to understand Marx. Is *Das Kapital* to be considered his definitive work? Is his earlier more philosophic writing inconsistent with his later economic emphasis? Is there a young Marx and an old Marx or are his works all of one piece of cloth? The answers to these questions will significantly affect our presentation and discussion of Marx's ideas, so some of the scholarly controversy concerning the "true" Marx must be examined.

Marx's Writings and the "Real" Marx

One of the great difficulties in having a successful revolution proclaimed in your name is that the leaders of that revolution become self-appointed authoritative interpreters of your ideas. With the Bolshevik success in

³Alfred G. Meyer, *Marxism: The Unity of Theory and Practice* (Ann Arbor, Mich.: Ann Arbor Paperbacks, 1963), p. 108.

Russia in 1917 all future leaders of the Soviet Union found it necessary as well as expedient to interpret Marx's ideas to fit changing times.
As we shall see in chapter 3, Lenin began the process of *authoritative*
interpretation and addition to Marxian thought. It was under Stalin's
reign, however, that Soviet scholars began to treat Marx's works more as
rigid dogma, and placed greater emphasis on certain writings. We have
referred to the *Manifesto of the Communist Party* as Marxism's "creed";
for classical Marxist scholars *Das Kapital* is its Bible. The classical
Marxist view tends to emphasize the concepts of dialectical materialism,
the labor theory of value, and Marx's theory of the state as developed in
Das Kapital. Some would say it greatly neglects Marx's earlier writings,
which are characterized as more philosophical and humanistic. Coexist-
ing with the orthodox interpretation of Marxian thought, a small group
of scholars emphasized differences between a young and an old Marx,
and placed greater weight on his earlier writings; Marx the humanist-
philosopher was contrasted with Marx the scientist-economist. With the
decline in Stalinist orthodoxy in the latter part of the 1950s, this
interpretation of his work gained increasing acceptance, particularly in
Eastern Europe. In terms of Marx's writings, the young period includes
his doctoral dissertation, *Economic and Philosophical Manuscripts*, and
the *German Ideology*—all of his works up to 1844-45 (according to
other scholars this period extends to 1847-48). All later works, beginning with the *Communist Manifesto*, are then seen to be the product of
the mature scholar. In contrast to the classical scholars' emphasis on
materialism and economics, the revisionist scholars take as central the
notion of alienation as developed in his early works. This controversy
still rages, though in a somewhat muted form today.

Our presentation assumes that while undoubtedly there are differences
of emphasis in the young and old Marx, all of his works can be seen as
a whole. The concept of human alienation, while mentioned infrequently
in the later works, still is a key element in Marx's analysis of the decline
and fall of capitalist systems. This does not mean that the later economic
arguments are to be discarded as outmoded or that dialectical materialism is not important in Marxism. If it is necessary to take a position in
this ongoing debate, the attempt here is to present both sides in the
belief that some sort of synthesis is possible. We have, however, been
using concepts and ideas which have not been fully explored or even
defined—it is time to look at Marx's ideas.

The Human Condition

Marx and Engels lived and wrote during the period of European history
generally called the Industrial Revolution. With the possible exception

of Russia, all European countries during the latter part of the eighteenth and throughout the nineteenth century experienced a rapid growth of industrial production which involved the introduction of machinery, establishment of factories, and the development of a specialization of labor. This period of industrialization is properly called a revolution in that it resulted in profound changes in the values and way of life of vast numbers of people. The craftsman who formerly produced objects with his own hands to be consumed or exchanged now found himself toiling on a production line in a factory, placing bolts in a complex piece of machinery. The introduction of mass production techniques forced individuals to become far more specialized in their work and to become part of a vast production process rather than fabricators of whole objects. The former craftsman of a pair of fine shoes now found himself operating a machine which cut out the soles for thousands of shoes, to be assembled later by other workers in the factory. There is little doubt that the industrial revolution produced tremendous hardships for members of the working classes. History books are full of examples; twelve- and fifteen-hour work days, women and children forced to work under intolerable conditions, disease unchecked, and poverty everywhere. Even today, one of the best descriptions of the excesses of the industrial revolution is to be found in Friedrich Engels's *Condition of the Working Class in England in 1844,* an early pamphlet which greatly impressed Karl Marx.

Given these deplorable conditions it is easy to see how sensitive and sensible men could condemn the results of industrialization and the capitalist economic system which brought them about. Marx and Engels were by no means alone in their violent reaction to these conditions. Yet where others fought for reform within the capitalist system and sought to bring about more humane working conditions, Karl Marx believed that such conditions were an inevitable part of capitalism. The condition of the working class led him to the conclusion that the entire capitalist system was wrong and must be radically changed. Marx's indictment of capitalism, while undoubtedly inspired to some extent by the human suffering it produced, is far more profound. It is his contention that capitalism as an economic system denies man his own humanity—it literally dehumanizes man. We can understand such a conclusion only by examining the Marxian conception of the unique role that laboring plays in human development.

Laboring, according to Marx, is not merely a process whereby man satisfies needs but it is man's existential activity. It is the way in which he achieves his true nature. Man is seen as an actor, one who is capable of altering the world for his own uses. The individual confronts the external world, goes out into it and alters it by mixing himself with it. In this process, the individual (subject) comes to realize what he is and to appreciate his potential as actor by discovering what he is not (i.e. the external world; the "object"). Thus, man in the process of mixing himself with the environment can be said to come to know himself—he becomes conscious of his own selfhood. This concept of self-realization or the achievement of self-consciousness was central in German philosophic thinking for a considerable period prior to Marx. The great German philosopher G.W. F. Hegel, whose ideas dominate the early part of the nineteenth century and who had a great influence on Marx, constructed an entire philosophical system designed to bridge this subject/object gap and define man's relationship to his environment.

History to Hegel consisted of a process of the embodiment in the spatio-temporal world of rationality which he called Absolute Idea— that is, the world and men in it were becoming increasingly rational. Within this broad historical process the individual human being is constantly trying to attain consciousness of self, and the process by which he achieves this is interaction with the environment. When interacting, however, man perceives the rationality which is embodied in the external world, hence becoming more rational himself. The process of attaining self-realization is thus also the path toward increasing rationality. Further, human freedom, for Hegel, can be achieved only when all men are capable of achieving self-consciousness and rationality; hence, complete rationality would be the same as total freedom and all men would be completely self-conscious. In this scheme, man is obviously limited in his ability to achieve personal freedom by the temporal period in which he exists. If he is living during a historical period in which little rationality is present in the world, he is not capable of finding true freedom. The important point here is that *all men* must be capable of achieving freedom and no one man may possess it at the expense of others. Thus there must be human institutions, particularly political institutions, which permit all men to achieve self-consciousness and freedom. Prior historical epochs were limited by the degree of rationality embodied in the world and by corresponding human institutions which permitted only some men to achieve freedom (not true freedom, of course, for all must be free in order for one to be free). Hegel spoke of an Oriental stage of human history where only one man, the Oriental despot, could achieve freedom, and a Graeco-Roman stage where only a few were capable of freedom since the Greeks and Romans had slaves. In his view, the rationality embodied in the world now provided for another stage in human history, the German-Christian stage, during which, for the first time, all men could achieve rationality and freedom.

We have briefly mentioned why human labor was an essential activity for Karl Marx; in Hegel's thought it plays an equally crucial role.

Through labor man transforms himself from a pure subject into an object; that is, by creating things he puts part of himself in the object, thus obtaining objective status for himself. The subject-object relationship apparently inherent in nature is thus transcended or synthesized—the subject (self) becomes objectified (object). In Hegel's rationalistic universe this process was sufficient to provide for true self-consciousness and its corresponding freedom. The German-Christian state, by permitting all individuals to engage in this appropriation of the environment, provides the basic condition of human freedom for all.

Marx, while thoroughly accepting the basic Hegelian analysis of human freedom, contended that his solution to the problem of the self-conscious man was a mere "paper" solution. Where Hegel believed that the mere objectification of self which occurred in the production of a thing (product) was sufficient to produce self-consciousness, Marx asserted that the future status of the *product of labor itself* was equally important. Man had placed part of himself in the object, thus it was part of his very being. It is man's ability to appropriate the actual product of his labor that results in self-consciousness, not merely the process of creating it. For Marx, then, the retention of the physical object of labor (which, remember, is part of himself) is crucial in obtaining human freedom. He therefore comes to attach particular significance to the process of the allocation of resources in a society and thus Hegel's philosophic studies must become economic matters. If the product of man's labor cannot be appropriated by the individual, he can in no sense be free. Hegel's freely interacting individual, unless he is capable of retaining the object of his creative act (the product of his labor) is not free at all! The system of private property which Hegel believed to be a liberating force in human history actually produces a denial of human freedom, for there existed under such a system an entire class of individuals who were forced to sell the product of their labor to other individuals. This class, the proletariat, cannot achieve self-consciousness or freedom and, if these men are not free, no man can be truly free. The essential matter for study is not philosophy, as Hegel would have us believe, but economics and the class system which capitalism produces.

Marx uses the term "alienated" to describe the condition of human beings existing under a capitalist economic system. This word has become all too common in modern usage—we speak of alienated youth, voters, workers, artists, using the term to indicate some sort of vaguely perceived disenchantment with one's lot. Indeed, alienation can be and has been used to describe almost anything. For Marx, however, it came to have a specific meaning. As we have seen, the act of laboring is the process by which human beings attain self-realization and the product of their labor is an integral part of that process. The sculptor who fashions a statue from a formless block of stone has endowed that stone with part of his person. Something of him is there in the statue. The hallmark of a capitalist economic system is that one class of individuals (capitalists) possess a monopoly of the means used to produce things, i.e., they own the machines and capital necessary for production. Under such circumstances the noncapitalists (workers) are forced to sell their labor to the capitalists so that they can engage in productive relations. They then work for the capitalist to produce objects which he sells for profit and pays the worker a wage for his work. The relationship between capitalist and workers is necessarily exploitive. As we shall see more fully in the later discussion of capitalist economics, the only way a capitalist can make a profit, i.e. produce capital, is by exploiting his labor force. Thus, by laboring for the capitalist the worker is giving him more power to be used against him and his fellow workers. Under the capitalist system, then, the product of labor, which is the only source of human development, is taken away from its fabricator (maker) and used to exploit him. Part of the worker's own being which is embodied in his product is now used against him. Instead of recognizing the object of his creation as a part of a process of self-development, the worker sees it as an alien object, something which has become independent of its producer.

In a very real way, part of the laborer's self is being taken away and used to hurt him. The product of his creative power becomes a weapon in *alien* hands. Thus Marx concludes that man is irrevocably alienated from himself under a capitalist economic system. Further, under capitalism that joyous creative act of laboring which is the uniquely human gift becomes an activity which is to be dreaded. Labor under capitalism becomes forced labor, time spent away from the job is considered free time when it should be just the other way around. Under capitalism, man's liberating activity, that which makes him free, becomes the negation of humanity: it is slave labor.

Capitalism produces still another dimension of alienation which completes the process of negating a truly human existence. Man is not only alienated from himself, but from his fellow human beings as well. This is because capitalism turns all human relationships into dollars and cents terms. Men treat each other as commodities, as objects to be used and manipulated; their labor becomes something to be bought and sold. Under such a system men are related to one another only through the commodities they exchange; they treat each other as things, not as fellow humans. Human beings are forced into constant competition with one another and the things they produce come to take an objective status and prevent human interaction. Commodities become symbols and attain a status different from their production and use. Larger and more flashy cars, "keeping up with the Joneses," "clothes are the mark of the man"—these are the more modern examples of Marx's meaning. One relates to "Jones" not as a human being but as a competitor in the accumulation of status-laden products; one looks at the clothes of a man but not at the man.

Marx has drawn a picture of a society where man is prevented from becoming human—man's alienation is complete. Even members of the exploiting class (capitalists) are not free because of cut-throat competition and because of the wage-slave status of the proletariat. Given the Marxian definition of freedom, no one class can ever attain that status; all must be free before any one can be. Having said all this, it must now be noted that in Marx's eyes the capitalist system is, in a limited sense, a good thing. It is an essential phase of an overall historical process which will eventually result in a society where all men can realize their true potential. Capitalism is the penultimate stage in the necessary historical progression from a condition of impotence and limitation to one of power and freedom. In order to understand such statements, we must now explore Marx's view of this historical process and examine the role of dialectics in his thinking.

Dialectical Materialism and History

We have seen how Marx was greatly influenced by the Hegelian conception of self-development. Another of Hegel's themes, that of dialectics, had an even more enduring impact on the young Marx. It was Hegel's contention that all prior philosophical thinking was incomplete, a limited form of analysis due primarily to its reliance on formal Aristotelian logic. This logical form forced men to think about their environment in a particular, highly abstract fashion. One of the central rules of formal logic, known as the principle of noncontradiction, held that a concept could not be both itself and its opposite at one and the same time. That is, something could not be said to be both "A" and "non-A" and convey any meaning. This type of formal logical rule led earlier philosophical thinkers to develop systems of categorization whereby objects in the real world were abstracted into categories of genus and species; something either existed or it did not, it was absurd to conceive of both "being" and "nonbeing" at the same time. Hegel believed that this formal logic resulted in a distortion of the true complexity of both the way human thinking occurred and the real world. It was not at all absurd to think of something being both itself and its opposite; indeed the key to understanding reality was in seeing that everything in existence in some sense contained within itself its opposite or negation. What Hegel was attempting was the transformation of the very meaning of the term logic. Formal or traditional logic consists of a system of rules by which we test the validity of our own thinking. We say that a conclusion is logical if it has been reached from its premises by using the rules of logic. It was Hegel's contention that this involved a distortion of the complexity of events and that man was forcing reality into an artificially contrived system. Rather than a set of rules devised to test the validity of thought processes, Hegelian logic purports to be an actual description of those processes, as well as an accurate reflection of events in the real world. Hegelian logic, then, is not a logic at all, but an ontology or an explanation of existence. By using it we can accurately describe the true nature of reality. The dialectical process is thus imbedded in the world of real events, and can provide the only accurate explanation of that world. It was this belief that led Hegel to assert that he had discovered the only correct way of "explaining the world."

The dialectical process is said by Hegel to contain three basic elements, or stages of development. While he never used the terms, the words *thesis, antithesis, and synthesis* have commonly been used to describe this triadic or three-stage process. At the thesis stage an event is said to be determinate, that is, it is primarily itself but contains within itself at least potentially its negation or opposite. With the passage of time this negation gradually becomes manifest, leading to the second stage, antithesis. At this point the thesis and the antithesis are said to exist in contradiction; "A" and "non-A" struggling for supremacy. Indeed, this contradiction and struggle is the element which insures a continual development in the world—it is the motive force of the entire universe. This contradiction is ultimately resolved when the thesis and antithesis stages are taken up into a third stage, the synthesis, which retains the best elements of the two prior stages. Hegel makes a difficult notion even more complex by using the German word *aufheben* to describe this taking up process, for it has at least three differing meanings: (a) to eliminate, (b) to lift or take up, (c) to preserve. Thus, while the contradiction of the prior stages is in some sense retained (c), it is also eliminated (a) in a higher unity. But the process does not end here for the synthesis stage in turn generates its own negation which eventually becomes a new antithesis, which will then become synthesized. This process will go on in history, with no end in sight. Perhaps the best way to explain this very difficult notion is to use one of Hegel's examples of the process, drawn from his description of the development of the nation-state.

Hegel's final triad in the development of the modern nation-state consists of a thesis stage of the Family, an antithesis of Civil Society, and a synthesis of the State. The Family stage is characterized by relationships of love and affection existing among members of the family unit; here is an entity in which all members are freely associated under communal norms—it is a cohesive unit. Gradually, however, the family unit generates its own negation in a stage called Civil Society. This is characterized by a more intense individualism and competition than the thesis stage; brother begins to compete with brother, largely in the economic realm. The cohesiveness and unity of the Family are lost and replaced by the particular wills of individuals in competition for self-development. These two stages are then synthesized by the institution of the State which takes the unity and general will aspect of the Family stage and combines it with the best of Civil Society, that is, the individual appropriation of the environment. We thus have a society which unites both particular and general will, the individual and the society, man with his fellow men.

Several things should be apparent from this example. Initially, the stage of synthesis has elevated what Hegel deems to be the best elements in the prior stages; hence the process is said to be moving upward toward some goal. It is teleological. Secondly, while retaining aspects of both prior stages, the synthesis is something quite new. It is a different entity which will now be capable of generating its own negation, keeping the dialectical process moving. Finally, the example illustrates some of the numerous difficulties of dialectical reasoning. Why, for example, is Civil Society the "negation" of the Family? Surely one could think of other institutions which could be similarly seen as contradicting the unity of the Family. Further, why should the nation-state be the synthesis of the two prior stages? Why not a world state or some kind of international organization? Whatever the arguments that can be raised concerning the dialectical method, and they are numerous, Hegel believed he had discovered the explanation for historical development, progress, and human freedom.

In our earlier discussion of Hegel, we saw that he believed the world was becoming more and more endowed with the rationality of the Absolute Idea. If we combine this notion with Hegel's conception of a teleological dialectical process, it is evident why each stage of synthesis was considered better. It was better because it was more rational. Thus, the history of the world as well as human history is appropriately described as a process constantly moving in dialectical fashion toward a free and rational community. The culmination of this process, at least in terms of political institutions, is to be found in Hegel's notion that the State will guarantee true freedom for all men. This notion of a rationally "becoming" universe had found many critics by the time Karl Marx came to study Hegel's ideas. Notable among those critics was Ludwig

Feuerbach whose criticisms of Hegel's abstractions were thoroughly assimilated by the young Marx, and whose ideas eventually led Marx to reject Hegelian idealism for something called *dialectical materialism.*

Feuerbach contended that the entire Hegelian system was an unconscious attempt to divert human attention from the real problems of existence. The notion of a rational Absolute Idea (really almost equatable with God) gradually manifesting itself in history was seen by Feuerbach as nothing more than the invention of an abstract entity which was then endowed with all of the attributes missing from real human existence. What man found lacking in his life was made part of something eternal, an attribute of the Absolute Idea. The difficulty with this form of reasoning was that it turned attention away from human beings and their predicament, and made this highly abstract Absolute Idea the true subject of history. Man was reduced to a small element in the overall patterns of things where, to Feuerbach, he was actually the central figure in all history. The entire Hegelian system focused on such abstractions and diverted attention from the true human condition. After all, if one can find intellectual satisfaction in such a fashion why worry about the insufficiencies of everyday life? Absolute Idea, rationality, and freedom became, to use Marx's word, "opiates," abstract ideas which satisfy without attempting to solve problems.

Marx thoroughly accepted Feuerbach's criticism of Hegel and was determined to apply his critical insight in the realms of politics and economics. Recall that we spoke of Hegel's triad of Family, Civil Society, and the State which synthesized the contradictions of the two prior stages. It was Marx's contention that Hegel's notion of the State was exactly the same sort of abstract solution to real human problems as Feuerbach had found in Hegel's religious teachings. Civil Society in Hegel was the antipode of the cohesive Family unit in that it permitted individuals to appropriate freely objects in the environment. This process would inevitably lead to conflicts between individuals desiring similar things and eventually, if unchecked, to much inequality. The major source of this inequality, recognized as such by Hegel himself, was to be found in private property. Private property, while an essential part of human self-development in that it permitted man to mix himself with the environment, would lead to inequality because some persons would be able to accumulate more than others. Hegel realized all this and declared that the individual, ego-dominated stage of Civil Society must be transcended in an ethical entity called the State which would solve this inequality and provide for a truly cohesive human community. The State would be a neutral agent which would only express the general will of the entire state; it would be the personification of the will of all the members of the community.

In the eyes of Karl Marx, the Hegelian State was but another example of the insufficiencies of this abstract system. The State was a projection of all of the problems of Civil Society and provided only an intellectual solution, leaving untouched the real world problem of inequality and lack of freedom. Further, anyone who took a clear look at the actions of existing states could readily see that they were anything but the neutral agents that Hegel envisioned. Indeed, a more appropriate description of state action would be that it served to perpetuate and enhance the existing inequalities. For these reasons Marx demanded a rejection of abstract philosophizing *à la* Hegel and a concentration on the real world forces which produce the human condition. Men must no longer be concerned with abstract *explanation* of the world, they must attempt to *change* it. Rejecting Hegelianism, Marx's concern turned to the real determining factor in all human experience; that is, he abandoned philosophy to study economics. Hegel's dialectical process is thus no longer an abstract rational process, but is imbedded in the material world of economics and politics. Dialectics remain, but as a materialistic dialectical process, with man the true subject of history.

History, Class, and the Development of Capitalism

Relieved of his Hegelian idealistic blinders, Marx was now prepared to reexamine the role of individuals and institutions in the historical process from a new perspective. Where Hegel sought to use the rationalistic Absolute Idea as the determining force in the historical process, Marx saw the central element to be ownership of the means of production and distribution of goods. He outlined five basic stages in human history: primitive community (primitive communism), slavery, feudalism, capitalism, and socialism. In each stage the determining factor is the control of the productive forces within the society, and when those means of production are owned by a particular group within the society they will exploit some other segment of the population. Thus, slavery, feudalism, and capitalism are necessarily oppressive societies, for they insure that one group will be able to control the means of production, thereby forcing the remaining individuals in the society to sell their labor in order to continue to exist. In each instance there are two principal classes which exist in opposition to one another; under slavery it is the masters versus the slaves, under feudalism the lords against the serfs, and under capitalism the capitalists against the workers. Both the primitive community and socialism are nonexploitive in that there is community ownership of the means of production and therefore no particular group can maximize its interests at the expense of others. Marx is far too sophisticated to believe that this two-class analysis (i.e. oppressers versus oppressed) is a completely accurate description of the real world at any point in time. In all real-world situations there will be a mixture of different classes. Under capitalism there will still be groups within the society whose relationship is primarily feudal, or even master-slave, but the prevailing relationship in the society can be appropriately characterized in terms of the workers versus the capitalists. Without going into a detailed description of the development of each of these stages, let us concentrate, as Marx did, on the situation under the capitalist mode of production.

Marx was one of the earliest social scientists to place great weight on the conditioning effect that economics has on all phases of human activity. While today it is commonplace to assert that human thought and action are greatly conditioned by upbringing, socioeconomic status, and the values of a particular culture, in Marx's time the general tendency was to place far greater weight on the effect of ideas in shaping human behavior. This is especially evident in the thought of Hegel where ideas and rationality determine the existence of the world. To Marx the fundamental conditioning factor in human action is essentially economic. The class structure of a society is a direct reflection of its distribution of wealth. Under the three antagonistic modes of ownership of the means of production (slavery, feudalism, and capitalism), all institutions, values, morality, and religion are conditioned, if not determined, by the class structure. These institutions and values occur as the result of the ruling class's desire for continued domination and nothing more. Under capitalism, for example, the state, far from being the neutral agency seen by Hegel, is a device invented by the capitalist class to further its own interests. Religion is the "opiate of the masses" in that it is designed to provide comforting rationalizations for the oppressed classes, so that they will become resigned to their lot. These institutions, part of what Marx called the *superstructure*, are but reflections of the underlying *substructure* of economic relationships. Under capitalism, then, all morality is capitalist morality, religion is bourgeois religion, and the state is nothing more than an instrument of oppression. It is in this context that Marx will later speak of the "withering away of the state" in a communist society, for the state will cease to exist once the class relationship which it perpetuates is abolished.

There remains some ambiguity as to the precise relationship between the substructure and the superstructure in Marxian thought. Marx at times speaks as though the relationship is casual in nature, i.e., the substructure can only effect the superstructure and not vice versa. This would deny the possibility, for example, of the political system in a capitalist country materially altering the process of allocating resources within the society. This position is commonly referred to as that of the "vulgar Marxist." At other points Marx seems to be saying that, while the economic substructure is the major determinant in all relationships, there is at least some interaction between substructure and superstructure and that superstructural institutions can alter the economic base. While it seems obvious that the latter interpretation is the only plausible one, for our purposes it is sufficient merely to emphasize the tremendous weight Marx placed on economic factors as determinants of all human activity. Many persons will assert that Marx's major contribution to social science was his recognition of this preponderant role that economic matters play in human affairs. However, today few would place quite as much weight on economic factors as Marx did.

While Marx substantially altered Hegel's dialectical process by imbedding it in the material world, he did not forsake the general notion of gradual progress in world history. Thus, each of the stages in history mentioned earlier is appropriately seen as part of a dialectical process moving toward the goal of a pure communist society. In another more important sense these societal stages can be viewed as part of the process of man achieving greater and greater control over his environment. We have seen that the fundamental fact of human development is man's ability to mix himself with the environment, to interact with it and to change it. Indeed, it is not inappropriate to view Marx's conception of human development as involving an ever-increasing control over the natural world. Man moves through varying historical stages from a condition of scarcity to one of abundance; from a state of lack of control to one of power. Herein we can see the major difficulty Marx saw in his nonantagonistic stage of the primitive community. While it was a classless society in that the means of production (however primitive) were possessed by all, man could not labor freely because he was totally preoccupied with satisfying the basic needs of subsistence. He had not achieved sufficient control over the environment to enable him to develop his nature without being constrained by the simple need to survive. If the laborer under capitalism can be said to be forced to work because of the exploitive class structure, in the primitive community men were in a similar sense forced to labor for their very existence. In the primitive community, despite its lack of class antagonisms, men could not achieve true self-consciousness or freedom because they were hampered by the natural environment. The dialectical process thus moves on to other stages whereby men achieve greater and greater control over their lives. It is for this reason that the capitalist stage is particularly important and the capitalist or bourgeois class is crucial for eventual human freedom. Capitalism was particularly effective in unleashing individual human wills to exploit the environment for their own personal benefit. In so doing it provided the technology which would permit men in the future to achieve a new society.

There is little doubt that Marx had tremendous admiration for the bourgeois class even while he was predicting its eventual overthrow. Under capitalism the bourgeoisie had succeeded in throwing off most of the values of traditional cultures and had further developed a technological base hitherto unknown in human history. Although this technology was based in the end on the exploitation of other men (proletarians), this does not alter the fact that the capitalist system provided man with the tools at last to control his environment.

> The bourgeoisie, during its rule of scarce one hundred years, has created more massive and more colossal productive forces than have all preceding generations together. Subjugation of Nature's forces to man, machinery, application of chemistry to industry and agriculture, steam navigation, railways, electric telegraphs, clearing of whole continents for cultivation, canalization of rivers, whole populations conjured out of the ground—what earlier century had even a presentiment that such productive forces slumbered in the lap of social labor?[4]

Using England as his model, Marx believed that eventually capitalism would spread throughout the world and provide the economic preconditions for a truly human existence. The internal dynamics of the system itself would force it to gradually spread around the world in search of new markets and new sources of raw materials. In doing this the capitalist system destroys all of the traditional values and mores and provides the preconditions for a new society for all men. Yet, by unleashing individual egos in cut-throat competition and exploitation (the very thing which made it so successful), capitalism insures its own demise. In pitting man against man in economic competition, capitalism denies the fundamental equality of all men, making some superior to others while prohibiting vast numbers of individuals from achieving their true nature. Capitalism must therefore be transcended in a pure communist state which will utilize the technological expertise of the capitalist stage to provide a "post-scarcity" economic situation. Here man for the first time in history can engage in the free conscious activity of labor for its own sake. No longer will it be necessary for human beings to struggle at a mere subsistence level as was the case in the primitive community. Man will no longer be buffeted about by the

---

[4]Marx and Engels, *The Communist Manifesto,* p. 85.

forces of nature, for he now can control them. The inequalities and suffering which capitalism produced will vanish once the ownership of the means of production is given to the entire community. Men's relationships will once again be harmonious. They will freely interact with the environment and each other in perfect accord.

Such are the broad outlines of the Marxian vision of a communist society. We shall speak at greater length of this at another point, but first it is essential to describe in detail Marx's analysis of the contradictions inherent within capitalist society which lead to its eventual downfall.

The Capitalist Economic System: Its Decline and Fall

We have seen how the young Marx described the dehumanizing and alienating effects of a capitalist economic system. The system itself inevitably produces a vast class of nonhuman wage slaves. This philosophical analysis is by no means Marx's only method of attacking capitalism; after all, one who asserts that the economic substructure of any society is the prime determining factor in its development must deal at length with the economic structure of that system. Marx's analysis of the decline and fall of capitalism is to be found primarily in *Das Kapital*, a work which is both brilliant and boring, insightful and repetitious.

The two key concepts in Marxian economics, concepts which are the building blocks for his entire analysis, are the *labor theory of value* and the *theory of surplus value*. Given what we know of Marx's regard for man as a "laboring animal," it is not surprising that he, along with most of the classical economists (Adam Smith, David Ricardo), regarded the amount of human labor involved in producing an object to be the sole source of any value that product might have. Simply, the amount of labor necessary to produce any object determines its economic value. If it takes three hours of human labor to produce a pair of shoes, and labor is priced at one dollar an hour, the shoes have a true value of three dollars; if a suit takes six hours to produce it will be valued at six dollars. In a purely competitive capitalist system, the market value of a product is determined by the amount of human labor it took to produce it. Marx is by no means unaware of the effects of supply and demand in establishing the market price of an object, but he asserts that in the long run that price is ultimately reducible to the true value of the product, i.e. the amount of human labor in it. Furthermore, the labor involved in a product need not be merely the direct physical labor of an individual. It can be indirect labor, such as conceiving of a more efficient design for the product or a better way of packaging it. Despite these qualifications, all value is in the end reduced to what Marx called "simple average labor" which, it seems, is somehow determined by convention.

The labor theory of value was an attempt by economists to find some common element which would provide a measure of value for products that was more objective than the fluctuations of supply and demand. The demand for a particular product is, after all, a subjective thing, subject to the taste and preferences of the individual. While most non-Marxian economists today would declare that the labor theory of value is at best an awkward way of explaining capitalist economics, Marx did succeed in using it to point out some basic facts about capitalism. As Robert Heilbroner puts it:

> ... by going through an even worse tangle of mathematics one can make the Marxist equations come out "right"—one can, that is, explain a correspondence between the prices that really obtain in life and the underlying values in terms of labor time. ... regardless of its mathematical purity, the Marxian rigmarole is at best a cumbersome and difficult framework and an unnecessarily laborious method of getting the required understanding of how capitalism works.[5]

Despite this, Marx's analysis grounded in the labor theory of value did lead him to an amazingly acute understanding of the dynamics of capitalism, and to a host of farsighted predictions. With the above difficulties in mind, let us then return to follow Marx's argument.

If everything is ultimately reducible to the amount of labor necessary to produce it, and the prices of objects in the long run reflect the amount of labor in the object, Marx then asks where the capitalist's profit comes from. If the price of a product is equal to its actual value, there can be no such thing as profit, at least for the system as a whole. Granted, one individual capitalist might benefit from a temporary variation between the actual value of a product and its current market price, but this is not sufficient to explain the existence of profit in the entire capitalist system. The only explanation of profit in capitalism is to be found in the monopoly of the means of production that the capitalists possess. Because they control the means of production the capitalists can force the working class to produce a profit for them. The analysis goes like this. Labor power, like anything else, has a certain value, defined in terms of the amount of labor necessary to sustain and reproduce it. The true value of an individual laborer can be seen as that amount of human labor which is necessary to keep that worker alive and to reproduce

---

[5]Heilbroner, *The Worldly Philosophers,* p. 137.

him; hence, to support a family. If it takes five hours of human labor to produce the goods necessary to keep one laborer alive (food, clothing, etc.), then the value of the laborer is five. This is what Marx called *necessary labor*, the amount of labor time necessary to sustain one worker. Because the capitalist class possesses a monopoly of the means of production it can force the workers to labor longer than is necessary for their own existence or more than their necessary labor. Let us say the laborer signs a contract with the capitalist to work ten hours a day; five of these ten hours are involved in necessary labor. The rest of the time is spent, in effect, working to produce a profit for the capitalist because the worker receives wages only for his necessary labor. The worker is producing five hours of extra value for the capitalist, five hours of *surplus labor*, which is the source of the capitalist's profit. The worker has no choice but to do this. If he refuses to work for the capitalist this additional period of time he has no livelihood, for the means of production are controlled by the the capitalist class. Surplus value, the difference between the actual value produced by a worker in a laboring day and his necessary labor, is the source of profit in a capitalist system. Small wonder that Marx declared all labor under capitalism to be forced labor!

The most pervasive aspect of capitalism is its emphasis on competition. Members of the bourgeois class are in constant competition with one another to maximize profit. We have seen how the only means of acquiring profit is through the exploitation of the laborer; the capitalist, then, increases his profit margin by driving his workers harder and harder, still paying them a subsistence wage. If we can say that the hallmark of capitalism is the acquisition of profit and capital by private individuals it is now evident why Marx saw this type of system as necessarily exploitative. If the laboring class were to receive the true value in wages for their labor, capitalism would literally cease to exist for there could then be no private profit. Capitalism must have a class of "wage slaves" in order to exist! One cannot overemphasize the necessity of constant competition which capitalism generates. The individual capitalist is constantly seeking ways in which he can increase his profit and this leads him to behave in ways which will eventually insure the demise of the entire system. Let us assume we have a capitalist operating within one industry which produces a single product. While the price that product can command on the open market may fluctuate slightly from day to day, the long-range price is determined on an industry-wide basis. Our individual capitalist then can attempt to increase his profit margin by driving his workers harder to achieve greater productivity from them during the time they are at work. Marx gives several examples of how this can be done, including such things as shortening the time allowed for eating and rest periods. In doing this our capitalist makes his position with respect to the whole industry more attractive. He is now producing a greater number of products with the same amount of workers and can thus either continue to sell this greater number of products at the industry-wide price, thereby adding to his profit, or he can lower the price of his products and attempt to undersell other firms, thus capturing a larger share of the market. While our hard driving capitalist now seems to be in a favorable position vis à vis the rest of the industry, it is really only a temporary solution. Initially, by the very nature of capitalist economics the other firms in the industry will respond to his initiative by driving their workers equally hard thereby reducing his competitive advantage. In effect, the industry-wide price is lowered so that our capitalist is no longer able to produce at a lower than industry cost. Further, there are physical limitations to the extent that this process of extracting more and more from one's laborers can continue—a man can be driven just so far. Still, the internal dynamic of capitalism demands that our owner increase his profit margin so he looks for other means of doing so. He accomplishes this through the introduction of labor-saving devices (machines) which make it possible to produce more products than the industry-wide norm. Once again, our capitalist is in a favorable position with respect to the industry as a whole. In addition, insofar as machinery is capable of performing the more complex tasks involved in the production process, the capitalist can reduce the quality of living laborers he employs. The skilled technician who was essential before the advent of the machine can now be replaced by an unskilled laborer, or eventually, even by women and children. As the necessary labor required for sustenance is based upon the family unit as a whole, the wages paid to such laborers can be further reduced, thus adding even more to the owner's profit. A final consequence is that working becomes increasingly boring and repetitious and the laborer loses all interest in what he is doing; he becomes a mere appendage of the machine he operates.

While the introduction of machinery does give the innovating capitalist a temporary advantage with respect to the rest of the industry, eventually the same forces we noted earlier will come into play and negate that advantage. In order to remain competitive other owners will have to follow the lead and replace their workers with machines, thus insuring the increasing mechanization of the industry and a growing pool of unemployed laborers. While machines may well bring increased profit to the innovating capitalist (and even this is not certain because of the high costs of invention) it is only a temporary thing, for competition will inevitably drive the industry-wide price downward. There are, however, further consequences for the industry as a whole which result from increasing mechanization. Machinery (Marx called it *constant capital*), like any other product, has a value equal to the amount of human labor necessary to produce it. A machine is appropriately seen as stored-up human labor and is capable of producing only as much value as human labor put into it. The "life" of a piece of machinery can be seen as a gradual process of spinning out the amount of labor in it. A machine cannot be exploited in the same way workers (*variable capital*) can. Further, the use of machines produces a great flood of products on the market and there is no one to buy them. As more and more machines are introduced, the number of unemployed workers greatly increases and even those who have jobs find their wages at the subsistence level. Thus they are unable to consume the machine-produced products. The system experiences ever more serious crises of overproduction and begins a frantic world-wide search for new markets for its products. In addition, the ever-increasing cost of machinery makes the competitive situation of many capitalists untenable. Because of the dramatically increasing costs of constant capital, many of the smaller capitalists are simply unable to continue the struggle and they are bought out by the more affluent. There is an ever increasing concentration of capital in fewer and fewer hands, and the marginal capitalists are forced into the ranks of the proletariat. Here is a second major Marxian prediction of capitalist development; it will tend inevitably toward *monopoly*. Finally, the system has succeeded in producing a vast army of unemployed workers who are living barely at the subsistence level and have little or no hope for a better future (Marx's *Law of Increasing Misery*). It is this vast, alienated, proletarian class which is to provide the negation of the capitalist system; capitalism has sown the seeds of its own destruction.

It is now evident why Marx saw the great proletarian revolution occurring in highly developed capitalist countries. Highly developed capitalist economies would inevitably produce this radical cleavage between the few remaining capitalists and the vast industrial proletariat, and the latter would gradually become aware of the fact that the only way they could improve their lot was through the overthrow of the entire system. Marx expected this revolution to be both spontaneous and violent. Although he did concede the possibility of a nonviolent revolution (perhaps in England), in general, his expectation was that the bourgeois class would fight for the existing system with all the weapons at its command. As the capitalists used more and more repressive measures to keep the proletariat in line, the workers, heretofore unorganized and impotent, would begin to see that their real enemies were the bourgeoisie and would begin to realize their collective power. In the Marxian jargon, they would develop *class consciousness,* a realization of their power as a unit and the firm conviction that their emancipation from slavery lay in the abolition of capitalism. Once they were possessed of this consciousness, the revolution would simply occur, a spontaneous uprising of the alienated. Although Marx became somewhat disenchanted with the revolutionary potential of the proletariat after the abortive revolutions of 1848, he retained throughout his life this belief in spontaneous revolution. This is particularly important in that Marx consequently had only a somewhat vague conception of a revolutionary communist party dedicated to producing a revolution. The idea of a group of dedicated revolutionaries constantly attempting to foment revolution, to light the "spark," is not Marxian in origin but a Leninist idea which produces many changes in the classical Marxian analysis.

Finally, it must be noted that there is very little that the bourgeois class can do about all this. They may attempt to placate the proletariat in a whole host of ways but ultimately the very nature of the capitalist system will, in proper dialectical fashion, insure its own destruction. It is this "scientific," inevitable aspect of the analysis that gives Marxism much of its revolutionary appeal. Capitalism is doomed; it is merely a question of time.

While Marx was somewhat vague as to the specifics of the society which would follow capitalism, the broad outlines should now be rather clear. The abolition of private property and community ownership of the means of production will insure a society where classes and exploitation cease to exist. Marx, and later Engels, talked specifically of universal suffrage and the direct responsibility of any leadership elements to the people through a process of referendum and recall. Any hierarchical power structure, whether based on class or expertise, was rejected. The technological base provided by the capitalist stage in history will provide man with the means to control his environment and make scarcity and poverty a thing of the past. Men will interact with their environment freely, treating each other as fellow humans all engaged in the common task of self-realization. The oppressive, superstructural state of capitalism will vanish, bourgeois morality will be replaced by a truly human morality, men will labor according to their ability and be rewarded according to their needs. Simply, he envisioned a community of peace, tranquillity, and power over nature which would insure true freedom for all mankind.

It is by now almost a cliché to say that Marxism possesses great appeal for masses of people because it promises the equivalent of a heaven on earth. Combine this ethical vision with a doctrine which promises scientific inevitability and one has a most powerful ideology. We shall not attempt specific criticisms of Marxism at this point largely because the two other ideologies to be discussed will provide us with a highly critical perspective of Marx. Yet it is appropriate to note the tremendously optimistic view of human nature built into the doctrine; man is by nature good; society, particularly capitalist society, at least temporarily corrupts him. In the end, criticisms of Marxism must deal with this view of man and evaluate it to determine whether a society built upon such premises is possible, or, for that matter, desirable.

Marxism did not, of course, die with Karl Marx. While his ideas to this day provide the building blocks for socialist and communist thought, one may no longer speak of Marxism but of Marxism-Leninism or perhaps Marxism-Leninism-Stalinism-Maoism. His ideas undergo great changes in the hands of his dedicated followers, changes which make the current doctrine quite different even while it retains the broad outlines of classical Marxism. We must now look at some of those changes, in particular those made by the leader of the first revolution proclaimed in Marx's name—Vladimir Ilyich Ulyanov, better known as V. I. Lenin.

BIBLIOGRAPHY

Balinky, Alexander. *Marx's Economics*. Lexington, Mass.: D.C. Heath & Company, 1970. The best short introduction to Marx's economic analysis available. The reading is somewhat difficult, but well worth the effort.

Findlay, J. N. *Hegel: A Re-Examination*. New York: Collier Books, 1958. A good modern introduction to the complexities of the Hegelian system as a whole. Difficult, but ultimately rewarding.

Gregor, A. James. *A Survey of Marxism: Problems in Philosophy and the Theory of History*. New York: Random House, 1965. A sophisticated analysis of Marxism from a more philosophical perspective.

Kaufmann, Walter. *Hegel: A Reinterpretation*. Garden City, N.Y.: Doubleday and Company, 1966. A groundbreaking study, notable for its insights into the totality of Hegel's work. Kaufmann also writes with clarity and verve.

Marcuse, Herbert. *Reason and Revolution: Hegel and the Rise of Social Theory*. Boston: Beacon Press, 1960. Probably the best study available of the Hegelian roots of Marxian thought as well as an examination of the broader impact of Hegelianism on social theory as a whole.

Meyer, Alfred G. *Marxism: The Unity of Theory and Practice.* Ann Arbor, Michigan: Ann Arbor Paperbacks, 1963. One of the best general introductions to Marx's thought.

Tucker, Robert C. *Philosophy and Myth in Karl Marx.* Cambridge: The Cambridge University Press, 1961.

————. *The Marxian Revolutionary Idea.* New York: W. W. Norton & Company, 1969. In these two excellent volumes Tucker provides a comprehensive study of Marxism as both a theory of man and society and as a revolutionary ideology.

Wolfe, Bertram D. *Marxism: 100 Years in the Life of a Doctrine.* New York: Dell Publishing Company, 1967. A distinguished Marxian scholar attempts to describe the evolution of the doctrine, paying particular attention to conflicting impulses in the early work of Marx.

Zeitlin, Irving M. *Marxism: A Re-Examination.* Princeton, N. J.: D. Van Nostrand Company, Inc., 1967. A good overall survey of Marxist thought from a modern perspective.

Original Works

Easton, Lloyd D. and Kurt H. Guddat, eds. *Writings of the Young Marx on Philosophy and Society.* Garden City, N.Y.: Doubleday & Company, 1967.

Feuer, Lewis S., ed. *Marx & Engels: Basic Writings on Politics and Philosophy.* Garden City, N. Y.: Doubleday & Company, 1959.

Marx, Karl and Friedrich Engels. *The Communist Manifesto.* Baltimore: Penguin Books, 1967.

————. *Selected Works.* New York: International Publishers, 1968.

Chapter 3

MARXISM
AND
LENINISM

By the time of Karl Marx's death in 1883 his doctrines had become common currency among European radicals; there was an established international communist movement, a quite strong Marxist party in Germany, and potentially serious stirrings elsewhere on the continent. Behind this façade of a united international movement, however, there were many arguments about the real meaning of the doctrines. To use Sidney Hook's phrase, "Karl Marx left a rich and ambiguous intellectual legacy."[1] Until his death in 1895, Engels, because of his status as a founding father of the movement, was able to keep some cohesiveness to the interpretations of the doctrine, yet even during this period warring factions were beginning to develop. This intellectual ferment about the true meaning of Marx's teachings was to continue until the imposed Stalinist orthodoxy of the 1930s, but the period between Marx's death and the Bolshevik success in Russia in 1917 shows the varying controversies in all of their richness. While it is impossible for us to go into great detail regarding these arguments and their effects on the international communist movement, we must have some basic understanding of the contending positions if only to set the stage for Lenin's contributions.

There are two major subjects which dominate the debate of this period: the question of violent or peaceful revolution and the question of

---

[1]Sidney Hook, *Marx and the Marxists: The Ambiguous Legacy* (Princeton, N.J.: D. Van Nostrand Company, Inc., 1955), p. 49.

the readiness of the industrial proletariat for the revolution. With respect to the first point, Marx's legacy, while seemingly ambiguous, is nevertheless rather clear. While admitting the slight possibility of a peaceful transition from capitalism to socialism, he expected that a violent overthrow of the system would be necessary. Given the class antagonisms which capitalism produced, one could not expect the bourgeois class to calmly sit back and preside over its own demise. Despite this rather clear teaching from the master, the years prior to World War I had produced a growing belief in the political power the working classes could achieve through democratic processes. Even Engels, although hardly renouncing the right of the proletariat to take up arms to insure revolutionary success, felt that significant changes were occurring via the ballot box. This position, that violence still might be necessary but that significant progress toward socialist goals was being made through legal means, is generally called Marxism of the center or *orthodox Marxism.* The major spokesman for this position was Karl Kautsky, the intellectual leader of the powerful German Social-Democratic party and a major theoretician of the time. While he emphasized the fact that Marxian political parties were indeed revolutionary in nature, he made a rather clear distinction between a party which tries to foment a revolution and one which reflects the inevitable historical progress being made toward the achievement of a socialist society. Placing great weight on Marx's doctrine of the historical inevitability of a socialist society, Kautsky cautioned against trying to speed up the process of history by reckless and clandestine revolutionary activity. He advocated open and active participation in the political processes of capitalist states, fully confident that the revolution would, in time, occur. If Marx was somewhat ambiguous regarding the violence necessary for the transition into socialism, the orthodox Marxist position seems much more so. Violence, they seem to say, may be necessary in order to achieve our goals, but only when dictated by history; we are revolutionary, but not actively engaged in the starting of revolutions. Perhaps the orthodox position may be explained by the general optimism concerning democratic processes which existed prior to the war. Unwilling to renounce the Marxian prediction of violent revolution, the orthodox wing of the movement is nevertheless very much in the position of not rocking the boat. They are appropriately called Marxists of the center, and perhaps their position will become clearer through an examination of the two extreme positions prevalent at the time.

Marxism of the right, or more commonly *revisionism,* does not share the ambiguity of the centerists, or, for that matter of Karl Marx. With Eduard Bernstein (1850-1932), a somewhat heretical member of the German Social-Democratic party, as their principal spokesman, revisionists simply abandoned the Marxian doctrine of violent revolution. While acknowledging that this was a significant revision of Marx's teaching, Bernstein asserted that the political power of the newly enfranchised proletariat made it possible to achieve most of the socialist goals by legal means. Instead of expending all of their energy theorizing about a communist society or dreaming of the violent overthrow of capitalism, true socialists should be working to improve the lot of the proletariat through trade unions and political parties. Bernstein and his allies (principally Jean Jaures, a French socialist), thus laid the theoretical groundwork for democratic socialist parties and the trade union movement throughout Europe. There is some question as to whether such a position is appropriately called "Marxist," for it implies that the capitalist superstructure (political processes) can be used to fundamentally alter the substructure (economic system). Yet Bernstein considered himself a dedicated follower of Marx, thinking only that he was making the doctrine compatible with changing times. Given the revisionist position, Marxism of the center perhaps makes more sense. Both the revisionists and the centerists were forced to deal with the increasing evidence that the demands of the proletariat were being realized within the capitalist system. The revisionist position acknowledged that fact and went on to assert that most of the goal culture of socialism could be satisfied in this way, and further that a significant improvement in the lot of the workers was more important than the achievement of some abstract and far-off goal culture. Centerists attempted to combat the revisionist position by declaring that some, but not all, demands can be achieved in this fashion, and affirmed the revolutionary nature of the struggle.

As might be expected, *Marxism of the left* completes our spectrum of positions on the role of violence in producing revolution. With V. I. Lenin and, to a certain extent German Socialist Rosa Luxemburg, as its leading advocates, left Marxism places great weight on the antagonistic nature of the class struggle under capitalism and declares violent revolution to be absolutely necessary in the realization of socialism. The revisionist and centerist positions can be seen from this perspective as denying the true Marxian vision of a socialist society and as distorting Marx's teachings on the relationship between substructure and superstructure. The supposed gains made by the trade union movement and by social-democratic political parties are nothing but sops given by the capitalists to keep the workers in line; a fundamental change in the system can only come about through a true revolution. Instead of allowing themselves to be used by the capitalists through participating in politics, true Marxians should be engaging in general strikes to paralyze the system, using terroristic activities to reveal the true repressive nature of capitalism, and constantly agitating for revolution. Left Marxism is, then, the position of the uncompromising revolutionary, who is dedicated to the overthrow of the system and refuses to believe that reformist measures of any sort will benefit the movement. Indeed, those so-called Marxians who believe in progress within a capitalist system are really helping the capitalists retain their superior position, for they lead the working class to renounce the necessity for radical action and inhibit the growth of class-consciousness. Action, agitation, and revolution are the cries of the left. Their position on the second of our two major questions of this period—the readiness of the proletariat for revolution—exhibits the same traits, and it is to that question we must now turn.

A considerable period of time had passed since Marx and Engels predicted the mass spontaneous uprising of the proletariat in highly developed capitalist states. While they attached no specific timetable to this prediction, there was a general expectation that revolution was imminent. The abortive revolutions of 1848 forced Marx to begin to think about the problem of working toward a revolution rather than just waiting for it to happen, but his confidence in the proletariat as the people chosen by history for this task never seriously wavered. It is important to note that the entire scientific nature of Marxian thought is at stake here. A large, alienated, class-conscious proletariat was the necessary outgrowth of highly developed capitalism and the fact that no uprising of major consequence had occurred cast Marx's entire set of scientific propositions in doubt. As we shall see later in this chapter, Lenin and other Marxists developed an ingenious explanation for this lack of proletarian activity in developed capitalist states, but for the moment it is sufficient to note that the entire question of the readiness of the proletariat for revolution was widely debated in the period prior to the First World War. As might be inferred from their position on the question of violence in the revolution, orthodox Marxists retained Karl Marx's basic belief in the spontaneous uprising of the proletarian class in highly developed capitalist countries. Because of this there was no need of a revolutionary activist party; class consciousness would naturally develop because of the inherent contradictions of capitalism, and no amount of "adventurism" or revolutionary agitation on the part of dedicated Marxists would help. Here again we see the reliance of the orthodox Marxists on the doctrine of historical inevitability and their faith in the scientific nature of Marx's predictions. They believed that Marxian political parties should be mass-based organizations which would provide some help in increasing the consciousness of the working class, but their prime function was to work by legal means for the betterment of the proletariat. In sum, the orthodox position was that the proletariat would become ready for revolution sometime in the future as a result of the internal contradictions of capitalism, and the task of dedicated Marxians was to work through mass-based political parties to gradually improve its lot.

The revisionist position on this question should be quite evident. Disavowing the violent nature of revolution, they advocated the recruitment of the entire working class in individual countries so that its political power would be enhanced. By developing a strong working class movement, they could force the capitalists to change the very nature of the systems and implement most of the goals of socialism. The question of whether the working class was ready for revolution was rather irrelevant to the revisionist. What was necessary, and immediately realizable, was the development of class solidarity in order to maximize the policy goals of the workers. It was in left Marxism, particularly in the thought of Lenin, that this question of proletarian readiness became particularly important and eventually led to profound alterations in classical Marxian teaching.

In order to explain Lenin's beliefs on this matter we must introduce, for the first of many times, the subject of the peculiar position of Russian Marxists. Most of the major figures in the international communist movement prior to the war resided in developed capitalist countries possessing a significant urban proletariat. In their eyes Russia was generally viewed as an anachronism; a country half-Asian, half-European, backward in industrial development and possessing an extremely small working class: hardly fitting Marx's model of a well-developed capitalist state. This is not to say that Marx was ignored in Russia. The Russian intelligentsia, a class of well-educated individuals cut off from participation in political affairs by the dictatorial rule of the Tsars, had a long tradition of radicalism, even anarchism. The first major Russian Marxist group was formed by George V. Plekhanov in 1883 and Marx found a ready ear in the highly alienated Russian intelligentsia. Despite this, the notion of a proletarian revolution in Russia was something of a joke, for there simply was no proletariat to speak of. This fact was to force Lenin and his followers to make many alterations in Marxian doctrine so that it fit the Russian experience, but for present purposes it also led Lenin to distrust the revolutionary potential of the working class. In contrast to the classical and orthodox Marxist position of waiting for the development of class-consciousness and the spontaneous uprising of the urban proletariat, Lenin came to believe that the proletariat, in alliance with other disaffected groups in the society, would require strong leadership to accomplish their revolutionary mission. Probably because of his Russian background, he was not optimistic about the possibilities of a spontaneous proletarian revolution. Even in a highly developed capitalist country such as Germany it seemed that the proletariat, under the influence of revisionists and orthodox Marxists, was losing its revolutionary potential and tending to adopt bourgeois values. However, for Lenin this did not preclude the possibility of revolution. These facts dictated a new strategy for committed Marxists—they required a new conception of the role of a party structure in the movement as well as an analysis of the place of other dissatisfied groups in the revolution. In formulating a new strategy, Lenin began the process of materially altering classical Marxism to fit the new circumstances of the twentieth century. We will treat these Leninist contributions to the doctrine under three headings: the Communist Party and its roles, state socialism and a socialist transfer culture, and the theory of imperialism. First, however, let us meet Lenin, the man and the revolutionary.

Lenin the Revolutionary

Vladimir Ilyich Ulyanov, who later adopted the "party" name Lenin, was born in 1870 in Simbirsk on the Volga River, the son of a moderately prosperous director of provincial education for the Russian state. Vladimir was the third child in a family of seven and the second eldest son. He and his elder brother Alexander were rather close, the younger Vladimir always trying to duplicate the intellectual and athletic feats of his brother. Both were excellent in school, earning the highest marks throughout their academic careers. During this period, Russia was undergoing a severe political reaction to the assassination of the reformist Tsar Alexander II, in 1881. His successor, Alexander III, proceeded systematically to repress dissent, discourage education, and make more absolute the famed absolutism of Russian rulers. The intelligentsia was understandably unhappy with this turn of events and prepared to make use of their favorite political weapon, another assassination. The Ulyanov family became intimately involved in these political affairs when Alexander, in St. Petersburg to continue his studies, was arrested by the police for plotting the bombing of Alexander III. Because of his knowledge of chemistry he had been assigned to make the bomb. After an eloquent defense of revolutionary action at his trial, Alexander was convicted, executed by the Tsar's police, and young Vladimir began, according to his sister, to think seriously about revolution. The next several years saw the Ulyanov family move to the larger city of Kazan and then to the city of Samara on the Volga. The young Lenin completed his gymnasium education and briefly attended the University of Kazan only to be dismissed for being involved in protest activities. There is still a good deal of disagreement as to when Lenin began serious study of Marxism. We have his sister Anna's statement that while the ill-fated Alexander was reading Marx in 1886 the younger Vladimir was preoccupied with the works of Turgenev and had no real political views. The period in Kazan and in Samara undoubtedly provided him with the opportunity to read extensively and think about his future since he did not have to work to maintain himself. He did, however, pursue a degree in law during this time and was admitted to the bar in 1892. Although he was permitted to practice law, Lenin spent much of his time at various radical meetings where he eventually developed a reputation for debating skills in defense of Marxist ideas. Whenever he came to accept the Marxian credo fully, by 1893 he was an identifiable advocate of its doctrines. In 1895, Lenin took what had by now become a customary trip for Russian radicals through Western Europe, meeting most of the leading Marxists of the time. Returning to St. Petersburg, he joined several other young radicals in the formation of a revolutionary action group, designed to put some of the ideas of the radical "debating societies" into practice. The experience was short-lived; they were arrested by the police in December 1895. Lenin spent more than a year in prison in St. Petersburg using the time to begin a major book, *The Development of Russian Capitalism,* until the authorities decided he should spend three years in exile in Siberia. The years of exile provided a rather pleasant interlude for the budding revolutionary. He had a good deal of freedom of movement, time to read and write as well as to plan strategy for his return. The situation was further enhanced when he was joined by a young comrade, Nadezhda Krupskaya whom he had met earlier in radical circles in St. Petersburg. She became his wife and life-long collaborator. By the time he left Siberia in February of 1900 he was a dedicated revolutionary with a rather clear plan of how to accomplish his goals. This well-formulated strategy distinguished him from most other radicals, who tended to be vague regarding the methods of achieving their ideals.

With the exception of a brief return to Russia in the revolutionary period of 1905-7, Lenin spent the entire time prior to 1917 in political exile. For a man of action, this was a particularly trying period; cut off from events in Russia, he could only spend his time in forming a group of dedicated followers who would be ready to seize opportunities as they arose. It is a testament to Lenin's dedication to the cause of Russian Marxism that during all of this time, spent in a great number of European cities, he thought of nothing but the coming struggle. Lenin had by now become one of the major figures in the movement, and the leading spokesman for its left wing. At the Second Party Congress of Russian Marxists in 1903, Lenin led a fight to establish the party as a close-knit organization of dedicated revolutionaries and succeeded, after several splinter factions had withdrawn from the Congress, in achieving a majority for his position. Because of this, Lenin was thereafter able to refer to his group as representing the majority (*Bolshevik* in Russian) position even though it was actually one of many splinter factions warring for domination of the Marxist movement in Russia. Such was the condition of Russian Marxism when, in reaction to an extremely unpopular and unsuccessful war with Japan, revolution broke out in St. Petersburg in 1905. Beginning with the massacre of peaceful demonstrators in February ("Bloody Sunday"), the revolt spread to most of European Russia with councils ("soviets") of workers attaining a great deal of power in the major cities. During this time, Lenin and his followers attempted to turn the general discontent of the population toward Marxian ends only to see the revolution brutally crushed by troops still loyal to the Tsar and by the granting of numerous concessions, notably the October Manifesto of 1905, which established a parliament. Alternately impressed by the potential power of the discontented Russian masses and convinced that only through his tightly organized party could any revolution be a success, Lenin withdrew once again into exile.

The years after the abortive revolution of 1905 saw Lenin and his Bolshevik faction increasingly split off from the other more moderate Marxists in Russia. They held their own conferences, published their own newspaper (with the now familiar name of *Pravda* or "truth" in Russian), and in general took a standoffish attitude toward the international Marxist movement. Lenin's final break with the more moderate socialists of the international movement came with the start of World War I. Confirming his worst fears of the moderates and revisionists, he found most European socialists supporting their respective national governments in the war effort. Castigating them for supporting a bourgeois war, Lenin, now in Switzerland, could only consolidate his Bolshevik faction even further and hope that the strain of a major war would finally topple the Tsarist regime. That hope, perhaps dream is a better word, was fulfilled in March of 1917 when, with the country completely out of control, the Tsar at long last abdicated.

For Lenin, however, this was but the beginning. Hearing in Switzerland of the Romanov abdication, he immediately made arrangements to return to Russia. The Germans, only too eager to have a revolutionary like Lenin causing further trouble in Russia, arranged the famous ride by sealed train through Germany and Finland. The exile returned to a triumphant celebration at the Finland Station in St. Petersburg, in April of 1917.

The remaining events of that fateful year are far too complex to summarize here. Our intention has been to understand something of Lenin the man and to describe briefly the society with which he was dealing, rather than to attempt a history of the Russian Revolution. Our prime interest is in Lenin the contributor to Marxist ideology; thus it is to his ideas that we must now turn.

The Communist Party and Its Roles

If there was one thing which made Lenin stand apart from his Marxist colleagues prior to 1917 it was his unique conception of a communist party. Most commentators would rate the notion of the party as Lenin's foremost contribution to Marxist thought, if only because it turns highly abstract doctrine into a revolutionary movement. In another sense, Lenin's party provides an excellent example of the direction of all of his thought, which was to make Marxist doctrine compatible with the facts of the twentieth century and with the particular conditions in Russia.

As we have seen, Karl Marx had at best a rather vague notion of a revolutionary party because of his belief that the contradictions of capitalism would produce a spontaneous revolution of the proletariat. His orthodox followers, still retaining the belief in spontaneity, felt that a mass workers' party operating within the bourgeois political system could provide material gains for the working class and develop in the proletariat a sense of its potential power. While Lenin in his early days accepted this notion, he gradually came to the belief that such mass-based workers' organizations were ineffective and tended to impede the goal of revolution. Partially owing to the lack of a large proletariat in Russia and partially because the proletariat in more highly developed countries tended to adopt bourgeois values as it gained even limited political power, Lenin called for the establishment of a small, tightly organized band of dedicated Marxists whose task was to lead the alienated groups within a country to revolution. In adopting such a position Lenin more or less stood by himself. Rosa Luxemburg, who shared many of his radical tendencies in interpreting Marx's thought, retained the belief in a spontaneous revolution. Even Leon Trotsky, a trusted lieutenant of Lenin's during the revolution, did not come to share this view until 1917. The reason for this lack of acceptance was that Lenin, at least implicitly, was advocating a large alteration in Marxian doctrine. Simply, he was saying that it was not necessary for the proletariat to possess class consciousness in order to have a revolution. Given a country where there was a good deal of discontent with the existing regime, it would be possible for a dedicated band of revolutionaries to seize upon the peoples' "alienation" and turn their energies toward Marxist ends. This is not to say that Lenin believed in the possibility of a palace revolution, engineered by a few men in strategic places. He was firm in the belief that a revolutionary movement had to have mass support and argued at great length with those who advocated such a *coup d'état* strategy. Even so, the important point here is that class consciousness on the part of the proletariat is not a prerequisite for revolution. If this is the case, one can see all sorts of opportunities for revolutionary agitation opening up. If class consciousness is not necessary, the party could attempt to use any dissatisfied group within society to further its ends. All kinds of alliances with different groups would be possible, depending upon the degree of capitalistic development in a particular country. If an alienated proletarian class, conscious of its own plight and potential power, is no longer a prerequisite for a Marxian revolution, then it is quite appropriate to advocate a revolution in countries which do not possess the characteristics of the classical Marxian model.

We have earlier spoken of Russia as a most unlikely place for a classical Marxist revolution, because of her lack of economic development. While this remains true it must be noted that Russia had made very rapid strides toward industrialization during the latter part of the nineteenth century. The success of the workers' soviets in the revolution of 1905 indicated the presence of a growing proletariat in major Russian cities. Still, the country was primarily rural, and her population mostly composed of peasants. Most Marxians considered Russia a feudal society, where the economic substructure was beginning a rapid movement into industrial capitalism while the state superstructure lagged behind, retaining its feudal elements. In such a situation it would be necessary to have not one, but two revolutions; the first bourgeois, the second communistic. Leon Trotsky had earlier advanced the doctrine of *permanent revolution* which contended that in Russia the two revolutions could take place within a very short period of time. Even while the bourgeois revolution was occurring, Marxists should be organizing and agitating for the proletarian revolution—the two revolutions could be telescoped. In such a situation, the task of Marxist revolutionaries was to speed the success of the bourgeois revolution and then attempt to foment a proletarian one. Consistent with this principle, Lenin, prior to 1905, advocated an alliance between the proletariat and the liberal bourgeoisie, so that the aims of the bourgeois revolution might be accomplished. The proletariat's role was temporarily that of assisting the bourgeoisie in the overthrow of the autocracy of the Tsar. The revolution of 1905 changed all that. The bourgeoisie, by accepting the Tsar's liberal October Manifesto had, in Lenin's eyes, sold out to the forces of oppression; they had denied their own revolution. Further, the events of 1905 had produced a situation which must have wet the lips of a true revolutionary such as Lenin; there had been a temporary alliance between the small urban proletariat and the vast Russian peasantry. These events led Lenin to abandon the Russian bourgeois class and rely increasingly upon an alliance between the peasants and the proletariat. Once again, we observe Lenin altering Marxian doctrine to suit the conditions of semifeudal Russia. Karl Marx, basing his observations on the developed capitalism of Western Europe, had concluded that the peasant class was one of the most conservative forces in society. However, the situation of the Russian peasantry was quite different. Achieving emancipation from serfdom only in 1861, the average peasant found his lot was unbearable and not at all dissimilar in revolutionary potential to that of Marx's alienated urban proletariat. After 1905 Lenin spoke with increasing frequency of a revolution of the *masses,* allying the proletariat with all dissatisfied classes in the society. It must be remembered, however, that Lenin retained a clear conception in his mind of the role of these groups; they were subservient to the class-conscious proletariat.

The task of Lenin's small, tightly disciplined party is now quite clear. Its function is to coordinate the actions of these various groups, always keeping control of the situation. When the revolution occurs, the party, because of its discipline and organization, will be in a position to assume overall leadership. To Lenin's mind, one of the fundamental failures of the 1905 revolution was the lack of effective leadership and coordination, and he was determined not to let that happen again. To provide that leadership Lenin set up the decision-making process of the party to conform to the principles of a doctrine called *democratic centralism.* This doctrine presupposes that all the people involved in the process of making decisions for the party are committed to the Marxian goal culture. Given this, decisions still will have to be made regarding party tactics and there will undoubtedly be disagreements as to the right way of proceeding. As the name implies, democratic centralism theoretically allows for a full democratic discussion of alternatives, but once a decision is made all members of the party must agree to abide by it. There are no minority reports in the party. This doctrine provided Lenin with precisely the tool he needed for revolutionary action; it is democratic by taking into account all positions, but it also provides for the unswerving allegiance necessary for swift action. Many persons justifiably contend that the adoption of this decision-making process marks the beginning of a totalitarian party in communist thought, for the "democratic" of democratic centralism is so easily forgotten in the presence of a strong leader such as Lenin. Whatever the case, Lenin's communist party, organized in this fashion, provided him with the means of taking control in the more chaotic days of the Russian Revolution. While others debated, the Bolsheviks acted.

Despite all of Lenin's attempts to alter Marxian doctrine to suit his special situation in Russia, the fact remains that he succeeded in presiding over a revolution which was distinctly un-Marxian in nature. The first communist revolution in the world occurred in a country which was singularly unprepared for communism, at least in Marx's sense. Directly contrary to Marxian teaching, the Bolshevik revolution was political, a superstructural revolution. As a dedicated Marxist Lenin knew this. With his success in Russia he was now faced with the task of using the political structure of the society to develop the economic conditions that Marxism decreed necessary for a pure communist society. To revert to jargon, Lenin had to develop a "transfer culture" which would lead toward the "goal culture" of pure communism. The communist party was to play a crucial role in this transfer period, but its activities after the revolution are best treated under the heading of the second of our "three themes of Leninism"—state socialism and the socialist transfer culture.

State Socialism

Marx had taught that the workers' revolution, once begun, would eventually spread around the entire world until all capitalist regimes were overthrown. Therefore the immediate problem facing the Bolsheviks after their takeover in November, 1917, concerned the relationship between the world-wide communist movement and the revolutionary regime in the Soviet Union. Many dedicated Bolsheviks wanted to carry the red flag of Marxism westward into the heart of Europe and at least partially fulfill Marx's prophecy. Initially Lenin agreed with this analysis, contending that the spark of the Bolshevik revolution would ignite the flames of revolution throughout Europe. The beachhead which had been established in Russia would be secured through the overthrow of other capitalist regimes. In the euphoric days immediately after the Russian Revolution Lenin apparently expected an immediate rise of the proletariat throughout Europe, making the Soviet experience a sort of trigger for the revolt in more highly developed capitalist countries. Such events did not occur and it became increasingly obvious that some new analysis of the situation was needed. Characteristically, Lenin shifted ground and began to argue that even though the Russian Revolution was inextricably linked to the international movement there would probably be a lag in time between the initial success of the Bolsheviks and the revolution in other countries. Although he continued to believe that this lag would be of short duration, possibly a few years, admitting of its existence forced the young Soviet regime to develop policy for the interim period and to address itself tentatively at least to the question of the existence of a Soviet state surrounded by capitalism. On a more practical level the Bolsheviks were surrounded by chaos; the years of war and revolution had reduced the army to a disorganized mass, a civil war was raging, and the regime was in real danger of losing control completely. The optimism of the immediate postrevolutionary period, which saw a quick transition to economic socialism at home and the rapid spread of revolution abroad, was replaced by a grim struggle for existence. Whatever the ideological costs, the situation required that Russia get out of the war, and after a good deal of argument this was accomplished through the treaty of *Brest-Litovsk* which ceded large portions of European Russia to the conquering Germans. Lenin was simply unwilling to sacrifice the Bolshevik success in the name of an immediate world-wide revolution. Still, consistent with the broad Marxian analysis, he similarly refused to abandon the international struggle for the sake of an independent Soviet nation-state. Confronted with the potentially conflicting goals of the Russian Revolution and international Marxism, Lenin characteristically opted for both. The long range goals of the international movement were not inconsistent with the idea of a Soviet state for the latter would serve as an inspiration to proletarians the world over. Since the time lag between the Russian Revolution and the world uprising would be of short duration, the Soviet Union could exist as an entity even though it was surrounded by hostile capitalist states. Marx's prophecy of an international movement was never in doubt. It was simply a question of time. While the international movement was by no means ignored, the Soviet leadership could now expend some energy in securing the gains of the revolution within Russia.

As we have said, the Russian Revolution was of a political nature, accomplished by a small band of revolutionaries supported by a variety of discontented groups in the society. From the viewpoint of classical Marxism, the two things most conspicuously lacking in Russia were economic development and the presence of a class-conscious proletariat. Unless these two goals were achieved it would be impossible to think of a truly communist society. Lenin's task inside the Soviet Union was to develop institutions and a value structure which would achieve these two goals; he had to develop a transfer culture. Because the people at large lacked true consciousness and had lived for so many years under the false value structures of feudalism and capitalism it would be necessary to have a group of leaders to direct the economic development of the society and lead the people as a whole toward proletarianization. The Communist Party would provide such leadership after the revolution in its role as *dictatorship of the proletariat*. If the society as a whole was lacking in class consciousness, it would be absurd, from the Leninist perspective, to give all people an equal say in the running of the country. Thus, it would be temporarily necessary for the Party to act as the spearhead of the revolution and to assume a dictatorial role until the time when the last vestiges of capitalism were removed. We must stop and note the enormity of the task confronting the Bolshevik leaders. If they were to be true to their Marxian commitment they had to attempt to wipe out all of the institutions, values and habit patterns acquired under years of bourgeois and feudal rule. They had to attempt to reeducate an entire people. Of course, if the revolution had occurred in a highly developed capitalist country such problems would not have arisen for the vast majority of people would then have been proletarianized. Marx, for example, had at best a dim notion of the process of transferring from highly developed capitalism into communism. Certainly, he thought the period of transition would be brief. The Bolsheviks' situation was completely different. They had to use education, propaganda, even coercion, to achieve their goals.

The same situation obtained in the economic realm. Despite the rapid growth of capitalism in Russia in the three decades before the revolution it was appropriately called an underdeveloped country. Further, the revolution and civil war which followed it had destroyed much of the small industrial base which had existed in 1917. If extensive economic development was necessary to achieve the Marxian vision, the Soviet Union would have to go through a quasi-capitalistic phase, which would in effect substitute for the technological expertise achieved elsewhere under capitalism. The country, under the leadership of the Party and the state apparatus, must develop itself, but somehow without the excesses of capitalism. To do this Lenin developed the notion generally called _state socialism_. Initially, this concept involved the appropriation of the means of production by the state as a whole so that the capital generated in the economy could be directed to insure maximum economic growth. The word "capital" is appropriate here in that there was still exploitation of a sort under state socialism. The worker still labored longer than necessary to support himself, and therefore generated a profit. Under socialism, however, this profit went to the state, which used it for the benefit of the entire society, not for one particular class. Because of this it is appropriate to say that the workers exploited themselves for their own benefit; they were exploited individually to achieve greater rewards collectively. Without getting bogged down in such arguments let us remember what Lenin was trying to achieve, the technological expertise of capitalism without its class structure.

Thus, it is not surprising that there was very little in the way of radical change in the economic structure in the immediate postrevolutionary period. Nor is it surprising to see policies promulgated which encouraged some individual competition such as the New Economic

Policy (N.E.P.) of 1921. Where Marx's economic dictum for a communist society had been "from each according to his ability to each according to his needs," under Lenin's transfer culture this became "from each according to his ability to each according to his work." One might observe that better capitalist doctrine never existed. There were, of course, numerous attempts to form communal organizations, particularly in the area of agriculture, but nothing like the massive, forced collectivization which characterized Stalin's reign.

In summary, the objectives of the Soviet transfer culture were the attainment of a highly developed economy, similar to that in the west, which would provide the technology and expertise necessary for communism. In addition, because of the nature of the Bolshevik Revolution, the entire value structure of the people must be changed so that they would possess the consciousness necessary for pure communism. It may well be that these two goals are antithetical, that the achievement of one of them makes the other impossible. After all, Marx long ago recognized that the thing which made capitalism so successful was its emphasis on individual reward for increased effort, which eventually leads to some sort of class structure. Leninism requires the individual initiative of capitalism, yet must avoid its class divisions—a difficult thing indeed. We shall meet this problem again in our discussion of Mao Tse-tung in the form of the question of "red" and "expert" (proletarianization and economic development), but for the moment it is necessary to move to a discussion of the theory of imperialism, Lenin's third major contribution to Marxian doctrine.

The Theory of Imperialism

We have seen how Lenin and numerous other followers of Karl Marx attempted to make his teaching more relevant to the twentieth century. In many respects this was not a difficult activity, for Marx had made some amazingly accurate predictions about the decline of capitalism. His assertion that capitalism would spread around the world seemed confirmed in 1917; in accordance with his second law of capitalist development, the monopolistic nature of modern capitalism was increasing; various business crises with world-wide implications seemed to be occurring more frequently; and the First World War seemed to confirm the hypothesis that capitalists would struggle mightily with each other for economic advantage. Despite the apparent correctness of these predictions, the key hypothesis of his entire analysis—that the lot of the proletariat would become increasingly worse and inevitably lead to revolution—simply was not happening. Indeed, proletarians in highly developed capitalist countries seemed every year to grow more content with their lot as they shared in the benefits of the expanding economies. This fact led some Marxists to adopt the revisionist position of working within the system, and others such as Lenin to foment revolution in an underdeveloped country, but the fundamental question remained—why was the proletariat in developed capitalist systems becoming increasingly passive? Addressing himself to this question in 1916 Lenin published a book entitled *Imperialism as the Highest Stage of Capitalism* which set out the basic ideas of the theory of imperialism. Before exploring these ideas it must be noted that the theory of imperialism was by no means original with Lenin. Many other Marxists, and some nonbelievers, had earlier advanced similar explanations for the decline in revolutionary activity by the proletariat, and Lenin borrowed freely from them. Still, Lenin's position as head of the only Marxist state in the world probably made it inevitable that his explanation would become *the* theory of imperialism.

At its broadest, the theory asserts that, despite the accuracy of his predictions concerning capitalism, Marx failed to see that it would move into a final stage of imperialism before collapsing. Although he clearly saw the world-wide spread of capitalism, Marx did not foresee some of the implications this would have, particularly on the working class of the industrialized countries. As Marx noted, the dwindling number of capitalists would be forced into a mad scramble for new markets because of overproduction and diminishing profits at home. Saddled with a great amount of nonexploitable constant capital (machinery) they would also seek out new sources of cheap raw materials and labor. They found these inexpensive raw materials and a brand new source of exploitable labor in the underdeveloped countries of the third world. With the armies of the capitalist states leading the way, they carved out different spheres of influence and proceeded to exploit the resources of these areas, both material and human, for all they were worth. With this seemingly inexhaustible labor supply, they could force the native population to work under deplorable conditions for tiny wages and extract tremendous profits. Some of the *super profit* derived in this manner could then be used to bribe their own internal proletariat with higher wages and better working conditions, thereby increasing consumption of the capitalists' products. Therefore, the internal proletariat of highly developed capitalist countries was bought off with the profit from the exploitation of the third world. Instead of the vast army of unemployed workers that Marx predicted, what resulted was an increasingly affluent middle class largely content with its lot, and a firm defender of the bourgeois status quo. Here we see the major reason for the lack of revolutionary activity on the part of the proletariat in industrialized countries. Their condition was not growing worse, but actually improving because of the exploitation of underdeveloped countries. This results in a new exploiter-exploited relationship; it is no longer the bourgeois class versus the proletariat but highly developed capitalist *countries* pitted against underdeveloped ones. Marx's class analysis had changed under the imperialistic stage of capitalism to a situation in which nation confronts nation.

This change to a nation-state orientation under the theory of imperialism cannot be overemphasized. Lenin had long ago recognized the revolutionary potential of nationalist slogans, and had utilized all classes within Russia to achieve the revolution. Still, classical Marxism was avowedly internationalistic, and all good Marxists thought of nationalist ideology as nothing but another capitalist attempt to keep the workers in one country from allying with those in another. Furthermore, the nation-state was a uniquely capitalist invention whose major purpose was to enhance the power position of the bourgeoisie; it would, after all, vanish under pure communism. The theory of imperialism united these seemingly contradictory goals of nationalism and internationalistic communism, and in the process provided a completely new revolutionary strategy for modern communism.

With the internal proletariat in industrialized countries bribed by super profits, Marxists now looked elsewhere for revolutionary groups. Under imperialism, revolutionary potential lay not with a particular class or alienated group within a society, but with entire exploited countries. Revolutionary activity would take place in the form of *wars of national liberation* which would unite nationalistic groups and communists within underdeveloped countries to throw off the capitalist yoke. Once successful, these nationalist movements should be controlled by communists who would then lead the country into a socialist transfer culture, following the pattern of the Soviet Union. It is easy to read too many things into the theory of imperialism; the revolutions in China, Cuba and Viet Nam, for example, fit perhaps too neatly. Nevertheless, contained within this theory are all the implications of most of the communist revolutions which have since occurred. Lenin had turned backwardness into a virtue; underdevelopment was now almost a prerequisite for revolution. What, we might now ask, of the old Marxian prophecy of an international class-based revolution? Obviously Marx's predictions had been greatly changed under imperialism; class revolt had become national revolution, and underdevelopment was a virtue. Despite these changes Lenin, once again, remained true to the broad outlines of Marx's analysis. As we saw in talking of socialism in one country, Lenin both altered the time sequence of Marx's predictions and used somewhat different means. Ultimately, however, the overall

Marxian analysis remained unchanged. Similarly, the wars of national liberation in underdeveloped countries were but the initial events which would eventually lead to world-wide communism. As these nationalist revolutions met with increasing success, they would cut off the source of cheap labor and raw materials from the capitalists. The super profits that the capitalists formerly reaped from these countries would no longer be available to them and in order to continue to make a profit they would have to go back to exploiting their own internal proletariat. Once this occurred, all of Marx's predictions concerning highly developed capitalism would come to be: overproduction, vast army of unemployed, crises, and revolution. The world-wide revolution would occur, although in a way not envisioned by Marx; even so, his overall analysis would be vindicated.

The changes wrought in classical Marxism by Lenin's revolutionary experience are obviously great, so great that we must now speak of Marxism-Leninism. It should be emphasized that we have only skimmed the surface of Lenin's contributions and neglected many aspects of his thought that others might deem crucial. He was, for example, most interested in the concept of dialectical materialism and wrote a goodly amount on that subject. Yet in his thoughts on the party, a socialist transfer culture, and the theory of imperialism, we clearly see the tremendous impact this man had upon the development of the doctrine. In a sense V. I. Lenin was a perfect Marxian man; a thinker and a revolutionary, a dedicated (almost doctrinaire) Marxist and an opportunist, unscrupulous yet idealistic. If, as Karl Marx said so many years ago, the point of philosophy was not to explain the world but to change it, Lenin surely was a success, for the world has not been the same since November of 1917.

BIBLIOGRAPHY

Deutscher, Isaac. *The Prophet Armed: Trotsky, 1879-1921.* New York: Oxford University Press, 1954.

_____. *The Prophet Unarmed: Trotsky, 1921-1929.* New York: Oxford University Press, 1959.

_____. *The Prophet Outcast: Trotsky, 1929-1940.* New York: Oxford University Press, 1963. This three volume study of Trotsky illuminates not only the career of one of the most brilliant of the "old Bolsheviks" but is an examination of the relationship between ideas and power politics which have no peer.

Fischer, Louis. *The Life of Lenin.* New York: Harper and Row, 1964. Believed by some to be the best biography of Lenin available.

Gay, Peter. *The Dilemma of Democratic Socialism: Eduard Bernstein's Challenge to Marx.* New York: Collier Books, 1962. A study of Bernstein and the German Social Democratic Party which is both good history and a penetrating analysis of the "dilemma" of a democratic socialist political party.

Hook, Sidney. *Marx and the Marxists: The Ambiguous Legacy.* Princeton, N.J.: D. Van Nostrand Company, Inc., 1955. Despite its date of publication, Hook's work remains one of the best studies of the richness of the communist movement after Marx. Contains both analysis and selected readings.

Meyer, Alfred G. *Leninism.* New York: Frederick A. Praeger, 1963. Meyer's study remains the best analysis of both the theory and practice of Leninism.

Wilson, Edmund. *To the Finland Station: A Study in the Writing and Acting of History.* Garden City, N.Y.: Doubleday & Company, Inc., 1953. A sweeping, somewhat journalistic study of various aspects of the history of ideas which culminated in the Russian Revolution. Written in a style which is both clear and enjoyable to read.

Wolfe, Bertram D. *Three Who Made a Revolution: Lenin, Trotsky, and Stalin.* New York: Dell Publishing Company, 1948. A brilliant study of the revolutionary personality as well as a description of the strategies involved in the Russian Revolution.

Original Works

Connor, James E., ed. *Lenin on Politics and Revolution.* New York: Western Publishing Company, 1968.

Lenin, V. I. *Selected Works.* 3 vols. New York: International Publishers, 1968.

Chapter 4

SOVIET
MARXISM

After the successes of 1917, Lenin's position as the leader of Russian Marxism was virtually unchallenged. He was, after all, the "father" of his country and, in spite of the many difficulties which confronted the Bolshevik regime during its early days, Lenin's stature could only be enhanced. Indeed his preeminence was such, particularly after the successful conclusion of the civil war in 1920, that the dictatorship of the proletariat became virtually the dictatorship of Lenin. While it is perfectly understandable that this would be the case, it provided a dangerous precedent for the development of Soviet Marxism; Lenin's tightly knit, highly centralized Bolshevik party provided all of the preconditions for the Stalinist totalitarianism which was to dominate the Soviet Union for almost thirty years.

It may seem strange that Stalin, in spite of the indelible imprint he left on present day Soviet life and despite his long tenure as head of the state, made at most minor contributions to the development of Marxist-Leninist ideology. Yet from another perspective such a situation makes perfectly good sense. The broad outlines of the Soviet transfer culture had been described by Lenin and what was now required was a practitioner to transform those outlines into reality. Whether a Lenin would have had the determination, patience, or, for that matter, the stomach to pursue the type of policies that characterized Stalin's reign of terror is, of course, a moot point. There is some evidence which we shall explore later which indicates that Lenin had real misgivings about the direction the regime was taking. Still, if a total transformation of the Russian

economy and the radical alteration of the beliefs of an entire people
were the stated prerequisites of pure communism, a good argument can
be made that some sort of Stalin-like era was a natural outgrowth of the
Bolshevik Revolution. If Lenin had provided all of the theoretical tools
for the future development of Soviet Marxism, Stalin used them with a
vengeance.

Stalin's rise to the pinnacle of power in the Soviet Union is an
extremely complex tale, one which is largely outside the confines of our
concern. However, during his early life and his rise to power he exhibited most of the personal traits which were to constitute his major
contributions to the doctrine. For almost thirty years Stalin *was* the
Soviet Union, his personal whims governed the state, making it impossible to ignore his personality.

Stalin was born to poor peasant parents in 1879 in a small village in
the Caucasus Mountains of Georgia. His father, Vissarion Djugashvili,
was apparently a rather bitter man who, it is sometimes said, took much
of his frustration out on young Josif (the pseudonym "Stalin" was
adopted later in his life). His father died when Josif was quite young,
leaving his upbringing and schooling to his mother. Through tremendous personal sacrifice she was able to provide the means for her young
son to study in Tiflis, the major city of Georgia, where he received his
education in a seminary. Whatever the quality of this education, Stalin
was to be plagued throughout his life by his Georgian background,
notably by his difficulties with the Russian language and by the general
"provincial" nature of his upbringing. The seminary apparently was a
center for the dissemination of liberal if not radical ideas, and the young
Stalin gradually came under the sway of them. He got into increasing
trouble with the school authorities and was finally dismissed for reading
banned books. By 1899, the year he was expelled from the seminary, he
considered himself a committed Marxist, although many commentators
doubt whether his knowledge of the doctrine was at all thorough. Stalin
was to spend much of the time between 1900 and 1917 in prison,
mostly in Siberia, a fact which surely indicates his dedication to the
cause. With the split between Lenin's Bolsheviks and the Mensheviks
occurring at the Second Party Congress in 1903, Stalin was increasingly
drawn to the Leninist notion of a tightly organized, revolutionary action
party. Some observers have noted that this was a perfectly natural
development in that Stalin was always a man of action, a practitioner,
and Lenin's call for agitation instead of discussion must have greatly
appealed to him. When he was not in prison Stalin became a major
Bolshevik figure in the Caucasus, organizing strikes and leading raids
against the Tsarist establishment. His relationship with Lenin during this

period was apparently that of a trusted functionary who could be counted on to carry out party directions to the letter. Certainly he was not well known, even in Russian Marxist circles. Writing theoretical treatises was the means by which young Marxists enhanced their reputations within the movement and although Stalin had done some writing it was not of the sort to attract much attention. Leon Trotsky, while not the most objective of observers, later asserted that he hardly remembered Stalin's name in May of 1917. He was, however, exactly the type of person that Lenin needed. He was tough, efficient, brave, and above all, loyal. It was not a coincidence that this was precisely the sort of person that Stalin himself found useful in his later rise to personal power.

Stalin's part in the revolution remains subject to a good deal of divergence in interpretation. Later Bolshevik accounts, written under the watchful eye of Stalin himself, place him at Lenin's side throughout the events of that year. While this seems to be an obvious fabrication, Stalin was a member of the Central Committee during the revolutionary year and later played an important role during the civil war. Throughout this period he accumulated a variety of titles and posts, the most important being the General Secretary of the party in 1922. Most of these positions added to the personal power of Stalin, but as long as Lenin was alive the figure of the latter dominated the revolution and its aftermath. When Lenin was taken ill in 1922 however, these offices proved quite useful in Stalin's bid to be his successor.

During the last several years of his life Lenin's relationship with Stalin began to sour. The leader became increasingly distressed with the problems of overbureaucratization and the arbitrary use of power by some of his subordinates. Stalin, in particular, seemed guilty of these offenses. In an early indication of what was to become a persistent theme of Stalinism, he had rather ruthlessly removed some Georgian Bolsheviks who favored more local autonomy for Stalin's native state. Stalin, whom one might think was ill suited at least by birth for the role, had become an advocate of Russification, that is, the spreading of Russian culture and language throughout the ethnically diverse country controlled by the Bolsheviks. Some commentators feel that the motivation behind such action was Stalin's mania for centralized bureaucratic control rather than any love of the Russian culture, but the results were the same.[1] Stalin was accused of "Great Russian Chauvinism" and castigated by Lenin for his high-handed tactics. These events in Georgia

---

[1] Varying opinions on this matter may be found in T. H. Rigby, ed., *Stalin* (Englewood Cliffs, N.J.: Prentice-Hall, Inc., 1966).

coupled with several others led Lenin to a growing distrust of Stalin which culminated in his famous last testament to the party in which he criticized Stalin's actions and recommended that he be removed from his position as General Secretary. This recommendation was never carried out. Stalin's position as General Secretary had given him sufficient power to prevent widespread circulation of Lenin's views and the ailing leader could not summon the strength to implement them. With Lenin's death in January of 1924 Stalin was very much in position to contend for power.

The period between 1924 and 1930 when Stalin achieved complete control is marked by a tremendously complicated series of maneuvers by various aspirants to Lenin's mantle. While we cannot discuss these events in any detail, some mention of them is necessary if only to indicate how different Stalin was from the other major Bolshevik figures. Stalin's primary rival, particularly during the early years, was Leon Trotsky, who probably had the best credentials to succeed Lenin. While he was a late convert to Bolshevism, Trotsky had served admirably during the revolution and was in large part responsible for the successes of the civil war. Trotsky was everything Stalin was not; a highly respected Marxist intellectual, well known for his contributions to the doctrine, and steeped in the western liberal traditions of the movement. Indeed, Stalin was easily distinguished from most of his Bolshevik colleagues; he was less educated, always somewhat provincial in his outlook, and above all untouched by the western liberalism which was an important part of the Marxist heritage.

Despite the fact that Lenin had mentioned Stalin and Trotsky as his most likely successors, few persons in leadership positions in the Bolshevik regime felt Stalin to be a genuine contender. In a sense this was a real asset for him since anyone with aspirations for power saw Leon Trotsky as their main obstacle, which led to numerous coalitions within the major decision-making organs designed to "stop Trotsky." The period between 1924 and 1930 saw a constant shifting of alliances among the major figures of the party. Stalin's role in this maneuvering apparently was largely that of playing the moderate, all the while using his position as General Secretary of the party to advance the careers of younger Bolsheviks who were loyal to him. By 1927 Stalin had amassed sufficient power to have Trotsky and his followers dismissed from the Politbureau, the central decision-making organ of the party, and by 1929 that group passed a resolution expelling him from Russia. In the same year, Stalin began the process of collectivization and relocation of the Russian peasantry, a series of events which resulted in enormous loss of life and property. Thus began the Stalinist reign of terror which, with varying intensity, was to last for almost twenty-five years.

Marxism-Leninism-Stalinism

We have already noted that Stalin's contributions to the development of Marxist-Leninist theory were rather small, whatever the impact of his policies on the life of the average Soviet citizen. Indeed, at some risk of oversimplification, it could be said that all of his ideological contributions revolved around the intensification of the doctrine of *socialism in one country* and the resultant enhancement of the Soviet nation-state. Stalin had exhibited his penchant for Russification and centralized control in his dealings with Georgia in 1923, acts which evoked Lenin's displeasure. Now he was in a position to apply the same types of devices throughout the entire Soviet state. From the ideological point of view it was essential that the young Soviet state develop the industrial base necessary for pure communism, as well as provide for the proletarianization of the people. Whether his motivation was born of a desire for a powerful Russian nation-state or from a commitment to Marxist ideas, Stalin was determined to industrialize the nation rapidly and was willing to inflict the costs that this action might entail upon the Russian people. With a planned economy directed from Moscow, it was possible to reinvest the capital generated throughout the country in heavy industry at the expense of consumer goods and general creature comforts for the people. Persons who dissented from such policies were easily dealt with through slave labor camps and the secret police. Whether such policies were necessary and whether the industrialization of the country would have occurred as rapidly with other economic measures are questions we cannot answer here. It is enough to say that, while the cost in human lives was tremendous, with Stalin's death in 1953 the Soviet Union had emerged as a major industrial power.

Industrialization was, however, only one of the two goals of the Leninist transfer culture and Stalin was equally interested in proletarianizing the people. It would be necessary to eradicate all bourgeois values, to remove those people who continued to hold them, and to develop a new "Soviet man," loyal to the regime and dedicated to the advancement of the Soviet state. Utilizing the same sort of centralized control, with the Communist Party and the secret police as the primary tools, Stalin produced what is generally recognized as the first truly totalitarian state the world had seen. Everything became a political matter; the heretofore private affairs of men were now matters of state concern. A gigantic propaganda machine, youth organizations, art, music, were all used to impose proletarian consciousness from above. With the party as the vanguard of the proletariat leading the way, every aspect of human experience was examined for its political import. School books were rewritten to reflect proletarian values and to correct bourgeois falsifications; socialist realism in art became the only permissible form; and a rigorous system of censorship was instituted to insure that no deviation from the party line occurred. Capping this gigantic system of state control was Stalin himself, a kind of giant puppeteer, pulling the strings to manipulate every aspect of Soviet life. The worship of Stalin as a great man became an integral part of the ideology. Indeed, there is evidence to indicate that Stalin believed that this sort of dictator worship was to become a permanent part of the ideology, even after his death.

It is almost impossible to describe the impact of these policies on the Soviet citizenry, peasants and high-ranking party members alike. The policy of forced collectivization in agriculture radically altered the lives of millions of peasants, while purges, capped by obviously staged trials systematically removed any potential dissenters from the society. By 1939 Stalin had achieved a true cultural revolution, forcing thousands of old Bolsheviks into slave labor camps, retirement, or death. The effect of all this was to develop a mass of people conditioned to respond to Stalin's personal notion of the correct path to socialism and to endure any hardships that journey might entail. All of the horrors of Stalin's domestic policies were rationalized as being necessary to the development of a strong Soviet state. This value of Soviet nationalism dominated the Stalinist ideology in other ways as well, notably in the area of foreign affairs.

At an earlier point we have noted some of the difficulties that Lenin faced in reconciling the goals of the Soviet nation-state with those of the international communist movement. After some equivocation, he opted for strengthening the socialist safe area in Russia while temporarily ignoring the world-wide revolution. Stalin, faced with the same set of problems, adopted a similar solution and expanded it to the extent that he is justifiably famed for his emphasis on the doctrine of socialism in one country. The implications of such a position both in terms of international communism and Soviet foreign policy are so vast that they constitute a genuine Stalinist contribution to the ideology and generate problems which remain to this very day.

Given what we know of his nationalist proclivities stemming from the early days of "Great Russian Chauvinism," it is perhaps not surprising to find that Stalin placed the interests of the Soviet nation-state above those of the international communist movement. Some of his earliest battles with Trotsky had resulted from Stalin's reluctance to involve the Soviet Union in "international adventurism." This does not mean that he doubted the eventual triumph of communism on a world-wide scale, but that he regarded the Soviet nation-state as being the prime vehicle for insuring that eventual victory. In its simplest terms, Stalin's policy was that the interests of the Soviet Union came first. When the base in the

USSR was reasonably secure, more aggressive action in the international area was in order: but if Soviet national interests were threatened, the international activity was suspended. This policy, in effect, made the international movement (the formal body of which was called the Comintern), a tool of Soviet foreign policy and made Communist parties in other states agents of the Soviet Union. Stalin's penchant for centralized control, which was manifested in so many ways within the USSR, was applied to the international movement. Everything was directed from Moscow. While other Communist parties throughout the world were theoretically equal, Stalin made it quite clear that the Communist Party of the Soviet Union (CPSU) was first among equals. This situation posed some very interesting problems for the parties in other countries; they were accused not only of advocating the overthrow of legitimate capitalist regimes, but of being the active agent of a foreign power dedicated to that goal. Further, they were constantly subjected to rapid shifts in the party line when it suited Stalin's plans for Soviet foreign policy. The most notable of these shifts occurred in 1939 when, after years of active opposition to Hitler's regime in Germany, Stalin signed the Nazi-Soviet Pact making the USSR and, consequently, the international movement, a temporary ally of a doctrine dedicated to the destruction of Marxism. Strange bedfellows indeed, but a quite logical manifestation of Stalin's "Soviet Union First" foreign policy.

Even more interesting were the consequences of this policy in countries where indigenous communist movements were in open rebellion against existing regimes. We shall explore the somewhat special case of China more fully at a later point but a brief mention of Chinese difficulties will illustrate the problems of running a world revolution from an apartment in the Kremlin. Following the current Moscow line of collaboration with other dissident groups within a society, the young Chinese Communist movement had allied itself with the bourgeois nationalists of Chiang Kai-shek only to have Chiang turn and slaughter thousands of communists. When the Chinese Communists, now under Mao Tse-tung, finally succeeded in 1949, it was largely without Soviet help and as the result of a strategy far removed from the model of the Bolshevik Revolution. Owing little to the Soviet Union, it was perhaps inevitable that the Chinese would begin to think for themselves in matters of doctrine as well as strategy. Further evidence of cracks in the monolithic façade of the Moscow controlled international movement was apparent during the 1940s. Joseph Broz Tito had succeeded in establishing a socialist regime in Yugoslavia through the use of a partisan army formed to combat the Nazi enemy. Tito simply refused to follow Moscow at every turn or to become a satellite of the USSR and this led to his expulsion from the international movement by Stalin.

All of these difficulties were to produce monumental problems for international communism after Stalin's death; in many ways the present warring factions within the movement can be seen as direct results of Stalin's conception of the role of the international movement. From the Stalinist perspective, the ideal situation was the general condition of Eastern Europe after the war which was a fortuitous blend of expanding the international movement and serving Soviet national interests. These satellite states were creations of the Red Army, clearly subservient to the USSR both materially and ideologically. They provided a buffer for the Soviet nation, ever fearful of German military might, while partially serving the ideological goal of spreading communism throughout the world.

From the ideological perspective perhaps the best word to use in summing up the career of Josif Stalin is consistency. From his earliest days his vision of the path to pure communism required a Soviet nation-state, economically and militarily powerful, and he was prepared to sacrifice anything to achieve that goal. Internally, this resulted in the slaughter of thousands, perhaps millions of people, many of them dedicated Bolsheviks. Externally, this vision reduced the once potent international communist movement to a puppet of the Soviet Union, a mere caricature of the movement of Lenin's time. It is quite tempting to see the mass horrors of the Stalinist era as a tragic mistake, the product of an insane mind bent on achieving tremendous personal power. Yet from an ideological perspective there was a cruel logic to his actions, a method to his madness. His task was to drag the young Soviet state into the twentieth century, to develop a strong economy, and to eradicate any vestiges of bourgeois life. By the time of his death in March of 1953, he had in many respects succeeded.

Soviet Marxism Since Stalin

Common sense tells us that when a dictator dies the country he was ruling ought to fall into mass confusion. When the one identifiable center of power ceases to exist, one might expect the people to feel a sense of great liberation and the beginning of an immediate and bloody struggle for power. While there was some of this type of reaction in the USSR at the death of Stalin, apparently the most general response was a feeling of relief, coupled with disbelief and disorientation. In a sense, the fact that there was no uprising and little chaos following his death is a tribute to the success of Stalin's policies. Vast numbers of people, if not happy with the Soviet regime, were conditioned to accept its rule, and even the demise of the "master conditioner" was not enough to produce outright rebellion. It is also a tribute to the rapid action and common sense of the remaining members of the ruling elite. The word "members" is appropriate, for Stalin had left no heir to his throne and there was no one man with sufficient power to establish authority. In many ways the situation was similar to that which occurred after Lenin's death, and the solution of the leadership elements of the state and Party was much the same. They reestablished the principle of collective leadership of the state and began an involved struggle for power which was to last ultimately until 1961. This leadership group, composed initially of Molotov, Voroshilov, Kaganovich, Mikoyan, Malenkov, Bulganin, Beria, and Khrushchev, was quick to realize that their collective safety as well as any personal aspirations they might have depended on having Stalin quickly forgotten. Thus a process of "silent de-Stalinization," as Wolfgang Leonhard calls it, began almost immediately.[2] A new purge which was begun by Stalin in his final years was halted and the principal figures in this so called "doctors' plot" were declared innocent. The number of members of the collective leadership was reduced by one when Lavrenti Beria, long hated as chief of Stalin's secret police, was declared an enemy of the state and removed from power.

These events are indicative of the general relaxation of totalitarian controls which followed Stalin's death. It can be argued that such a process was inevitable in order to secure support of party members and the people for the new regime. Nevertheless, few persons in the Soviet Union or, for that matter, in the world, were prepared for the total rejection of the Stalinist years which was to become the dominant theme of the latter 1950s. In pointing to these events and in marking their effect on Soviet ideology we have, for once, a rather clear benchmark— the Twentieth Party Congress of the CPSU held in February 1956.

If the period prior to the Twentieth Party Congress can be called the time of silent de-Stalinization, the Congress marks the beginning of overt and vociferous de-Stalinization. The dominating theme of the entire Congress was the errors of the former dictator. Beginning with speeches decrying Stalin's economic policies and censorship control, it culminated with Khrushchev's famous "secret speech" denouncing Stalin's cult in all of its manifestations. This Congress has been called the most important one held since the time of Lenin and from an ideological point of view that is correct. In the process of a wholesale renunciation of the Stalinist era, the collective leadership, dominated more and more by the figure of Khrushchev, adopted a series of policies which were to change the face of modern communism. For our purposes

---

[2]Wolfgang Leonhard, *The Kremlin Since Stalin,* trans. Elizabeth Wiskemann and Marian Jackson (New York: Frederick A. Praeger, 1962), pp. 63-119.

we can once again summarize these changes using the categories of internal and external reforms.

The most far-reaching alteration in internal policy was the rejection of the one man leadership which had been the cornerstone of Stalin's personal dictatorship. Khrushchev pictured Stalin as a man with a mania for absolute control who presided over the slaughter of millions of loyal citizens only to gratify his desire for personal power. Stalin was portrayed as the perverter of the Soviet state, a butcher who forced the Soviet people to conform to his personal whims in matters as far-ranging as architecture and economics. Quoting from Lenin's last testament, Khrushchev contrasted the democratic party of Lenin's day with the autocratic rule of Stalin, declaring the latter to have betrayed the goals of Bolshevism. One could go on, but it is enough to note here that this remarkable speech constituted a wholesale renunciation of the Stalinist regime and demanded a return to the true principles of Leninism.

Further attempts at reform on the domestic front saw the institution of some types of decentralization in decision making, and a gradual movement away from Stalin's emphasis on heavy industry in the economy. Once the Stalinist censorship system was loosened, all types of criticisms of his regime began to appear in print. All of these measures contributed to the period which is generally called the "thaw," a gradual movement away from the total political control of the prior era. We must note, however, that the type of criticism which emerged in the USSR after Stalin's death has to be taken in context. Stalin was condemned for denying the principles of Leninism and perverting the role of the party in building a socialist society. There was never any public doubt about those principles or, more importantly, about the ultimate control of the party as the carrier of revolutionary consciousness. However strange it may have seemed to Russians who thought Stalin and the party were one, or wondered why other dedicated party members had not seen Stalin's perversions at an earlier date and removed him, such was the new party line. Indeed, the very leaders who were now condemning Stalinist practices had achieved their positions of leadership under Stalin. Needless to say, this produced some rather difficult moments for the new leaders, to say nothing of problems in explaining their various roles under the dictator. Still, it was a liberalization of considerable magnitude when contrasted with the previous twenty-five years, and in a groping, limited way a return to some of the principles of Leninism.

In the international sphere the same general relaxation of control occurred, but here it had much more far-reaching consequences for Marxist-Leninist theory. Almost immediately after Stalin's death the collective leadership began making overtures to Marshal Tito of Yugoslavia in an effort to bring his country back into the international movement. Tito had been expelled from that movement in 1948 for refusing to follow Moscow's line in international affairs and for numerous heresies on the economic front. Even during the last years of Stalin's reign it had become obvious that Tito was not going to knuckle under to Moscow, and that the only way the monolithic façade of international communism might be preserved would be by invading the country. Short of this, Tito's brand of socialism might be seen as an attempt to apply the principles of Marx and Lenin under circumstances different from those in the Soviet Union and his experiment applauded as another way to build a socialist society. Stalin could not possibly have taken such a position for it would have denied his control of the international movement. If he could not control Tito, the latter must be declared illegitimate! Stalin's successors had no such qualms and saw a rapprochement with Yugoslavia as one method of establishing their legitimacy as rulers of the international movement. In May of 1955, a high-level delegation, headed by Khrushchev, went to Belgrade in an attempt to patch over grievances between the two countries and discovered that Tito was as adamant as ever about pursuing his own course. All that could be done was to recognize Tito and the Yugoslavian Communist Party as legitimate socialists and declare that their regime was striving for the same basic goals as the USSR. Once it was admitted that there might be ways to achieve socialism that were different from the Soviet pattern, a host of possibilities presented themselves. At the Twentieth Party Congress, Khrushchev and several other speakers formally proclaimed the doctrine of *different paths to socialism* which struck the final blow to Stalin's monolithic façade. Appealing with justification to the writings of Marx and Lenin, the speakers declared that there were numerous ways a socialist society might be achieved. At least three different paths were recognized: the traditional Russian Revolution model (by now idealized into an urban proletarian revolution), a nationalist oriented partisan army type (like Tito's), and a democratic revolution. While the last might seem to be a vast departure from the doctrine, we must recall that Marx himself admitted of the possibility of a democratic revolution in countries like England. Whatever the case, Moscow seemed to have given up its monolithic control of the international movement and the reactions to this action were almost immediate.

The combination of de-Stalinization and the rehabilitation of Marshal Tito's brand of socialism brought about revolutionary changes throughout the communist world. This was particulary the case in the Stalinist satellite countries of Eastern Europe where reformist groups began clamoring for radical changes. The agitation culminated in the summer of 1956 when workers' strikes broke out in Poland and, with ominous overtones, a new government in Hungary proclaimed itself in favor of a whole series of reforms including free speech and a type of multi-party system. The reformers in Moscow were losing control; eager for mild reforms in Stalin's policies, their actions had produced a revolutionary situation. Faced with the crumbling of empire in Eastern Europe and growing liberalization at home, they acted swiftly and decisively. The Hungarian regime was crushed by an invading Red Army, many Stalinist control devices were reinstituted, and reaction set in within Russia itself.

The announcement of different paths to socialism and the renunciation of complete control of the international movement had impaled the Soviet leadership on the horns of a dilemma. If complete control from Moscow was no longer possible, or, perhaps even desirable, did that mean that the Soviet Union was giving up its role as the leader of world socialism? Obviously it did not, and the question now was *how much* deviation from Moscow's wishes was possible; how much independence could be tolerated. This remains one of the central problems for the USSR today and has resulted in a pendulum-like movement with respect to international communism; at one time the hard line, as in Hungary or Czechoslovakia in 1968, at other times a toleration of experimentation or deviance within the movement. Short of a new type of Stalinist control, which seems impossible, the problem of the relationship between the USSR and the international movement will remain, for it involves the conflicting aims of Russian nationalism and international communism. A final ideological change which emerged from the Twentieth Party Congress exhibits the same general characteristics and has produced additional problems for modern Soviet communism. This is the doctrine of *peaceful coexistence*.

It was a long established Marxist tenet that communism was locked in an unceasing battle with the capitalist forces of oppression throughout the world. While the doctrine of socialism in one country and the alliance with western capitalist powers during World War II can be seen as deviations from this general policy, on the ideological level the doctrine remained firm: constant struggle and the eventual triumph of world-wide communism. While many of the other ideological changes of the Twentieth Party Congress could be justified as a return to Leninism, any change in this doctrine would be counter to the words of both Lenin and Marx who forsaw unceasing wars during the capitalist phase. Still, the reality of Soviet foreign policy for many years had been the tacit acceptance of coexistence, and at times cooperation with the enemy. To justify these actions, the leadership group now proclaimed that socialism had achieved sufficient power whereby it was no longer threatened with annihilation by the capitalist powers or, if it were, it would be a process of mutual annihilation. Modern weaponry, particularly the development of nuclear devices, made the prospect of all-out war between the two camps less than desirable. Thus, cooperation with the enemy was seen as necessary in the second half of the twentieth century. This did not, however, alter the basic premise of Marxism-Leninism that communism would eventually triumph. It was described as a change in tactics in that competition with the capitalists would be carried on in other ways. Later Khrushchev would declare that socialism would beat capitalism at its own game by outproducing it, and achieving world economic domination. Further, the Leninist doctrine of imperialism was given greater emphasis and small wars of national liberation in the third world were seen as sapping the strength of the major capitalist powers. Given these alterations in tactics, it became perfectly consistent for Khrushchev to proclaim coexistence and cooperation on the one hand and declare that socialism would bury capitalism on the other.

Still, the elevation of peaceful coexistence to the level of dogma displeased many loyal Marxists throughout the world. Indeed, as we shall see in the following chapter, it constitutes one of the main ideological arguments between the Soviet Union and China. Many Western observers see the doctrine of peaceful coexistence as the major symbol of a general deradicalization of Soviet Marxism and there is some basis for this view.[3] As a large and powerful nation-state, the USSR is bound to have a stake in preserving the status quo, irrespective of its ideology. But before we accept a view of the Soviet Union as growing fat and complacent, willing to join hands with capitalist countries in preserving their positions of mutual power, we must remember that the Marxist-Leninist ideology has had a great effect on the actions of the leaders of the Soviet Union, and that ideology requires further revolutionary changes in the world.

The more than fifty years of Soviet Marxism have produced numerous and far-reaching changes in Marxist-Leninist ideology. Still, one can contend that the broad outlines of Marxism-Leninism remain fairly intact, and that the alterations made by numerous leaders of the USSR have been merely tactical adaptations to fit changing circumstances. We have made no attempt to spell out the more recent twists and turns of Soviet policy largely in the belief that the ideological structure has remained fairly stable since the early years of de-Stalinization. Furthermore, without the perspective afforded by time it is difficult to know when such alterations are merely temporary. Finally, we have avoided extensive discussion of the prime problem of modern communism—the existence of another major interpreter of Marxism-Leninism who claims

---

[3]See the interesting discussion on deradicalization in Robert C. Tucker, *The Marxian Revolutionary Idea* (New York: W. W. Norton & Company, Inc., 1969), pp. 172-225.

that today's Soviet Marxism is a perversion of the original doctrine. That extensive discussion can no longer be avoided and we must turn to the political thought of Mao Tse-tung.

BIBLIOGRAPHY

Conquest, Robert. *Russia After Khrushchev*. New York: Frederick A. Praeger, 1965. One of the best of more recent attempts to assess the Soviet Union under Khrushchev's rule and to make predictions as to the future.

Crossman, Richard, ed. *The God That Failed*. New York: Bantam Books, 1965. Six eminent former sympathizers describe the reasons for their attraction to, and ultimate rejection of, communism.

Deutcher, Isaac. *Stalin: A Political Biography*. New York: Random House, 1960. A biography of Stalin which is actully a detailed analysis of Russian and Soviet society in the years encompassed by Stalin's life. First published in 1949 it has withstood not only the test of time, but of numerous carping critics.

Djilas, Milovan. *The New Class*. New York: Frederick A. Praeger, 1958.

———. *Anatomy of a Moral*. New York: Frederick A. Praeger, 1959. In these two volumes Djilas, a former Yugoslav official and dedicated Marxist, describes how the master's teachings have been perverted. *The New Class* is undoubtedly the more important of the two in terms of its impact and analysis.

Leonhard, Wolfgang. *The Kremlin Since Stalin*. New York: Frederick A. Praeger, 1962. A somewhat dated yet still interesting analysis of the critical period after Stalin's death. Noteworthy for its excellent description of Khrushchev's rise to power.

Lobkowicz, Nicholas, ed. *Marx and the Western World*. Notre Dame, Ind.: University of Notre Dame Press, 1967. A large collection of essays by eminent Marxist scholars focused upon, but not confined to, Marxism's relationship to the Western world.

Marcuse, Herbert. *Soviet Marxism*. New York: Random House, 1961. A high-level analysis of the Soviet conception of the transition to communism, including some interesting comparisons with the Western world.

McNeal, Robert H. *The Bolshevik Tradition.* Englewood Cliffs, N.J.: Prentice-Hall, Inc., 1963. A brief introduction to the period from Lenin through Khrushchev, including short biographies as well as a description of Bolshevism in power.

Petrovic, Gajo. *Marx in the Mid-Twentieth Century.* Garden City, N.Y.: Doubleday & Company, Inc., 1967. Petrovic, a Yugoslav, in this short volume attempts to synthesize the scholarship on the development of Marxian ideas and to determine the relevance of classical Marxism for contemporary times.

Original Works

Anderson, Thornton, ed. *Masters of Russian Marxism.* New York: Appleton-Century-Crofts, 1963.

Christman, Henry M., ed. with intro. *Communism in Action: A Documentary History.* New York: Bantam Books, 1969.

Stalin, Josif. "The Foundations of Leninism." In *Essential Works of Marxism,* edited by Arthur P. Mendel. New York: Bantam Books, 1961.

Trotsky, Leon. *The Revolution Betrayed.* New York: Merit Publications, 1937.

Chapter 5

THE
POLITICAL
THOUGHT
OF
MAO
TSE-TUNG

In spite of the fact that Lenin's theory of imperialism has prepared us for the phenomenon of a Marxist revolution in an underdeveloped country, the notion of Chinese Marxism still seems a bit strange. Indeed, the implanting of a technologically based Western European ideology in an economically backward Oriental culture has produced some interesting results. Having said this, one must still admit that the total impression of Chinese Marxism is quite consistent with the basic doctrines of classical Marxism-Leninism and that the political thought of Mao Tse-tung can be seen as a logical outgrowth of those classical doctrines. Some commentators would even argue that Mao has contributed very little to Marxist-Leninist theory and that any additions he has made are in the realm of the tactical application of classical ideas to the particular conditions of China.[1] However, if we attach any weight at all to the Marxist notion of the unity of theory and practice, even tactical adaptation of the doctrine will have a great effect on the theoretical base. Without getting deeply involved in the question of the originality of Mao's thought, let us simply say that his ideas are worth examining and that an understanding of Marxism-Leninism in the second half of the twentieth century seems impossible if we ignore Mao.

Mao's thought and personality do present us with a host of difficulties. Much as in the case of Stalin, Mao's works have been edited and

---

[1]Arthur A. Cohen, *The Communism of Mao Tse-tung* (Chicago: The University of Chicago Press, 1964).

changed at various times in order to establish his credentials as a major
Marxist theoretician. Further, his thoughts on even the most prosaic
matters are treated by the Chinese as absolute dogma and elevated to
the position of commands of God. To Western minds many of these
thoughts seem silly, if not simply absurd. Still, there is little doubt that
the figure of Mao Tse-tung has loomed large on the world scene, and
that his brand of Marxism has had great influence on many persons
outside of China itself. During a time when the rising aspirations of the
so-called "third world" have produced widespread instability and revolution, the Mao-led Chinese Revolution has become a major symbol of
success. To communists troubled by the apathy of the proletariat in
highly developed capitalist countries, Mao's model of a successful revolution in an underdeveloped country has become a source of hope for
the future of international communism. To Western capitalists, the
spread of Chinese influence under Mao has become one of the major
obstacles to world peace. If their assessments differ, both groups could
agree on his importance. Both groups could also probably agree on
Mao's central contribution to modern communism—the rural strategy.

Mao's Rural Strategy

It has often been said that China provided a nearly perfect test case for
the Leninist theory of imperialism. Here was a country which had long
dominated its neighbors, both militarily and culturally, only to succumb
to the superior technology and military strength of European colonial
powers. Carved up into spheres of interest by expanding Western capitalists, subject to the machinations of great power politics, the beginning
of the twentieth century saw China subservient in every sense of the
word. Faced with this condition of impotence, some Chinese saw a
solution in the wholesale importation of Western technology and culture, cthers in the return to the basic strength of a superior Chinese
culture. Given what we know of the process of cultural transformation
and rejuvenation, it was perhaps inevitable that certain Western values
were imported and altered to fit traditional Chinese patterns. Prime
among those Western idea systems was Marxism.

The Chinese Communist Party was established in 1921 in Shanghai;
Mao Tse-tung dates his personal conversion to the doctrine in 1920,
with an incubation period in Marxist ideas beginning in 1918. While the
history of the movement from its formation to final success in 1949 is a
fascinating study in modern revolution, we must confine ourselves to
only those aspects of that experience which have theoretical relevance.
However, there are several events in the history of the party and in the
intellectual development of Mao Tse-tung which set the stage for later

theoretical advances, notably the revolutionary strategy which evolved between 1920 and 1930.

Throughout its early days, the Party operated as if the classical model of a Marxian revolution had a direct application to China. That is, their efforts were largely concentrated on recruiting members of the proletariat and their organizational work was primarily in the larger cities. While Lenin's example in the Russian Revolution made the establishment of peasant *cadres* possible as well, there was no question in Lenin's mind that the proletariat retained its role as the leading element in revolutionary activity. Mao Tse-tung, although he was of peasant origin, held rather strictly to the classical line advocating an urban-based, essentially proletarian revolution. Indeed, his peasant background made him quite skeptical of revolutionary action on the part of the Chinese peasantry, a position closer to Marx than Lenin. Further than that, the urban-based activities of the Chinese Communist Party were at odds with the revolutionary advice of the Comintern emanating from Moscow—advice which emphasized the central role of the peasant class in underdeveloped countries. Both Lenin and later Stalin declared the peasantry to be a prime asset in revolutionary activity in China. While it is difficult to date precisely, Mao's position on this matter apparently began to change during 1925 and the change became decisive with his report on peasant activities in Hunan province in 1927. In that report Mao emphasized that most of the revolutionary activity in the province was being carried on by the poor peasants and that in the future they would play *the major role* in the Chinese Revolution. Indeed, Mao began to speak of the increasingly important role that the Chinese peasantry would play in *leading* the revolution, eventually coming to the position that the leadership elements of the Party would be drawn from the peasantry. Whether such a position constitutes a genuine contribution to Marxism-Leninism or not, Mao had definitely altered the tactics of revolutionary activity. Even Lenin, who used the Russian peasantry extensively and emphasized their role in revolutionary activity, never granted them leadership status. To Lenin's mind the peasantry constituted an allied force which was always to be subservient to the control of the class-conscious proletariat. Given the leading role of the Chinese peasants it was a natural, if not logical, step for Mao to declare that the focus of revolutionary activity ought to be carried out on the peasant's home ground— in the countryside, rather than the cities. Here then, are the three major elements of the rural strategy: a revolution led by poor peasants, a base in the inaccessible countryside, and the advocacy of guerrilla warfare. They constitute genuine Maoist contributions to the doctrine.

It can be argued that Mao's entire rural strategy is but an extension of the doctrine of imperialism, but if that is so it is a most important extension. Under imperialism, the stronghold of the foreign capitalists is bound to be in urban areas where their monopoly on the use of force is most effective. If this is the case, the urban area is the least likely place for revolutionary activity to occur, and the small urban proletariat, whatever the extent of its consciousness, is easily suppressed. In much the same fashion as Lenin's imperialism, Mao advocated gradually gaining control of the countryside where the capitalist armies were most vulnerable, assaulting the capitalist citadels in the cities only at the end of the revolution. Just as Lenin would have revolution in underdeveloped countries cut off the mother country's source of super profit and force internal exploitation, so Mao would surround the urban areas, thus insuring the eventual capitulating of the imperialist power. In support of this strategy, Mao urged the development of rural safe areas, where peasant support was assured and supplies were plentiful, to which the revolutionary army could retreat in the face of concentrated opposition. The essential element in guerrilla warfare is the ability of the armed forces to live with the people and to be able to fade back into the mass of peasants when required. From this rural safe area, the guerrilla forces would launch periodic attacks on the enemy, avoiding major confrontations where the enemy's superior firepower would prevail, all the while expanding the area under their control.

Guerrilla warfare against major Western powers has become common practice during the past several decades and, while there have been numerous refinements in the tactics of this type of military action, the basic strategy for this type of communist revolution originated with Mao Tse-tung. From the theoretical perspective the entire rural strategy can be seen as an adaptation of the basic teachings of Marx and Lenin to Chinese circumstances. The leadership role of the peasantry was undoubtedly dictated by the large number of peasants in China whose support was necessary for a successful revolution. In a sense, Mao was altering the doctrine to maximize his support, but the alteration in Marxist-Leninist theory nevertheless remains. Similarly, in an effort to gain further support from the Chinese people, Mao developed a concept of the advancement to and through socialism which differs from the Soviet model, and may be seen as another contribution to the doctrine.

The Path to Socialism

Owing to the extremely backward state of the Chinese economic base, it was generally conceded that the country could not immediately move into a socialist phase after a successful revolution. Further, Mao realized that it would be necessary to retain the technical skills and the general support of many classes in order to develop the industrial base necessary for the march to communism. We have seen that Lenin had similar problems in the USSR and tolerated a degree of bourgeois capitalism, particularly under the New Economic Policy. Still, Lenin was never very happy with the existence of a small bourgeois class, however weak, for he was sure that they would eventually try to subvert revolutionary goals. Stalin later solved this problem by eradicating all bourgeois elements in the society. Because of the semifeudal nature of China, Mao contended that it would be necessary to adopt a somewhat different solution. He proclaimed the existence of a People's Democratic Dictatorship which would unite all anti-imperialist elements within the country in support of the revolutionary regime. Particularly noteworthy was his treatment of the bourgeoisie in Chinese society. He made a distinction between the *national bourgeoisie*, who were anti-imperialist and the *international bourgeoisie,* who were deemed lackeys of the imperialist powers, labeling the latter intractable foes of the regime. The national bourgeoisie were, however, to be considered part of the class bloc which would lead the country through a presocialist phase into the establishment of a socialist society—they were to be considered legitimate members of the People's Democratic Dictatorship. Here we see another attempt by a Marxist to integrate the values of nationalism and communism for the purposes of revolution. Mao is willing to tolerate the existence of bourgeois elements within the society, even to declare them an integral part of the process of developing socialism.

Although this is a significant departure from earlier thought it must not be overemphasized, for the national bourgeoisie must be *nationalist* and ultimately will be assimilated into a single class society. Indeed, the economic developments within China from 1953 on can be seen as a continuing process in reducing the power of these bourgeois elements. The significant fact is that this will be accomplished through the reeducation of the bourgeois group within the society. Articulating what seems to be a recurring theme of Chinese communism, Mao declared that the bourgeoisie would be gradually reeducated so that they would gain the *people's perspective*, thus becoming full-fledged members of the socialist regime. In discussing this matter of the reeducation of the population Mao gave great emphasis to the process of proletarianization. Recall that the two major difficulties for any modern communist regime are the establishment of an industrial base and the development of a class-conscious proletariat. While Stalin's totalitarian state attempted to propagandize the entire population and was somewhat successful in that endeavor, there is little doubt that the Soviet Union had expended most of its effort on the development of an industrial base. On the contrary, throughout his writings Mao placed heavy emphasis on the proletarianization side of the coin. People of all classes are called upon to struggle with themselves to cast off old bourgeois values and to approach their everyday problems from the perspective of the new morality. In support of this there has been extensive experimentation with thought control ("brainwashing," to Western eyes), where the individual is guided through a process of renunciation of his old life to the affirmation of a new existence wherein all problems are approached from the people's perspective. The ultimate goal of this process of self-criticism and reevaluation is to produce an entire population which views its world from a Marxist-Leninist perspective and uses the example of the life of Mao as a guide to everyday action. Simply, the desired result is an entire population which is a carbon copy of Mao Tse-tung. It is in this way that Mao's every thought is seen as an application of Marxism-Leninism to Chinese circumstances, something to be copied by all good communists.

Emphasizing what Mao calls the red side of the *red/expert* problem (i.e. proletarianization/industrialization) does not mean that industrialization is to be ignored. No good Marxist could infer that. On the economic front the Chinese Communist regime has engaged in numerous experiments in an attempt to advance industrialization. Indeed, Mao advanced the thesis that because China was so backward it could leap forward economically at a faster rate than even the Soviet Union, with the use of vast peasant communes and backyard industries. Still, Mao seems above all concerned that the population shall become red and if the industrialization of the country must suffer slightly in order to insure that goal, so be it. As we shall see in the forthcoming discussion of the Sino-Soviet rift, one of Mao's persistent criticisms of the leadership of the Soviet Union is that it has lost its touch with the people, becoming a bureaucratic class which advances its own interests at the expense of the ongoing revolution. This general theme of struggle, self-criticism, and interaction with the environment can also be seen as manifesting itself in another of Mao's developments in Marxism-Leninism: the notion of contradiction.

On Contradiction

While Mao is generally given credit for his contributions on the question of a rural strategy for revolution in underdeveloped countries, the Chinese, apparently stung by the charge that this was merely a tactical adaptation of Leninism, have attempted to emphasize other more theoretical contributions of their leader. Following a long and distinguished line of Marxist thinkers, Mao is said to have made genuine theoretical breakthroughs in the study of dialectical materialism, notably through his ideas on contradiction in socialist societies.

In detailing his explanation of the Chinese path to socialism, Mao said that there would be different classes in the society united primarily by their opposition to imperialism. Given this, Mao asserted that there would naturally be conflict and struggle between these groups as they pursued their goal. This raised no real difficulty, for these groups were united in moving toward a socialist society. However, Mao went on to contend that these contradictions between people would continue even under socialism and, in addition, that there would be increasing contradiction between man and nature as the industrial base was advanced. This doctrine of *nonantagonistic contradictions* constituted a specific denial of existing Soviet ideology and, despite some Leninist precedents, seems to be a genuine addition to the doctrine.

In classical Marxism the major source of conflict in the world was the struggle which was constantly occurring between antagonistic classes. A basic Marxist teaching was that once the source of such conflict was eliminated through the institution of a classless society, peace and harmony would prevail throughout the world. Mao reaffirms the basically antagonistic nature of class conflict or *antagonistic contradictions*, and asserts that this type of conflict can only be resolved through complete victory of the proletariat: there must be no compromise in the unending battle with capitalist powers. There are however, other types of contradictions which exist among the people which are not antagonistic (nonantagonistic contradictions) and which may be peacefully resolved. Perhaps we can characterize this type of conflict as resulting from a disagreement of the means to be pursued in achieving socialism. All agree on the goal, but differ, and are in conflict, on how to get there. In any case, the Soviet Union, adhering to the classical line, had long ago asserted that conflict and contradiction had ceased to exist within its territory, and the Maoist notion of the necessity of nonantagonistic contradictions during the building of socialism was a direct refutation of that assertion. Further, Mao seems to be saying that this contradiction is a rather desirable thing for it would produce, in proper dialectical fashion, a series of *qualitative changes* in the society, since the tension of the conflict would produce a synthesis which was notably better than that which preceded it. Thus a socialist society would be in a state of *permanent revolution* with the results of these contradictions constituting qualitative changes or revolutions. Even after the establishment of a communist society, the conflict between the forces of production and the relations of production will generate conflict and that, in turn, will produce conflict among the people. What Mao has done is to remove class as the sole source of contradiction in Marxist-Leninist theory; surely this is a significant alteration in the doctrine. Before we make too much of it however, let us remember that the type of conflict to which

Mao is referring is a different thing from antagonistic class conflict. While nonantagonistic contradictions will continue to generate conflict even after the establishment of pure communism, there will be no further changes in social or economic forms, i.e. no antithesis to pure communism, for the basic dialectical process in history will have ended. Parenthetically, it is interesting to note that one of the major sources of this conflict will be man's continuing interaction with nature. This idea of a perpetual war against nature in an effort to harness its power is, of course, an essential part of Marx's Promethean image of man, but it is somewhat strange to have it emphasized by a Chinese whose traditional culture, at least in part, preached basic harmony with natural forces. Whether this subject/object, man/nature juxtaposition in Mao's thought is a result of Marxism or not, it is a theme which persists in his writings. Another theme of Chinese communism, which at least since 1957 can be called persistent, is an ongoing conflict with the other major socialist power in the world. We have mentioned several points of disagreement between the Soviet Union and China in the foregoing discussion, now we must look more systematically at the Sino-Soviet split.

China and the USSR

The Sino-Soviet split must be called one of the most important events in the history of international communism. The prospect of the two major socialist powers in the world, supposedly friendly allies in the fight against capitalism, lashing out at one another on ideological grounds, even engaging in fighting on their common border, is rather difficult to understand. Marx or Lenin, to say nothing of Stalin, would have been horrified by this apparent breakup in the international communist movement. Whether the ideological and great power difficulties between these two countries are a permanent facet of modern communism is a question beyond the scope of this book. We can say, however, that despite numerous attempts at accommodation, the disputes rage on with little hope for complete resolution in the near future. For the student of political ideologies this presents a fascinating area for study because the battle for ideological supremacy brings out numerous contradictions and variations in the doctrine which might otherwise be papered over in the name of a united front. Once again, we shall emphasize the ideological nature of the conflict, largely ignoring the very real interests of the two nation states in competition for territorial and economic domination. While there are commentators who will defend the proposition that differences between China and the Soviet Union began as early as 1949 with the success of the Chinese Communist Party, a far more concrete benchmark appears to be the death of Josif Stalin and the emergence of de-Stalinization in the Soviet Union.

The Chinese response to the de-Stalinization policies of the Twentieth Party Congress of the CPSU was rather ambivalent. Reacting to the wholesale denunciation of the Stalinist era by his successors, Mao agreed that Stalin had made some errors; in particular he denounced the Stalinist cult of the hero. Still, the tone of Chinese de-Stalinization was far more muted than the same process in the USSR. Despite his errors, Mao asserted that Stalin was a great leader of Marxism-Leninism and had performed a most valuable role in developing the Soviet Union economically. In retrospect it is obvious that the tone of Chinese responses to Stalin's death was far more laudatory than that of the USSR, undoubtedly presaging the much more acrimonious ideological splits of recent years. In a sense, however, one might argue that some sort of contest for ideological supremacy was inevitable from the beginning. As far back as 1936, Mao declared that he was not fighting a revolution in China only to turn the country over to Moscow. Further, the Chinese revolution was successful without a great deal of Soviet support and it evolved a strategy for revolution which was far different from the classic Russian model. This being the case, it was only natural for Mao to declare that his revolutionary model was more appropriate for Marxists in the third world, and that the winds of revolution would blow much more strongly from the East during the imperialist phase of capitalism. Implicitly, then, merely by existing as an alternative to the Soviet model, the Chinese Revolution offered a different way. It is, of course, a long way from the establishment of an alternative revolutionary model to the acrimonious exchanges which marked relations between the two socialist powers in the 1960s, but in a sense it all revolves around Stalin's figure and his policies.

Faced with increasing denunciation of Stalin by the USSR, Mao found himself in a difficult position. He believed that strong party leadership was necessary in order to achieve the goals of a socialist state and knew that a good deal of suffering on the part of the Chinese people would be part of that process. One can argue that under such circumstances it is necessary to invent an almost superhuman leader who can act as a symbol for the struggle of all the people and serve as a source of inspiration. Briefly, Mao needed a new "cult of the hero" in order to speed the development of China, yet he was faced with constant denunciation of that concept from the Soviet Union. This, as much as anything, seems to be the reason for the Chinese emphasis on Stalin as a hero of Marxism-Leninism. They were going through a process similar to that of the Soviet Union from 1930 to 1953 which necessitated tremendous sacrifice and iron-handed control. While Stalin could be condemned for certain excesses, a wholesale denunciation of his type of regime might lead to an undermining of Mao's position. Much of this is, of course, in the realm of speculation, and there are other ideological points where the split between the two powers is more obvious and more ominous. Using one of the nastiest words in Marxist-Leninist jargon, the Chinese accuse the Soviet Union of a general policy of *revisionism.*

There are many facets to this particular charge but the most general statement that can be made is that the USSR is seen as pursuing a policy of conciliation with capitalism, and denying the goals of Marxism-Leninism. Specifically, the Chinese simply refuse to accept the doctrine of peaceful coexistence with capitalism. We have seen that Khrushchev's notion of peaceful coexistence does not deny the ongoing struggle with capitalism but affirms that all-out war would be mutually destructive and must be avoided. Adopting a pugnacious stance, at least ideologically, Mao declared that Khrushchev was selling out to capitalism, denounced the West as a "paper tiger," and asserted that China with her vast population would survive a nuclear war. This is a particularly difficult notion to understand for we are forced to compare public statements with actual practice. Despite his denunciation of the capitalist powers as "paper tigers" and however often he calls for all-out war, Mao's actions have not been much more bellicose than those of the USSR. We cannot go into the various armed conflicts that the Chinese have had with the West, nor can we examine the Chinese role in fomenting revolutionary movements in other underdeveloped countries. What Mao seems to be trying to achieve by denouncing peaceful coexistence and adopting this belligerent stance is the unification of the Chinese people in the face of outside enemies. Furthermore, such a position places Mao in the fore-front of revolutionary ideology in modern times and permits him to call the Chinese the true carriers of the revolutionary idealism of Marx and Lenin. Perhaps he is only scoring some ideological points at the expense of the Soviet Union but the image of Mao, the eternal revolutionary, has great attraction for dissatisfied people throughout the world.

Peaceful coexistence is not the only manifestation of Soviet revision-ism condemned by the Chinese. They see the USSR illicitly experiment-ing with various economic reforms at home, and attempting to advance Soviet national interests abroad at the expense of world revolution. Most important from the ideological perspective, they accuse the leader-ship elements of the USSR of divorcing themselves from their own people, constituting a leadership elite which advances its interests at the expense of the Soviet people. We noted earlier that Mao viewed classes and nonantagonistic class conflict as part of the process of building socialism in China. From his point of view, the Soviet Union, while declaring that it had achieved a single class society, was actually covering over the existence of a vast bureaucratic class which was so eager to preserve its position of privilege that it had become counterrevolutionary. This is, of course, a most serious charge. If the Soviet Union after fifty years of building socialism has succeeded only in producing a society based upon a different class relationship, there must be something wrong with the Soviet model. In criticizing the class-based nature of the Soviet Union, Mao exhibited two additional traits that seem to be persistent in his thought.

Despite his repeated exhortation to his countrymen to reeducate themselves, Mao has considerable dislike for formal education. There are numerous references in his writings to the basic wisdom of the uneducated masses, and warnings against producing a technologically sophisticated elite that is divorced from that wisdom. Related to this is his fear of producing a Soviet-like managerial class which advances the economy at the expense of proletarianization. There is now evidence to show that the Cultural Revolution of 1966-69 was in part instituted in an effort to break down growing class stratification in China. By sending the most radical elements in the population, the students, out to destroy pockets of bourgeois influence throughout the country, Mao was giving an object lesson to those who might stray from his model. Furthermore, by insisting that these student groups then retire to rural areas to work with their hands among the peasants, he was again emphasizing the innate wisdom of the common worker. Through all of these actions Mao shows, by implication at least, what is wrong with the USSR.

In summary, let us stray briefly from the ideological plane to say that much of the Sino-Soviet conflict seems to be the result of the differing perspectives of a developed nation-state and one that is still in the early stages of economic development. From the Chinese perspective the Soviet Union has become antirevolutionary because it is basically satisfied with its position in world affairs. As a major power, the USSR seems to support the maintenance of the status quo, both by accommodating competing capitalist powers and by supporting existing regimes irrespective of their ideology. Insofar as support of the status quo means keeping China in a relatively powerless position, the USSR is bound to be condemned by Mao as reactionary. It is in this sense that Mao can speak of the possibility of an alliance between the USSR and the United States designed to keep China in its present condition of relative impotence. From their "have-not" perspective the Chinese demand change and revolution throughout the world and condemn their fraternal socialists in the Soviet Union for collaborating with reactionary capitalists. Here, for the final time, we observe the difficulty of reconciling the aspirations of nation-states with the internationalism of Marxism-Leninism. This is a persistent problem of modern communism which shows no signs of being solved in the near future.

Mao Tse-tung as a Symbol

We cannot leave the subject of Chinese communism without briefly commenting on the appeal Mao Tse-tung seems to have for self-declared revolutionaries around the world. Despite the apparent silliness of many of its pronouncements, the little red book of Mao's thoughts is waved and quoted at all sorts of protest demonstrations. The most obvious reason for such veneration is that Mao constitutes a symbol of a dedicated revolutionary, constantly struggling against overwhelming odds to achieve his goals. While this is a rather overdrawn picture, there is a good deal of truth in it and as such it is an important phenomenon of modern communism. To put it too simply, Mao has seized the revolutionary initiative from the Soviet Union and he, along with figures such as Fidel Castro, Ho Chi Minh, and Che Guevara, is seen as the true carrier of revolutionary consciousness in modern times. In a way, Mao's notion of struggle summarizes all of the romantic appeal of his character—struggle against nature, struggle against tremendous odds, struggle to retain the purity of the revolution—all these are popular themes with those who desire radical change.

Also, his reliance on youth, willingness to experiment with all sorts of techniques to advance his cause, and his emphasis on the contribution of every individual in a society seem to be popular themes throughout the world. In the end, however, it is the Maoist model of a successful revolution in a terribly underdeveloped country that provides Mao with his greatest claim to fame. While highly developed countries are scarcely free from strife in the second half of this century it is in underdeveloped countries, as they say, "where the action is." Here Mao's thought provides clear guidelines for action and his teaching has significantly influenced most of the revolutionary figures in the third world. In contrast to the rather staid, "fat" communists of the Soviet Union, Mao Tse-tung provides a somewhat romantic example that radical change is still possible.

This is no place for a summary of the teachings of Marx and Engels as they have been developed and applied over the past century. In a very real way the four previous chapters provide only the bare outlines of the development of Marxist-Leninist ideology, thereby in themselves constituting a summary. Neither is this the place for an attempt at an extended critique of those doctrines. As was stated in the introductory discussion, the major aim is an understanding of the ideology as a prelude to evaluation. Still, there are numerous problems of communism which have entered the discussion, ranging from the lack of a truly communist revolution anywhere in the world to the difficulties of integrating nationalist values with Marxist internationalism. These problems surely are the beginning of a critique for anyone who feels the need to attempt one. Indeed, if there is one thing we possess in abundance in the West it is authoritative, and, in many instances, well-reasoned criticisms of communist thought. Finally, as we move on to the second of the three idea systems under consideration, we will find that these other ideologies will afford us an excellent critical perspective of communism. In many ways one could look a long while before finding a more vehement critic of Marxism than a reformed Marxist; fascism offers us just such a person in its founding father, Benito Mussolini.

BIBLIOGRAPHY

Cohen, Arthur A. *The Communism of Mao Tse-tung.* Chicago, Ill.: University of Chicago Press, 1964. In this tightly reasoned volume Cohen argues that most of Mao's so-called contributions to Marxism are but extensions of earlier doctrines advanced by Marx, Engels, and Lenin. It is one of the few books available dealing explicitly with Mao's thought.

Lifton, Robert J. *Thought Reform and the Psychology of Totalism.* New York: Norton, 1961. A ground-breaking study of Chinese attempts at thought control, based upon the author's interviews with refugees who went through the process. Notable not only as a psychological study, but for its presentation of certain apsects of ideology.

Schram, Stuart R., ed. *The Political Thought of Mao Tse-Tung.* New York: Frederick A. Praeger, 1963. Selections from the writings of Mao and other Chinese communist leaders follow a lengthy historical introduction by Schram.

Schurmann, Franz. *Ideology and Organization in Communist China.* Berkeley, California: University of California Press, 1966. A fascinating attempt to show the interrelationship between Maoist ideology and the organization structure in China. Schurmann's discussion of Mao's "thoughts" is particularly enlightening.

Snow, Edgar. *Red Star Over China.* New York: Modern Library, 1944. The classic study of Mao Tse-tung and his movement.

Original Works

Chai, Winberg, ed. *Essential Works of Chinese Communism.* New York: Bantam Books, 1969.

Schram, Stuart R., ed. *The Political Thought of Mao Tse-Tung.* New York: Frederick A. Praeger, 1963.

For the student interested in exploring other aspects of the immensely complex phenomenon of modern communism, the following are offered as points of departure.

Debray, Regis. *Revolution in the Revolution?* New York: Monthly Review Press, 1967. A fascinating short work about the conflict in ideology and in revolutionary strategy between various warring communist camps in a Latin American setting.

Draper, Theodore. *Castroism: Theory and Practice.* New York: Frederick A. Praeger, 1965. The best introduction to both the thought and the application of the phenomenon called Castroism.

Fall, Bernard B., ed. *Ho Chi Minh on Revolution.* New York: New American Library, 1968.

Gyorgy, Andrew, ed. *Issues of World Communism.* New York: D. Van Nostrand Company, Inc., 1966.

Lowenthal, Richard. *World Communism: The Disintegration of a Secular Faith.* New York: Oxford University Press, 1964. A cogent discussion of the problems of the international movement from a theoretical perspective.

Scalapino, Robert A., ed. *The Communist Revolution in Asia.* Englewood Cliffs, New Jersey: Prentice-Hall, 1965.

Chapter 6

FASCISM

How does one begin to write about a set of ideas as apparently varied as fascism? To persons who lived through the Second World War the term itself is almost a synonym for evil, for the "war to defeat fascism" is a bitter memory. Even those who had no first hand experience with the fascist regimes of Italy and Germany invariably use the word with a bad connotation. When policemen are thought to be overzealous in performing their duty they are called fascist; sometimes people who deem themselves good conservatives are referred to in the same vein, and we speak darkly of fascist tendencies in the modern nation-state. It is probably inevitable that any word which is frequently employed in common language will lose some of its initial meaning and will be used in a vague or general way. Still, in the case of this particular word, the situation is rather absurd. Sometimes it seems that almost anything a person dislikes is arbitrarily labeled fascist. There are some reasons for such a situation. Fascism as a set of ideas was never as clearly formulated as Marxism-Leninism, although I believe there is more coherence among the ideas than is commonly supposed. Further, there is a tendency to refer to fascism as a rather peculiar phenomenon, existing only during a particular period in history and largely confined to two nation-states, Nazi Germany and Fascist Italy. Because of this identification with historical nation-states there is a tendency to refer to all of the actions of those states as somehow expressive of the phenomenon of fascism. It is as though every action of the Soviet Union were to be seen as expressive of the doctrine of Marxism-Leninism when we know that the Soviet nation-state is best seen as an attempt to apply certain ideas which exist independently of their application. There is a relatively coherent set of ideas called Marxism-Leninism and there have been several attempts to apply those ideas to different nations, but this is not to say that the ideas are to be equated with every practical policy of the particular nation-state. The same thing obtains with fascism. It can be viewed as a set of ideas which attempts to say something about man, his society, and his future development, and that idea set can be analyzed separately from the attempts to apply it to particular nations.

This difficulty is compounded by the fact that we have had surprisingly little scholarship on fascism as an ideology. There are numerous books on Mussolini's Italy or biographical studies of Hitler, or discussions of fascism in other countries, but there have been few attempts to look at the ideology per se. While recent scholarship has remedied this situation somewhat, notably through A. James Gregor's excellent study of the *Ideology of Fascism,*[1] the contrast between the number of studies of fascist ideology and of Marxism-Leninism remains quite striking. Again, there are reasons for this. Drawing support from statements of prominent fascists, many commentators have contended that there is no ideology of fascism, that it is a doctrine lacking in principle which celebrates irrational action for its own sake and that to analyze it as though it were a relatively coherent set of ideas is only to distort it. Such an interpretation of fascism sees it as a highly pragmatic form of nationalism and views any attempt to examine it using intellectual categories as doomed to failure. Other interpretations place great emphasis on the leadership element in fascist doctrine and assert that leadership is so fundamental to the movement that a study of fascism ought to consist of a series of political biographies.

There is some truth in both of these positions. The role of leadership in fascist regimes is crucial, so much so that Mussolini could declare late in life, "What would Fascism be, if I had not been."[2] Further, there is little doubt that fascism celebrated a form of irrationalism and that its doctrines changed considerably with the passage of time, making it difficult to apply the traditional tests of coherence and consistency to the idea system. Despite all of these difficulties it is possible to see certain common fascist traits and to develop a rather coherent fascist ideology.

A glance at the table of contents reveals an additional point concerning our treatment of fascism; four chapters are devoted to Marxism, three to democratic theory, and only two to fascism. Such a structure

---

[1] A. James Gregor, *The Ideology of Fascism* (New York: The Free Press, 1969).

[2] Benito Mussolini, quoted in Herman Finer, *Mussolini's Italy* (New York: Grosset & Dunlap, 1965), introduction.

reflects the author's judgment as to the importance of these respective idea systems for modern times, as well as an estimate of those persons most likely to read this book. Further it means that fascism will be treated largely in the reflected light of communism and democracy; that is, it will provide us with a critical perspective of the other two idea systems. As such, our treatment of fascism will be quite brief, although hopefully not overly superficial.

As a final introductory point, mention must be made of the rather strict separation herein made between fascism and national-socialism. In common language, fascism is often used as a general term to refer to the between-war political structures in Italy and Germany. As previously noted, such use is inappropriate in that a system of fascist ideas can be seen as existing independent of these two particular nation-states. Further complicating this matter is the fact that the founding father of the movement, Benito Mussolini, served as the leader of Italy during its fascist period. Hence, it becomes quite difficult to separate the doctrine from its applications in the Italian nation. While we should not see every action of Mussolini as head of the Italian state as an expression of fascist doctrine, in many ways Mussolini's Italy can provide us with an ideal type of a fascist regime. If this is the case, the actions of other so-called fascist leaders can be evaluated in terms of the degree to which they conform or deviate from the Italian model. From this perspective, Adolf Hitler, while his regime expressed many fascist traits, is not appropriately called a fascist. At best, National-Socialist Germany can be seen as an extreme form of fascism, at worst it can be viewed as the most virulent form of biological racism the world has ever seen. Such distinctions will become clearer as we pursue the subject matter, but for the moment the term fascism refers to the ideas of Benito Mussolini and their application in Italy.

The Evolution of a Doctrine

While it is certainly true that Marxism did not emerge full blown from the pen of Karl Marx at any particular date, we have argued that the development of that doctrine followed a rather consistent pattern at least from 1844 on. Such is not the case with fascism. There is a parallel between the doctrines in that they both were articulated largely by one man; thus we can speak of a founding father or at least a small group of founding fathers. At first glance, however, Mussolini's ideas seem to have undergone a great deal of change during his lifetime. He began his political career as a confirmed Marxian socialist, added some rather vague voluntarist and elitist elements at an early date, took a seemingly abrupt turn to Italian nationalism during the First World War, and emerged from that war proclaiming the existence of something called fascism. Even then the doctrine was by no means complete; further developments included the addition of an ethical dimension to the conception of the state, the insertion of a form of racism, and finally the advocacy of a rather radical form of socialism. What are we to do with such a grab bag of ideas? To many commentators the most radical change in Mussolini's intellectual development occurred in 1914 when, as editor of the major socialist paper *Avanti!*, he abandoned the socialist line of international class warfare and called for the intervention of Italy in the "bourgeois" World War. Whatever the reasons for this change, or however great a change it actually was, it provides us with an excellent vantage point for viewing the evolution of his ideas. Let us, then, look at the socialism of Mussolini prior to 1914 and then attempt to determine how orthodox he was with an eye toward partially explaining the radical change which occurred during the First World War.

As Ernst Nolte has observed, even today one can get cries of surprise or at least raised eyebrows by calling Mussolini a Marxist, yet there is no doubt that he was.[3] Indeed, his Marxism during the first decade of the century was quite similar to that of Lenin's. The battle against revisionist tendencies in the international movement found them on the same side. They were both vociferous in their advocacy of the necessity of violent class warfare. Both were disgusted by the nationalist sentiments which seemed to be undermining the internationalism of classical Marxism, and thought the adventurism of capitalist armies to be but a device for delaying the revolution. One could go on, but the significant point is that Mussolini during the period between 1902 and 1914 constantly used Marxist terms, cited Marx as the authority for his actions, and thought in categories which can only be described as Marxist. Having said this, however, we must recall that there were many different types of Marxism existing during the first decade of the century. Ranging from the outright revisionism of Bernstein to the radical revolutionary position of Lenin, Marxism was many things to many men. Where did Mussolini fit in this ideological spectrum? As mentioned earlier, his position was rather close to that of Lenin in opposition to revisionism and in calling for revolutionary agitation but, most importantly, he also shared Lenin's distrust of a mass spontaneous revolution.

Recall that Lenin advanced his conception of a small, tightly knit revolutionary party as a solution to proletarian apathy and as a device

---

[3]Ernst Nolte, *Three Faces of Fascism,* trans. Leila Vennewitz (New York: Holt, Rinehart and Winston, 1966), p. 151.

for fomenting revolution in a largely underdeveloped country. While we have not used the term in the prior discussion, there is little doubt that Lenin's party was an elitist organization. Its purpose was to maximize the latent energy of the mass of people and direct it toward appropriate Marxian ends. Mussolini shared this skepticism concerning the revolutionary potential of the masses, and spoke with increasing frequency of the need for a force to guide the supposedly spontaneous revolution. Numerous times during this early period of development Mussolini spoke with a good deal of contempt for the apathetic masses and emphasized the need for elite leadership. In doing this he was reflecting a rather deep seated trend in Italian intellectual circles. Two of the earliest advocates of elitist theories of the state, Gaetano Mosca and Vilfredo Pareto, had advanced theories of political participation which denied any leadership role for the masses in politics and thought that government was best seen as the rule of successive elite groups. While the direct influence of these men on Mussolini's thinking is a matter of some controversy, there can be little doubt that he shared the elitist tendencies of his time. Although this reliance on an elite leadership group was by no means uncommon with Marxists of this period, it does provide us with an early indication of a doctrine which later becomes central in fascist thought. If mass participation in political life was to become a fact of the twentieth century, there must be an elite leadership group to mobilize and guide it. Here, then, is an initial deviation from classical Marxism in Benito Mussolini's thought.

Another facet of Mussolini's early thought which was to have important consequences in the development of fascism was his emphasis on human will. This is a difficult thing to describe in that it is more a way of approaching reality and an affirmation of action rather than an intellectual category. Mussolini was desperately concerned with creative action, with making history, and with something which can only be described as "life philosophy." Looked at from a Marxist-Leninist perspective, this can be seen as a real deviation from the doctrine. By asserting that human will is capable of altering the environment by sheer determination to change it, Mussolini was implicitly undermining Marx's scientific laws of development. After all, for Marxism-Leninism, human consciousness and will are determined by the objective economic situation; the individual human being as a member of a class is largely limited by the circumstances in which he finds himself. In implying that the creative actions of men could radically alter history, Mussolini is saying that human will is independent of economic conditions. There is an emphasis on voluntarism, almost idealism, in the young Mussolini which is distinctly un-Marxian and emerges full blown in later fascism. Perhaps this reliance on will can be attributed to Mussolini's early interest in the writings of Friedrich Nietzsche who believed that a truly human man could transcend his environment, throw off his chains, and remake the world to conform to his image of what it should be. Whatever the case, this voluntarism led Mussolini to an interest in the role of myth in human affairs, and specifically to the question of how myths could be used to energize masses to perform acts of creation and change. These difficult notions of will and myth will be more fully explored later in this chapter; for the moment it is sufficient to note their presence in his early thinking.

In spite of his elitism and voluntarism one can only describe the Mussolini of the first decade of the century as a Marxist. Before moving to a discussion of his development after 1914, we must emphasize the centrality of an international revolution in his thought. Despite attempts of later fascist apologists to find elements of nationalism in the young Mussolini's thought, he can be properly viewed only as a thoroughgoing internationalist. There are simply too many instances where he condemned the state, called nationalism a bourgeois trick, or railed against the Italian monarchy. The major analytical category in his speeches as well as his writings was the class, and not the nation. His initial response to the First World War was thoroughly consistent with this Marxist internationalism; he counseled neutrality and fully expected the proletariat to refuse to fight in a capitalist war. Given this, his later actions in 1914 seem very strange indeed.

The Nation-State

Despite being bound by treaty to Germany, Italy remained neutral during the early stages of World War I. Socialists in Italy were in many ways more consistent than their brethren in other countries, for they agitated in behalf of neutrality and continued to proclaim the international solidarity of the working class. While the German proletariat and many of its intellectual leaders were rallying around the banner of nationalism, Italian socialists remained firmly neutralist. Given this, imagine the surprise when *Avanti!* under Mussolini's editorship appeared in October, 1914, calling for the abandonment of neutralism and the entry of Italy in the war. It was to be Mussolini's last editorial, for he was forced from his position as managing editor and eventually drummed out of the party.

How can we explain such an action—the flaunting of a basic tenet of Marxism by a dedicated Marxist? Before leaping to the conclusion that Mussolini was simply jumping aboard the bandwagon of growing nationalist sentiment in Italy, we must recall the dilemma that the First

World War caused dedicated socialists throughout Europe. The war provided the first real test of Marxism's internationalism, and in general the doctrine failed to pass the test. There were exceptions such as Rosa Luxemburg and Lenin, but for the most part European socialists supported their respective countries in the war. In a sense, then, Mussolini was in the mainstream of socialist action. Further, we have already noted some early tendencies toward voluntarism in Mussolini's thinking, where the human will is seen capable of performing tremendously heroic actions, remaking history. Given this, it must have been extremely difficult for a man of Mussolini's temperament to sit back calmly and assume a neutralist posture while the cataclysmic events of the war were occurring all around him. Whatever the case, the idea which forms the keystone of fascist ideology was now firmly established, and this concept of the nation-state was to dominate Italian political thinking for the next thirty years. We must now leave the historical development of Mussolini's intellectual and political career to concentrate on the major doctrines which comprise the ideology of fascism, remembering that these ideas emerged gradually over a twenty-year period. If there is one authoritative statement of fascist ideology it is Mussolini's *The Doctrine of Fascism* published in 1932, and that document appropriately emphasizes the notion of the nation-state.[4]

The change from the concept of class to the notion of nation involves a complete change in conceptual framework. In Marxism, the fundamental unit of analysis is class. Everything is defined in terms of its class base—one is either proletarian or bourgeois, institutions are bourgeois, consciousness is defined by class. In fascism the fundamental unit of analysis is the nation—you are either a member of it or you are not, values are national values, one achieves realization only in and through the nation. Much as in the case of class in Marxism, the nation is not simply the numerical summation of the individuals comprising it, but it possesses a history, a cohesiveness, and a destiny of its own. The nation is thus an entity which is both real and ideal; it can be physically defined in terms of boundaries and size of population; but it also has a past which differentiates it from other nations and a future potential which may or may not be achieved. Fascist spokesmen constantly used an organic metaphor in referring to the relationship of the nation to the individuals who comprise it. The nation is seen as an organism which lives, breathes, grows and, presumably, dies while individuals are seen as cells which perform their function and achieve fulfillment only insofar as the entire organism is healthy. The individual simply cannot live

---

[4]Benito Mussolini, "The Doctrine of Fasciscm," in John Somerville and Ronald E. Santoni, eds., *Social and Political Philosophy* (Garden City, N.Y.: Doubleday & Company, Inc., 1963).

without the state, for man is by nature a social animal and can realize himself as an individual only by being a member of a collectivity. Perhaps this conception of the state and the individual can best be explained by briefly recounting fascist arguments against so-called liberal democratic thought.

We will disscuss the intellectual origins of modern democratic thought at length in the final chapters of this book, but we must mention briefly some of its basic assumptions at this point so that we may understand fascist opposition to it. In general, the liberal democratic tradition saw man existing as an individual before the establishment of the state, possessed of certain rights granted to him by God or nature. Because of certain inconveniences of this presocial, prepolitical situation these individuals band together and give up certain of their natural rights to a collectivity so that they may, as individuals, live a more comfortable existence. State and society thus are established for a specific purpose, have limited powers and functions, and may be abolished if they exceed their granted powers. Democratic representative institutions are designed to translate the desires of individuals in the society, normally on a majority rule basis, into public policy. Representative institutions are, by their very nature, intended to express the *particular wills* of individuals within the society. Finally, democratic theory is quite clear about the locus of sovereignty in the society—it lies with each individual and the actions of the state must be with the consent of those individuals.

To the fascist all of this is simply absurd. The democratic tradition defines freedom largely as an absence of restraint on individual action, yet it requires man to give up some freedom, e.g. relinquish natural rights, in order to attain freedom. How, fascism asks, does one become free by giving up freedom? Indeed, a fascist would argue, in talking about giving up natural rights so as to achieve a more convenient situation, the democrat exposes the fallacy of his entire enterprise. What he is really saying is that freedom cannot exist without a stable body of laws and political institutions, and that the only way true freedom can be attained is through obedience to those laws. The myth of the isolated sovereign individual is thus destroyed and we come to understand that the individual can exist only in and through the state. Any rights that individuals may possess are granted to him and may be removed by the state; similarly the private interests of individuals must be subordinated to the general interests of the collectivity. Insofar as representative institutions, political parties, and all of the other trappings of parliamentary democracy are designed to reflect the particular interests of individuals, they must be discarded and replaced by institutions which will determine the *general will* of the nation.

One of the more common modern attempts to describe the functions of the state speaks of it as the "authoritative allocator of values for the society,"[5] meaning that political institutions can within limits control what is done by other institutions and individuals within the society. Fascist ideology takes this type of descriptive statement and adds an ethical dimension to it. The nation is the source of ultimate values for all members of the community and the political arm of the nation—the state—gives articulation to those values. There is, simply, no higher ethical authority. If this is the case, the individual human being fulfills his nature by insuring that the goals of the collectivity are achieved. Indeed, the terms "individual" and "state" are incorrect abstractions insofar as they imply differing perspectives—in fascism they are but two sides of the same coin. The nation is struggling to achieve actuality, to fulfill its potential; individuals are good when they contribute to that quest. Given this, it is obvious why fascism was opposed to liberal democratic thought, for the latter's major assumption is that the state is ultimately a creation of and subservient to the individual. Fascism contended that such thinking had led to disunity in the society and provided no feeling of national cohesiveness; liberal democratic thought was ultimately selfish and as such prevented man from living in a moral association with his fellow man.

If the basic fascist premise is that the nation-state is the ultimate authority in all matters, it must of necessity be in direct opposition to Marxism-Leninism. To the Marxist, nationalism is but another capitalist trick designed to prevent the formation of an international proletarian movement. From the fascist point of view, communism is one of the prime sources of disunity in the state for it preaches unending class antagonism and therefore divides the people. Further, communism is particularly dangerous in that it asserts that there is an authority which is higher than the state, and that nation-states are but a passing phenomenon on the path toward a world society. It was thus almost inevitable that fascism would adopt a radically anti-Marxist stance, despite the intellectual origins of its founding father. Indeed, the *anti-Bolshevism* of fascism is so vehement that it can be described as one of the central traits of the ideology. While fascism had little use for the excessive individualism of democratic theory, it was especially polemical about Bolshevism. The reasons for this should be obvious in that fascism was in general competing for the allegiance of the same sort of person as Marxism. Indeed, at many points fascists thought of themselves as

[5]This modern definition of the function of the state can be found in David Easton, *The Political System* (New York: Alfred A. Knopf, 1953), pp. 126-48.

improving upon the democratic form in order to more effectively combat the Bolshevik menace. It is for this reason that many people assert
that fascism was a conservative or reactionary movement. If Marxism is
on the radical left of the political spectrum, then some assume that any
movement which is violently opposed to it must be on the right wing. As
we shall see, however, fascism was in many ways as revolutionary as
Marxism ever hoped to be, and to dismiss it as simply a right-wing
reaction to communism is to deny its complexity and power as an
ideology.

Any attempt at comparison between fascism and the socialism of a
Lenin or a Stalin reveals a tangled web. While Mussolini was calling
for national strength to resist the "red menace" of Bolshevism, he
was adopting many policies within Italy that can only be described as
socialistic. From his early calls for destruction of the monarchy and his
battles with the Catholic Church to the nationalization of many sectors
of the economy in 1945 there was a definite socialistic thread in his
thought. This is not to say that deviations from this pattern did not
occur. As notable exceptions one need only mention his eventual accommodation with the Church and the monarchy. Still, fascist regimes
called themselves "national-socialist" and in the case of Italy there was
a consistent policy of intervention in economic matters. It was, however, socialism of a different kind, for any measures taken were not in
and of themselves instituted for the betterment of the working classes,
but to make those individuals better able to contribute to the economic
power of the state. Recalling the organic analogy mentioned earlier,
an unhealthy working class is a cancerous growth on the body politic
and must be cured so that it is able to cooperate with the other organs
of the state. Similarly, fascism was not against the ownership of private
property in the dogmatic fashion of Marxism. Private property was
something that was tolerated, even encouraged as long as it added to
the overall goal of maximization of state power. Finally, if we can loosely refer to the socialism of Lenin or Stalin as the complete control of
the economic sector by the state to increase the productivity and expand the economic base of the nation, there is little doubt that Mussolini's regime was appropriately called socialistic. Brief mention of the
fascist doctrine of the corporate state will add additional support to
that conclusion.

It is difficult although not impossible to find consistency in Mussolini's
pattern of action in economic matters. Throughout its period of
ascendancy in Italy, fascism was forced to accommodate itself to varying
pressures from other interest groups in the society. It could not simply
adopt a form of Marxian socialism, for that sort of precipitous action
would have destroyed the conservative propertyholder support that

Mussolini had acquired by his militant anti-Bolshevism. On the other hand, a simple continuation of capitalism was not possible for the fascists were convinced that the individualistic basis of capitalism led to disunity and that the economic system of capitalism was outmoded. If the overall goal of the regime was national unity and power perhaps that could be accomplished by retaining some capitalist elements, while reforming others along lines suggested by the Marxian critique of capitalism. To this end the doctrine of the corporate state gradually evolved. It involved a series of decision-making institutions which were instituted to effect a unity of purpose between capitalists and workers, under the watchful eye of the state. A corporative chamber, designed to replace parliament, would have representation from both labor and management and was empowered to make decisions on wages and amount of production on an industry-wide basis. We cannot go into the institutional details of this conception of the state; for our purposes it is primarily important as a device to eradicate the influence of selfish interest, whether expressed by a single capitalist or an entire working class. In a sense, the corporate state was Mussolini's answer to the five-year plans in the Soviet Union, which attempted to set production goals, centralize economic decision making, and rationalize the allocation of resources for the entire country. From the ideological perspective one thing stands out—whatever the institutional arrangements, and despite the existence of private property, the state is clearly in control of all aspects of the economy.

National Goals, Elitism, and Leadership

We have seen that one of the major goals of fascism is to supplant the selfish individualism of liberal democracy with national solidarity expressed in the form of the will of all the people. We must now inquire as to the source of that will, what it is and how it is to be found. Asking such questions immediately involves us in *voluntarism, anti-intellectualism,* and *elite leadership,* three additional doctrines in the constellation of fascist ideas.

If the state is to be seen as a type of organism, it must possess certain functions and have certain goals which it is to accomplish. While it is true that fascists constantly spoke of the spirit of the state and invoked the concept of a will which was general in nature, there was little in the way of systematic articulation of the goals of the Italian nation-state. There were vague references to the glory of ancient Rome and the potential greatness of the Italian people, but nothing as specific as the goal culture which we shall find in Nazi Germany. Perhaps it was inevitable that the concrete form of these vague references to Italian power resulted in various atempts to expand the influence of the nation in foreign affairs. Italian adventurism in Ethiopia and, for that matter, in the Second World War can be seen as an attempt to provide the material resources and physical boundaries necessary for national greatness. We should not, however, be surprised at the lack of specificity of goals to be reached by a great Italy, for Mussolini's celebration of action for its own sake is an important element here. He later declared that the fascist movement of the early twenties had no specific goals, and surely did not possess a well-formulated program for political action. The point is that achievement of certain goals is really not as important as the process of struggle to achieve them. In an almost Hegelian fashion, the state and its people come to know what they can be only by constantly testing themselves through ceaseless action. The exercise of national will is as important, if not more important, than the fulfillment of any set of goals; action and struggle are celebrated for their own sakes. In this case there is no substitute for Mussolini's own words:

> The years which preceded the march on Rome were years of great difficulty, during which the necessity for action did not permit of research, or any complete elaboration of doctrine. There was much discussion, but what was more important and more sacred—men died. They knew how to die. Doctrine, beautifully defined and carefully elucidated, with headlines and paragraphs, might be lacking; but there was to take its place something more decisive—faith.[6]

It should be apparent from the above quotation that fascism has little use for the rational quibbling of intellectuals. If action is what is desired there is little point in spending a great amount of time debating or spelling out logical systems of ideas. There is a very distinct and deep strand of anti-intellectualism in fascism accompanied by the belief that human emotions provide the true seat of wisdom and truth. Man, while he is a thinking animal, finds true wisdom in his emotional responses to words and actions and shows that wisdom through committing his will to action. As such, speeches and written statements are not used to communicate information but to induce certain emotional responses in the audience, to stir them to action. To a cynical observer, this means that the speaker or writer is merely using symbols for their propaganda effect. There is, however, evidence to indicate that both Mussolini and Hitler believed that the interchange of emotion which occurred during

---

[6]Benito Mussolini, "Facismo," included in Henry S. Kariel, ed., *Sources in Twentieth-Century Political Thought* (Glencoe, Ill.: The Free Press of Glencoe, 1964), p. 89.

mass rallies was actually a fundamental method of communication with the people. Here we once again encounter the elitist elements in fascist doctrine, for if the spoken word is seen as a device for inducing emotional response and is a fundamental method of communication between people, the person who is speaking those words becomes a most important man indeed. Hence, to fully appreciate the notions of emotionalism, will, and mass action we must look at the man who is to be the source of all of these—*the leader.*

The fascist leader is the person who discovers the general will of the nation, interprets it and communicates it to the people in a way which will lead them to fulfill its commands. As such, the leader is in many ways the key to all of fascism. To return to the organic analogy, the leader is literally the personification of the nation; his body and his will express the will of all of the people. We must emphasize that fascist doctrine asserts that the leader does not act in his own personal interest; that is, all of his words and actions are dictated by the general will. In a sense he is a captive of that will and simply could not act arbitrarily or on the basis of personal whim. We have already noted that the spirit of the people exists throughout time independent of any particular person, so that the leader is really discovering and being lead by a national will which already exists. Thus, we must ask how a particular person such as the leader comes to know what that will is. Fascist doctrine provides us with little in the way of explanation of this discovery process. The leader's communication with the general will is a mystical process—he simply knows it and is chosen by history to be the one person who gives verbal form to the national spirit. That will always existed in potential, but it required a great person to know it, translate it for the rest of the nation and mobilize the people to insure that the potential is fulfilled. How do the people know when a particular man, such as Mussolini or Hitler, is the authentic manifestation of the general will? Fascists asserted that the true greatness of the people is shown when they simply recognize the leader when he appears and agree to follow all of his commands. Again we see the emotional and irrational base in fascism. How does the leader know he is chosen to articulate the will of the people? He simply knows it! How do the people recognize the leader when he appears? They simply do, and thereafter follow his commands! There just is no rational explanation for these phenomena for they arise from the will and emotions of people.

From a more objective vantage point one can see the tremendous power that fascism gives to the leader, particularly when this concept is combined with other fascist doctrines. If the state is the final authority in all matters as we argued earlier, and if the leader is the personification of the state, his commands are by definition law. The masses show both their wisdom and exhibit their greatness by acknowledging the leader and following him. Here we see with greater clarity the elite-mass distinction observed in the thought of the young Mussolini. The leader possesses the truth, and it is his historical duty to communicate that truth to the masses and to insure that the nation fulfills its destiny. Fascism sees the masses as possessed of great potential energy; the problem is to mobilize them toward the proper goals. Thus, the question of the method of communication between the leader and the masses is of great importance. Here the elite finds the use of myth and propaganda extremely useful. Much as the "noble lie" of Plato, myths are used to communicate to the people a simplified version of the general will, and propaganda is used to direct their energies. Note that this does not mean that the leader is manipulating the masses for his own personal power— what he is doing is leading them on the proper path to personal and national fulfillment. If he is successful, the entire nation will be mobilized in pursuit of national glory and the will of the people, however vaguely defined, will be achieved.

Here, then, are some of the central traits of Mussolini's fascism: irrationalism, emotionalism, will, leadership, a vague sort of socialism, action for its own sake—all of these within the confines of that supreme value of national greatness. Before moving to a more explicit summary of the ideas of Benito Mussolini we must talk briefly about the role of racial doctrines in Italian fascism, for it provides one of the major distinctions between fascism and national-socialism.

Fascism and Race

It is difficult to encapsulate the racial doctrines of Fascist Italy for the issue is clouded by semantic confusion, lack of consistency, and most important, the alliance with Nazi Germany. Even after 1936 when Italy officially referred to itself as a racist society, there was a good deal of confusion as to exactly what the term meant. Further, several of the major theoreticians of the fascist movement, notably Giovanni Gentile, explicitly denounced German national-socialist racial doctrines as both simplistic and unproved. Finally, despite the existence of anti-Semitic legislation in Italy, there is a good deal of evidence to indicate that its application was half-hearted and that many major fascist figures gave covert assistance to Jews escaping the expanding German empire.

The confusion surrounding these doctrines revolves around the concepts of *race* and *nation*. Even in the early twenties Mussolini had spoken of the superiority of the Italian race and its potential for greatness. Yet it is quite clear from the context of his speeches that he used the word race almost as a synonym for nation. The entire notion of an

Italian race was simply impossible, for Italy was a country made up of individuals of myriad racial backgrounds—more of a melting pot of races than a homogenous body. Furthermore, while Hitler and the Nazis were proclaiming the existence of one particular race (variously referred to as Aryan, Nordic, and sometimes even Germantic) as physically and culturally superior to all others, Italy was in the position of having a very small proportion of so-called Nordics in its population. How can one refer to Italy as a superior state if superiority is defined in terms of the prevalence of Nordics in the nation? This is but a more complex way of saying that Italian racism was constantly associated with Italian nationalism, and that references to an Italian race generally included all Italians, irrespective of their actual racial background.

This is not to deny that there are theoretical bases in fascist doctrine for some sort of racial and cultural separatism. The entire concept of a people, or *volk*, immediately asserts that there is something distinctive and usually superior about a particular set of persons. If that group can be seen as separate and superior it is but a short step to assert that they should somehow dominate over other groups who are less fortunate. Further, fascism contained a distinct strain of anti-Semitism or, more precisely, anti-Zionism. Its opposition to Jews and to Jewish culture was, however, largely on grounds similar to its opposition to Marxism— Zionism preached a doctrine which placed the values of international Jewry higher than those of the nation-state. Given fascism's opposition to any doctrine which challenged the ultimate authority of the nation it is obvious why such sentiments had to be countered. Having said all this, what is apparent, once again, is that the central conceptual category in Italian fascism was the nation, and that any racism involved was usually defined in terms of the nation-state. Such, as we shall see, was not the case with national-socialism.

Perhaps the single most correct statement one can make concerning racism in Mussolini's doctrine is that it was part of an attempt to cement relations between Fascist Italy and Nazi Germany. How else can one interpret Mussolini's early attempts to dissuade Hitler from his racial policies? How else can one explain the prominence of men like Gentile in the fascist state, whose opposition to Hitler's racial policies was well documented? Racism in Italy is best seen as an *ad hoc* addition to the doctrine, instituted for strategic purposes, and never made fully compatible with the far more basic value of Italian nationalism.

A Tentative Summary of Traits

Before moving to a discussion of German National-Socialism it seems worth attempting a summary of the major themes of Italian Fascism, if only to serve as a source of comparison and contrast for further discussion. Little more need be said of the doctrine of the nation-state, for it has dominated our discussion throughout the chapter. Much as the notion of "class" in Marxism-Leninism, the "nation" forms the fundamental unit of analysis in fascist doctrine. One is tempted to dismiss fascism by simply asserting that anything which is good for the nation-state is, by definition, part of the doctrine. Yet we have seen that there are several general themes which were used to enhance that goal of national greatness and which reappear in further discussion of the ill-defined phenomenon of fascism. Let us attempt to summarize and clarify those themes by looking at some attempts at systematic definition of the fascist phenomenon. A recent dictionary definition reads:

> Any authoritarian, anti-democratic, anti-socialistic system of government in which economic control by the state, militaristic nationalism, propaganda, and the crushing of opposition by means of secret police emphasize the supremacy of the state over the individual.[7]

This definition seems reasonably accurate in that it contains most of the themes we have associated with fascism, but it suffers, perhaps inevitably, from superficiality and it is in the complex interrelation of traits that fascism acquires its power as an ideology. For example, fascism is surely "anti-democratic" if by that we mean that it opposes the excessive individualism of classical liberalism and the representative institutions associated with it, but only in the name of providing a better, more direct democracy achieved through the communication of the general will to all the people through the fascist leader. Further, fascism is indeed "anti-socialistic" if that means violent opposition to the internationalism and class framework of socialism. However, it did rely on many socialist measures in the economic realm, hardly saw itself as capitalistic, and had its intellectual origins in the mind of a confirmed Marxian. What about "the supremacy of the state over the individual"— is this good fascism? Yes, if by that phrase we mean that the nation-state defines the norms for action for all the people and admits of no higher authority. Still, a good fascist would declare that the implied opposition of the terms "state" and individual" in the definition is but another example of excessive democratic individualism. Man, being a social animal, can only fulfill himself as an individual in and through the nation-state and to imply that there is some sort of opposition between the two is to distort the nature of man. Finally, the dictionary definition

---

[7]Charles Earle Funk, ed., *New Practical Standard Dictionary of the English Language*, vol. 1 (New York: Funk & Wagnalls Company, 1954), p. 481.

suffers by ignoring other aspects which are central to fascism—where, for example, are elitism and leadership?

Another attempt at a "first definition" of fascism is offered by Ernst Nolte in his *Three Faces of Fascism:*

> Fascism is anti-Marxism which seeks to destroy the enemy by the evolvement of a radically opposed and yet related ideology and by the use of almost identical and yet typically modified methods, always, however, within the unyielding framework of national self-assertion and autonomy."[8]

The major virtue of this definition is that it correctly asserts the centrality of anti-Marxism and nationalism while attempting to show the complexity of the doctrine through the use of qualifying phrases. Still, this definition seems incomplete and suffers from vagueness. Perhaps we must conclude that no good definition of fascism is possible, and that the best we can hope for is a listing of fascist traits and anticipations. This is but to underscore the emotionalism and anti-intellectualism of the movement, for its dislike of rational argument makes systematic exposition of the doctrine most difficult. Such is not the case, however, with our next subject for discussion—Adolf Hitler was all too explicit about what he intended. The problem was, too few people believed him.

BIBLIOGRAPHY

Finer, Herman. *Mussolini's Italy*. New York: Grosset & Dunlap, 1965. A good standard account which concentrates somewhat more on the institutions of the Italian state than other works listed here.

Greene, Nathanael, ed. *Fascism: An Anthology*. New York: Thomas Y. Crowell Company, 1968. The best collection of essays available on fascist ideology. While concentrating on Germany and Italy it also contains material on Spain and France.

Gregor, A. James. *The Ideology of Fascism*. New York: The Free Press, 1969. The best study available of the ideology of Italian Fascism and its relationship to national-socialism. While some of Gregor's points are controversial, this is a well documented and thought-provoking book.

---

[8]Nolte, *Three Faces of Fascism,* pp. 20-21.

Nolte, Ernst. *Three Faces of Fascism.* New York: Holt, Rinehart and Winston, 1966. Perhaps the definitive work on all aspects of fascism. It is particularly noteworthy for its discussion of the *Action Francais* as a philosophical precursor of the German and Italian variations. However, it is not particularly easy reading.

Payne, Stanley G. *Falange: A History of Spanish Fascism.* Stanford, California: Stanford University Press, 1961.

Schneider, Herbert W. *Making the Fascist State.* New York: Oxford University Press, 1928. Without doubt *the* classical study of ideological origins of the fascist movement. However dated, its insights remain quite fresh.

Weber, Eugen, ed. *Varieties of Fascism.* Princeton, N.J.: D. Van Nostrand, 1964. Weber attempts, through use of a wide selection of fascist writings, to show both the breadth and complexity of the phenomenon. A good introductory volume.

Woolf, S. J., ed. *The Nature of Fascism.* New York: Random House, 1969. A collection of articles which attempts to show the impact of fascism on various groups and institutions. The section on fascism and the economy is particularly good.

Original Works

Gentile, G. *The Genesis and Structure of Society.* Translated by H. S. Harris. Urbana, Illinois: University of Illinois Press, 1960.

Halperin, S. Williams, ed. *Mussolini and Italian Fascism.* Princeton, N.J.: D. Van Nostrand, 1964.

Mussolini, B. "The Doctrine of Fascism." In *Social and Political Philosophy,* edited by John Somerville and Ronald E. Stantoni. Garden City, N.Y.: Doubleday & Company, 1963.

Weber, Eugen, ed. *Varieties of Fascism.* Princeton, N.J.: D. Van Nostrand, 1964.

Chapter 7

NATIONAL
SOCIALISM

"All that is not race in this world is trash."[1] With those words in *Mein Kampf* Adolf Hitler pointed at once to the prime difference between Italian Fascism and German National-Socialism as well as the major category of national-socialist thought. We have stated earlier that the idea of the nation provided the fundamental building block for fascist thought and that despite some rather awkward attempts to speak of an Italian race, Mussolini's doctrines were fundamentally nationalist. While it is a subject matter by no means free from controversy, it is here submitted that almost the opposite situation obtained in Hitler's doctrines of national-socialism. Despite his appeals to German nationalism and his constant references to German history and greatness, Hitler was primarily a champion of a particular racial group and the fruition of his plans would have led to the destruction of the German nation-state. To support such a conclusion we must once again enter into that murky area of the relationship between nation and race, or better, between the *volk* (people) and the racial group. In discussing these ideas with respect to Italian Fascism we found that Mussolini was rather obscure as to the history and composition of the Italian people, forced to make vague references to the glories of ancient Rome and the future potential of the nation. In the case of Germany we are dealing with a different situation for the celebration of uniquely Germanic myths, culture, and history

---

[1] Adolf Hitler, "Mein Kampf," included in Somerville and Santoni, *Social and Political Philosophy,* p. 452.

was very much a part of both the popular and intellectual traditions in that country. Tracing its roots back to the Germanic tribes who conquered mighty Rome, an entire line of writers was able to refer to a German volk which was unique insofar as it possessed characteristics which separated it from all other peoples. In our discussion of fascism we have noted that the concept of a people does not merely refer to the individuals populating an area at any given time. The volk consists of an entire tradition, possesses a will of its own, and has a destiny which is unique to it. In the Germany of the nineteenth and early twentieth centuries these rather vague ideas were given specific content through reference to a whole host of events in the history of the region. As such, the notion of a German volk received a far more concrete manifestation and provides us with a much better example of this type of thinking than its Italian counterpart.

The Romantic Tradition

The volkish or romantic tradition as it is sometimes called was in many respects a reaction to the complexities produced by a rapidly developing industrial economy. The urban areas which grew up around varying industrial complexes attracted thousands of people with promises of greater rewards and a new life. In many instances, however, they encountered the type of conditions that so repelled the young Karl Marx. Torn from the familiar surroundings of the rural village, performing the seemingly meaningless tasks of large industry, the alienation of which the young Marx spoke was a very real thing, even for those who did not share his vision of the future. One of the responses to this situation was an attempt to revert to a somewhat idealized past, where life was simple and a man had roots. If there was one central idea in the diversity that characterized German romanticism it was that man had somehow lost his bearings in modern civilization and had to return to a more natural setting to cure his sickness. Romantics of all stripes stressed the necessity of restoring a harmonious interrelationship between the human animal and the forces of nature. Further, this was particularly true for the German volk whose strength and wisdom lay in natural settings and whose greatness could only be achieved by remaining true to those origins. The volkish spirit was seen as manifesting itself in the natural environment—indeed, in the very landscape of areas populated by Germans. In particular, the Germany of mists, hills, and dark forests was viewed as being something uniquely German and an appropriate physical manifestation of the volkish spirit. Despite an overlay of the Christian religion there was a good deal of pagan pantheism in much of the romantic tradition. The spirit of the people was to be found in the very forests and streams which made up its ancestral home, and this spirit communicated with members of the volk through those natural objects. The image of the sun, for example, played a very important role in popular volkish literature as the symbol of the strength and power of the German spirit. Germans were seen as looking up from their dark mysterious forests to the sun for guidance and contrasted with other peoples whose existence was arid and devoid of mystery because of their origins in flat, treeless areas. This type of determinism by the natural environment was to play an even more important part in later racist literature, but it was an essential aspect of the volkish tradition as well.

Such a picture of the true German provided a stark contrast with the rootless urban laborer whose spirit had been corrupted by the supposed sophistication of civilization to the extent that he could only be described as a sick animal. If the greatness of the German spirit lay in the mystery and simplicity of the natural setting, the city could only be viewed as an artificial thing—as a corrupter of nature and of the volk. This juxtaposition of urban dominated *civilization* with true volkish *culture* produced a host of interesting contrasts as well as some real problems for the romanticists. Civilized man was seen as rather effeminate, preoccupied with the superficialities of life such as clothing styles, whereas the true German was content with simple functional dress which protected him from the elements. Urban man was caught up in a value structure which necessitated constant pursuit of material objects and the money necessary for their purchase, whereas the man of spirit worked the soil for his everyday necessities and harmoniously interacted with nature. Many writers contrasted the ideal German with a stereotyped Frenchman, the latter being materialistic, effeminate, and lacking the virtues of true humanity. Perhaps the best expression of this antimodern stance of the German romantics is seen in their proposals for economic reform, for in a sense the major cause of all the difficulties of urban life was a product of economic growth. There were numerous proposals to return to the equivalent of the guild system of the Middle Ages and to break up the industrial complexes and move them to rural areas. Here again, there existed the desire for a simple solution and a willingness to renounce the rewards of economic progress in the name of reuniting man with his natural environment. Some of the later literature of the tradition managed to accommodate itself to the necessity of large-scale industry in order to produce a strong nation-state, but the deepest roots of German romanticism rejected it.

It should not be surprising that a movement which placed great emphasis on reuniting man with nature tended to celebrate man's emotional reactions and to depreciate his rationality. Indeed, the mystical communication which occurs between the individual will and the volkish spirit cannot really be described with words—it is something which must be felt. Many of the problems that modern man encountered could be directly attributed to the overdevelopment of his rational capacities. As such, there was a need to return to the soil, thereby resurrecting the emotional side of the human animal so that he might once again become whole. Much as in the case of Mussolini's fascism, man's immediate emotional responses were considered more correct guides to action than lengthy deliberation or intellectualizing. Some writers in the tradition went to the extent of celebrating violence for its own sake, seeing the desire to inflict punishment on others as a natural manifestation of human emotion. Whatever, if the intellect and excessive rationality were the cause of most of man's problems, the simple response was to resurrect the human will as the prime vehicle for directing action. This effort is seen quite graphically in the attempts of several romantic thinkers to alter the Christian tradition to make it more compatible with volkish doctrines. Throughout the centuries Christianity had become institutionalized to such an extent that it was dominated by dogma—mere form with little substance. The doctrines had been rationalized and drained of their mystical origins. Christ was seen as much a symbol of the divine spirit as the originator of a body of doctrine and his experience exemplified exactly the sort of mystical communication that the romanticists envisioned existing between the volkish spirit and the people. To put it all too simply, the tradition placed a great emphasis on the irrational and mystical side of Christianity thereby making it quite compatible with their volkish themes. Further, there were several efforts to "Germanize" Christianity—to make it a national religion by de-emphasizing the more internationalistic aspects of the Christian tradition.

Here, then, is the romantic view of the human condition as well as an ideal type to which all members of the volk ought to aspire. There is a great danger in reading too much into this tradition, despite the apparently widespread dissemination of volkish ideas in both popular literature and in intellectual circles. To imply that the romantic tradition was the only major strain of thought existing in nineteenth and early twentieth century Germany and that somehow its existence caused the later developments of national-socialism is simply to distort reality. After all, the same region that produced volkish thinkers also generated the highly rationalistic Hegel as well as the scientific and materialistic doctrines of Karl Marx. Having dismissed the notion that romanticism and volkishness were somehow uniquely characteristic of a monolithic German mind we must note however, that the existence of this type of tradition provided fertile soil for the growth of national-socialism. With such ideas part of the popular and intellectual marketplace it was possible for national-socialists to pick and choose ideas from the tradition to suit their purposes. On the other side of the coin, then, it is also a distortion of reality to deny that romanticism and volkish thinking contributed significantly to German National-Socialism. Still, at least one additional element was necessary before the volatile mixture of ideas which characterized nazism was possible—the factor of racism.

The notion that a particular racial group is somehow culturally and spiritually superior to all others is surely not German in origin. Minimally, the distinction is as old as that between Greeks and barbarians, the latter being regarded in ancient times as really subhuman. Similarly, the singling out of a particular racial group for censure or as a scapegoat for all human ills was not unique to Germany. Indeed, a rather convincing argument can be made that during the nineteenth and early twentieth centuries France, rather than Germany, was the real hotbed of anti-Semitism. Yet it was in Nazi German that ideas of racial superiority and anti-Semitism became the official policies of the state and resulted in the slaughter of uncounted numbers of innocent people. Why in Germany? Obviously that question cannot be answered within the brief confines of this discussion—perhaps the final answer lies in the warped mind of the young Hitler. Yet, that would be too easy an answer, for there was a distinct tradition of racial ideas of which Hitler was an adherent and Nazi policies, however horrible, cannot simply be dismissed as manifestations of a sick mind. If, as we have stated, race is the core concept of national-socialism, we must examine prevalent racial doctrines in some detail however absurd they may seem.

It is a somewhat ironic fact that the man whose racial ideas had the greatest impact on late nineteenth century German thought was a Frenchman. Despite the existence of varying racial theories throughout continental Europe it was the publication of Count Arthur de Gobineau's *Essay on the Inequality of Races* in 1853 that gave the "scientific" study of race its most coherent form.[2] While Gobineau's work achieved fame in Germany at a somewhat later date there is little doubt that his theories had a great influence on most of the Nazi racial theorists and that his ideas provided much of the conceptual framework for subsequent thinking on such matters. In a manner strangely similar to that of Karl Marx's use of the concept of class, Gobineau asserted that race was the only significant variable that could be used to explain human progress and decline. Ideas, institutions, even individual accomplishments were, to borrow the Marxian phrase, but superstructural elements which were

---

[2]Joseph Arthur, *comte de* Gobineau, *The Inequality of Human Races,* trans. Adrain Collins, intro. Oscar Levy (New York: H. Fertig, 1967).

reflections of the more basic category of race. Indeed, the entire sweep of human history could be explained by the degree to which racial elements retained their purity. A race which allowed itself to become mixed with the blood of other races would inevitably insure its decline, while one which retained its racially primal elements in relative purity would triumph. Lacking the optimism of later racial doctrines, Gobineau's prognosis for the human race was rather gloomy in that he saw that the natural tendency of all races was to permit the intermixing of blood lines, thereby insuring cultural decline. In his own time he could identify but one race which had been relatively successful in keeping itself pure—a race called Aryan (or Nordic) which had its origins in a rather mysterious fashion in India (other theorists later saw Aryans originating from the lost continent of Atlantis!). However Aryan is defined (and there are some places where Gobineau seems to equate it with the "white" race) Gobineau saw this particular race as the true bearer of culture for all mankind. All human accomplishments were seen as a function of the degree of Aryan blood present in either the individual or the society and, of course, mixing of the Aryan blood with that of lower races, notably Slavs, inevitably led to a smaller and smaller amount of the Aryan strain in any particular group. Given such a racially dominated view of human history, small wonder that the good Count was pessimistic about the future. It must be emphasized that Gobineau did not view his theory as merely one theory about human history but the single explanation—a doctrine which was scientifically provable. Later racist thinkers expanded upon this scientism to the extent of developing various devices designed to measure the degree of Aryanism in any individual largely through examination of facial and bodily characteristics. It must also be noted, finally, that there is little overt anti-Semitism to be found in Gobineau's writings. The problem was maintaining the purity of the race and no particular racial group was seen as uniquely guilty of blood mingling.

As mentioned earlier, Gobineau's work lay dormant in Germany for a considerable period of time but eventually came to be accepted and popularized by a group of German intellectuals and artists who formed a circle centered in the small town of Bayreuth. Beginning in the last three decades of the nineteenth century Bayreuth became the major center for the dissemination and popularization of racist doctrines for all of Germany. Most of the individuals who later served as philosophers or intellectual apologists for Hitler's regime had some connection with the Bayreuth circle, so much so that the town became a religious shrine for the Nazi movement. The originator and major light of Bayreuth until his death in 1883 was the composer Richard Wagner, who gathered about him a group of people whose purpose was the celebration of the volkish tradition. Wagner's influence is somewhat difficult to assess and his works, both musically and politically, remain the subject of a good deal of controversy, even today. His operas served as vehicles for popularizing early German mythology and the image of a Teutonic Siegfried—a primitive German "beyond good and evil"—became a central symbol of the Third Reich. There is little doubt of the influence of his operas on Hitler; Wagner was his favorite composer and Hitler himself asserted that his early life was greatly influenced by the composer's operas. It was from Bayreuth that the clearest popular formulation of racial doctrines eminated, particularly after Wagner's death. The great composer had spelled out the broad outlines of racism in some of his political writings and his widow Cosima, son Siegfried, and son-in-law Houston Stewart Chamberlain expanded on the themes. It is in the work of the Bayreuth Circle that we can see the blending of German romanticism with doctrines of racial purity in a very clear fashion. Wagner himself asserted that the source of German woes was race mingling and that the only hope for the future was the resurrection of the pure Aryan strain. To accomplish this a leader would emerge, dedicated to German greatness and determined to purify the race—in particular to eradicate the French and Jewish elements. That Wagner himself would have approved of Hitler's final solution to the "Jewish problem" is doubtful in that there are many liberal themes in both his writings and his music, but he did lend his famous name to the anti-Semitism which culminated in nazism.

It is extremely difficult, if not impossible, to assess the influence of the Bayreuth Circle either in popularizing racist doctrines or in the thinking of the young Hitler. We know, for example, that Hitler met and talked with Houston Stewart Chamberlain shortly before the latter's death, but many of the racial doctrines Hitler adopted were at odds with Chamberlain's teaching. Some commentators assert that Hitler's ideas crystallized in conversations with Dietrich Eckhart while others assert that his ideas about race derived from Ludwig Woltmann and Hans F. K. Guenther.[3] We can make no attempt to show a causal relationship between the ideas of any of these men and later Nazi doctrines, but can only spell out several other aspects of the amorphous body of racist ideas that later influenced Nazi policies.

The Aryan race, however it was defined, was seen as the sole source of all of man's achievements. The existence of sophisticated civilizations in other parts of the world was explained by noting the migration of Aryan elements from Europe to those areas. Further, the English

---

[3]See the discussion in George L. Mosse, *The Crisis of German Ideology: Intellectual Origins of the Third Reich* (New York: Grosset & Dunlap, 1964), and in A. James Gregor, *Contemporary Radical Ideologies: Totalitarian Thought in the Twentieth Century* (New York: Random House, 1968).

achievement in building a world-wide empire was additional evidence of
the innate superiority of Aryanism, in that Britain contained a large
number of Aryans. Using the argument familiar to racists of all stripes,
they explained the existence of superior achievement in non-Aryan
countries by attempting to prove that Aryan blood flowed through the
veins of their leaders. Italians, Spaniards, and Frenchmen were, as
individuals, capable of greatness only because of the existence of Aryan
forebearers. The world-wide spread of Aryans, while providing truly
human values for other less fortunate races, did, however, tend to
produce blood-mingling and resulted in a gradual loss of the pure Aryan
strain. In modern times the major remaining strain of Aryan blood is to
be found in Northern Europe, particularly in Germany, and the destiny
both of the German nation and all of mankind lies with that group.
These Aryans must be identified and elevated to positions of leadership
so that they may lead men to further glories. The problem, then,
becomes the identification of those men possessing large amounts of
Aryan blood—surely all Germans do not possess it!

To aid in this identification process a list of typically Aryan traits was
drawn up; physical characteristics that gave evidence of an indwelling
Aryan spirit. These characteristics included a general lightness of skin
color (further indication of the tendency to identify Aryanism with the
"white" race), blond hair, blue eyes, a long narrow skull, and a perfect
proportion between head size and body length. This attempt to scientifically determine traits of Aryanism through external observation was
later to cause the Nazis some difficulty because of the obvious fact that
many of their leaders, including the Führer himself, did not have such
bodily attributes. This was circumvented by saying that physical traits
were not the only way of identifying the indwelling Aryan spirit, but
simply a good general rule of thumb. At any rate, the introduction of
this type of pseudoscientific façade to racial doctrine provided additional means by which the "chosen people" could be identified, and lent
a form of scientific credibility to the doctrine.

We must note here how the traditions of German romanticism and
nationalism are becoming merged with racial doctrines. The Siegfried of
ancient German myth has become the blond, blue-eyed bearer of the
Aryan strain of blood. Germany, although long dormant as a nation-
state, is destined for greatness because she possesses the largest amount
of the primal strain of blood in the modern world. Indeed, she will
fulfill her destiny as a nation through the leadership of the master race.
In much the same fashion, several other elements of the romantic
tradition were amalgamated with racial dogma and transformed to produce a more dynamic synthesis. The traditional romantic fear of indus-

trialization and the evils inherent in it was overcome by noting that non-Nordics had presided over past economic development. Industrialization, by itself, was not an evil as some of the romantics had thought; it had resulted in bad conditions because inferior men were in positions of power. Rapid economic growth and the development of an industrial base were now seen as positive benefits in the assertion of German greatness, provided, of course, that Aryans were supreme in the economic sphere. Similarly, the pessimism which had pervaded much of the earlier racial literature was circumvented. True, blood-mixing had led to a decline in the human condition, but this did not necessarily have to continue. Rather than pointing to a glorious but long-lost past, men of will and energy could work to resurrect the Aryan strain which would provide the precondition of an era of even greater human progress. In buttressing this argument, racial theorists appealed to the authority of a crude Social Darwinism, which held that the human race was in a constant struggle in which only the fittest survived. If this is the case, the Aryan who is, by definition, the most fit, need only assert his natural superiority and the future of mankind is assured. In effect, it became a self-fulfilling prophecy; Aryans are most fit, the fittest will survive, therefore Aryan culture will triumph over the forces of evil!

A final aspect of the general grab-bag of ideas of racism in the early twentieth century must be emphasized before we move on to a discussion of the young Hitler—a change in the stereotype of the Jew. Anti-Semitism, of course, existed in the world for a long period prior to the nineteenth and twentieth centuries, varying in intensity, one could argue, with the power Jews possessed in particular countries. Despite their ability to attain political and economic power, most earlier anti-Semitic doctrines pictured Jews as inferior beings who through some mysterious craft and cunning were able to succeed in spite of their innate failings. The difficult question of how a supposedly inferior race could achieve power at the expense of a superior one was seldom directly addressed in racist literature and was surely not answered. A rather ambivalent attitude toward Jews developed whereby on the one hand they were viewed as inferior objects of ridicule, and on the other as a potent force to be feared and demolished. Indeed, it was noted that Jews seemed to possess the solidarity as a racial and religious group that the supposedly superior Aryans lacked. Viewed in this fashion, history could be seen as a perpetual struggle between Aryans and Jews as the two purest racial groups; the one representing culture and progress, the other a synonym for evil and decay. The Jew is thus not merely a parasite and a debaser of culture, but a formidable foe to be treated most seriously. It is in this context that we meet full-blown the notion of a Jewish conspiracy against mankind, whereby Jews, through cunning and treachery, seek to control the world. Inferior and ridiculous though they be, Jews represent a threat to all that is human, and thus must be destroyed.

It was from this inconsistent mixing of racist ideas that the Nazis fashioned their racial doctrines. The fact that such doctrines were common currency around the turn of the century is surely more important than the writing of any one racist thinker. Whether the young Hitler ever read Chamberlain or Woltmann or any other academic treatise on racism is somewhat immaterial. These thinkers provided a respectable, scientific overlay for very deep-seated human prejudices and permitted a man like Hitler an appeal to authority in support of his own emotional reactions.

Hitler: Race, Leadership, and the National Socialist State

This is not the place for a political biography of Adolf Hitler. The facts of his life and the history of nazism in Germany are either well known or readily available. What is necessary is a brief summary of the ideas of the young Hitler to see how they incorporated the various intellectual traditions we have been describing, and to provide points of comparison with Italian Fascism. It is appropriate to speak of the *young* Hitler because in large measure the ideology of national-socialism was firmly set in his mind by his twenty-fourth year. Ernst Nolte in a deft phrase refers to national-socialism as "practice as fulfillment" asserting that the ideology was "pre-formed" in Hitler's mind and all that was necessary was its "fulfillment."[4] As such, the ideas of Hitler's youth can be used as keys to understanding not only the ideology of national-socialism, but the entire Nazi movement. Once again, we must note the centrality of racist ideas, for in Hitler's mind race explained everything.

His own description in *Mein Kampf* (My Struggle) of his conversion to anti-Semitism perhaps will help us to understand.

> Once, when I was walking through the inner city, I suddenly came across a being in a long caftan with black side-locks. My first thought was: Is that a Jew? In Linz they did not look like that. I watched the man stealthily and cautiously, but the longer I stared at the strange countenance and studied it feature by feature, the more the question in a different form turned in my brain: Is that a German?[5]

---

[4]Nolte, *Three Faces of Fascism,* pp. 365-401.
[5]Adolf Hitler, *My Battle,* abridged and trans., E. T. S. Dugdale (Boston: Houghton-Mifflin Co., 1933), p. 19.

From this early experience on the streets of Vienna, Hitler moved to the position of finding race at the core of all human affairs. In particular, it was the existence and widespread influence of Jews which served as an explanation of the sorry condition of Germany as well as a rationalization for Hitler's personal lack of early success in life. It is true that Hitler went on in *Mein Kampf* to spell out most of the major themes that we have associated with Italian Fascism. He condemned Bolshevism, class, democratic institutions, the liberal press, and spoke in glowing terms of national unity, organism, duty, and a vaguely socialistic economy. What differentiated Hitler from Mussolini, however, was that blood-mixing and the Jews were seen as the basic cause of all of the standard fascist list of problems. Marxism, for example, was viewed by both men as a dire threat to national unity and as a revolutionary doctrine which competed with fascism for recruits. For Hitler, however, Marxism was a doctrine invented by a Jew (remember Marx's father's early conversion to Christianity?) and used by international Jewry to prevent the German working class from realizing its prime allegiance to volk and state. Similarly, democracy and all of the so-called freedoms associated with it was a doctrine designed by and dominated by Jews. By asserting that political equality was a basic presupposition in governing, Jews had tricked the German people into believing that they were equal to legitimate members of the volk. Thus democracy as a political form insured the debasement of the volk and its superior culture while at the same time permitting Jews to rise to positions of power. Finally, free speech and press, two of the cornerstones of a democratic liberal society, were vehicles for international Jewry in that they spread equalitarian falsehoods, or at best, prevented a united volk by fostering differences among the people. Behind all of these things was the Jew, a member of a lesser race, a parasite living off the body politic, yet a clever and dangerous adversary. Given his presuppositions, there was simply no question about it; Jews must go, for the words German and Jewish were incompatible.

Having discovered his truth it became Hitler's self-appointed task to communicate it to the German masses so that the evils of Jewish control could be eradicated and a new Aryan culture established. Sure of his truth, Hitler's main problem was in communicating it to masses conditioned by false values, and it was in this area, perhaps more than anywhere else, that his genius lay. While we have discussed the notions of leadership, emotion, and mass psychology in connection with fascism, Hitler's contributions in this area were such that they merit additional attention. He, at one with Mussolini, had a good deal of contempt for masses of people, believing that it was the function of an elite to lead them. This leadership was to be achieved largely through emotional communication between the two and, in particular, through the spoken word. Mass rallies and emotion-laden speeches designed to achieve a religious-like catharsis for both speaker and audience were Hitler's major devices for insuring the success of the Nazi movement. There is a good deal of evidence to show that Hitler regarded his speeches as the fundamental means of communication between the leader and his followers. They were designed not primarily to communicate ideas or to convey information but to provide for a mystical exchange of spiritual energy.

As Alan Bullock has said:

> Speech was the essential medium of his power, not only over his audiences but over his own temperament. Hitler talked incessantly, often using words less to communicate his thoughts than to release the hidden spring of his own and others' emotions, whipping himself and his audience into anger or exaltation by the sound of his voice.[6]

This is, of course, thoroughly consistent with the antirationalism and emphasis on mystery and emotion that we have noted before. Hitler saw himself as the reincarnation of the ancient German rulers, returned by history to lead the people in fulfilling their destiny. In asserting these ties to historical Germany, Hitler was able to draw on large portions of the romantic tradition that had become so much a part of everyday culture. After all, his was to be the Third Reich, not the first, and this time it was to last for a thousand years. Ancient symbols were drawn upon to assert these historical ties, the simple strong man of the soil became an ideal German, even architectural styles copying the designs of the Middle Ages were in vogue. All this is but another way of saying that Hitler was a master at the new art (science?) of propaganda and mass psychology. Early in his life he was greatly impressed with the British efforts at propaganda during World War I and he realized the potential of mass communication. All of the media of communication were used to emphasize the Aryan ideal and to condemn the Jewish influence in German life. The art form of the propaganda motion picture was perfected by the Nazis even though the use of movies for such purposes had been discovered only recently. Poster art further served to celebrate the notions of duty to the state and the necessity of self-sacrifice in building a new Germany. Hitler's personal taste in art and architecture dictated aesthetic values for the entire society, while the whole educational structure was revamped to wipe out liberal values and Jewish influences. It is in this attempt to develop what George Mosse has called a "Nazi

---

[6]Alan Bullock, *Hitler: A Study in Tyranny* (New York: Bantam Books, 1961), pp. 323-24.

culture"[7] that we can see the truly revolutionary nature of Hitler's enterprise. He was attempting to change the values of an entire population and point them toward a new society, composed partially of elements of an idealized historical Germany but dominated by a vision of a new Reich. We have earlier used the word totalitarian to describe Stalin's efforts in the Soviet Union to produce a new Soviet man, and surely that word can be used with equal or greater force in describing Hitler's Germany.

There is another area, however, in which direct parallels may be drawn between Hitler and Stalin—something which distinguished both of their regimes from Mussolini's Italy. We have noted that Mussolini's fascism possessed no clear conception of a goal culture and tended to emphasize action for its own sake. Such is not the case with Hitler; he had a clear conception of his new society and the actions that would be necessary to achieve it.

At the beginning of this discussion on national-socialism it was asserted that Hitler was fundamentally an Aryan racist and that the fruition of his plans would have led to the destruction of the German nation-state. Hopefully by now we have established the importance that race had in Hitler's mind, but the full import of those doctrines can be seen only by examining his plans for the future society. Once again, perhaps it is better to let Hitler speak for himself.

> The main principle which we must observe is that the State is not an end, but a means. It is the foundation on which higher human culture is to rest, but it does not originate it. It is rather the presence of a race endowed with capabilities for civilization which is able to do this.[8]

Hitler asserts clearly that the state serves as a vehicle for the elevation of the Aryan race to a position of power—that is its prime purpose. Surely, one might say, but doesn't that mean greater glory and power for all Germans? By no means, for it must be remembered that the existing German nation has been corrupted by blood-mixing and therefore it contains impurities which must be eradicated.

> In its capacity as a State, the German Reich must gather all Germans to itself; it must not only select out of the German nation *only the best of the original racial elements* and conserve them, but must slowly and surely raise them to a position of dominance.[9]

---

[7]George L. Mosse, ed., *Nazi Culture* (New York: Grosset & Dunlap, 1968).
[8]Hitler, *My Battle*, p. 158.
[9]*Ibid.*, p. 161 (emphasis added).

Not only the state, but the existing German volk itself is a device for resurrecting the pure Aryan strain. In effect, a German whose blood is not completely pure is in the same position as a Jew! The only true German is an Aryan, and anyone existing within the state who has mixed blood is at best a second class citizen and at worst must be destroyed. Here we see Hitler's racism in full bloom. The thousand-year Reich will not be a German nation-state but an Aryan state in which any non-Aryans exist only to serve the interests of the culture creator. Given this, the expansionist military policies of Nazi Germany take on an even more horrible dimension. The ultimate objective of war with other non-Aryan nations was to subjugate their populations to the rule of the master race. Hitler's grand vision of the future paid no heed to the superficial boundaries of nations but was concerned solely with the dominance of one racial group over all others. In the end Hitler was almost as much an *internationalist* as Karl Marx!

Given such presuppositions many of the actions that Hitler took fit into a pattern which was rather consistent. His emphasis on education and attempts that were made to actually breed persons possessing Aryan characteristics with others of similar origin can be seen as direct means for achieving the goal culture. Further, during the latter days of World War II Hitler could declare that Germany had let him down without destroying the basic premise of his racism. That is, the fact that Germany was losing the war had nothing to do with the innate superiority of Aryans but simply showed that the Germans of mixed blood (which is, recall, somewhat a contradiction in terms) had not been strong enough to fulfill their task of achieving Aryan supremacy. Finally, with re-treating armies on all sides, Hitler could declare that he had, in truth, been successful, because his extermination camps and breeding policies would insure that from the ashes of a defeated Germany would rise a new Aryan-dominated society, free of Jews. His racial doctrines, with all of their horrifying consequences, remained with him to the end.

In conclusion we may once again ask a question posed at the beginning of the discussion: Is it appropriate to call national-socialism a type of fascism? While it must be granted that this discussion of national-socialism has emphasized the differences between that doctrine and Italian Fascism, the factor of racism was so crucial to the Nazi movement that the emphasis seems merited. Although most fascist traits were to be found in Hitler's thought, and became policies of the Third Reich, racism produced a phenomenon qualitatively different from the ideal type of Italian Fascism.

BIBLIOGRAPHY

Abel, Theodore. *The Nazi Movement.* New York: Atherton Press, 1966. A historical and analytical account of Hitler's rise to power, including six "life histories" of average men in Nazi Germany.

Bullock, Alan. *Hitler: A Study in Tyranny.* New York: Bantam Books, 1961. A biography of Hitler which is much more than mere biography. It is safe to say that this remains the best standard work on the subject. In addition, it is well written and entertaining.

Mosse, George L. *The Crisis of German Ideology: Intellectual Origins of the Third Reich.* New York: Universal Library, 1964. An account which is similar in intention to Viereck's listed below, but is a more balanced presentation. Mosse is particularly effective in discussing the relationship between German romanticism and nazism.

Mosse, George L., ed. *Nazi Culture.* New York: Grosset and Dunlap, 1966. A masterful job of editing to produce a picture of daily life under the Third Reich. Utilizing material ranging from prayers to official documents, Mosse demonstrates the effect of Hitler's policies on the entire culture.

Shirer, William L. *The Rise and Fall of the Third Reich.* New York: Crest Books, 1962.

Viereck, Peter. *Metapolitics: The Roots of the Nazi Mind.* New York: Capricorn Books, 1961. This study, first published in 1941, contains some amazingly accurate predictions as to the direction the Nazi regime would take. Despite excesses, it, more than any other work, probes the German intellectual origins of the national-socialist movement.

Original Works

Chamberlain, Houston S. *The Origins of the Nineteenth Century,* 1912-13. Translated by John Lees. London: John Lane Company.

Hitler, Adolf. *Mein Kampf,* unabridged. New York: Reynal and Hitchcock, 1939.

————. "Mein Kampf," abridged version included in Somerville and Santoni, *op. cit.*

————. *The Speeches of Adolf Hitler,* 1922-1939. Edited by Norman H. Baynes. 2 vols. Oxford: Oxford University Press, 1942.

Chapter 8

THE
DEMOCRATIC
TRADITION

We began our discussion of fascism by noting that the word is almost invariably used with bad connotations—not quite a synonym for evil, but close to it. With democracy, the situation is practically reversed. Even the most power-hungry dictator feels it is necessary to cloak his ambition in the rhetoric of democracy, producing such interesting word combinations as "guided democracy" and "authoritarian democracy." We have seen fascists refer to their regime as a "more perfect democracy" because of the direct communication that supposedly obtains between leader and follower. Similarly, any good modern day Marxist will assure us that the dictatorship of the proletariat in his country provides for true democracy in that the proletariat automatically does what is best for all of the people. What are we to make of such claims? Are they to be dismissed as mere rhetoric, and if so by what criteria? One thing is certain; in an age of mass participation in political life many of the ideas associated with classical democratic thought have become part and parcel of political discourse, whatever ideology is being espoused. Imagine if you can a political leader in the mid-twentieth century declaring that he will act without the consent of the governed or that the popular will on any matter is to be completely ignored. He may in fact believe that popular will ought to be ignored, but the pervasiveness of democratic words and ideas in modern times makes it all but impossible to say so. The only way the student of ideas can move beyond such rhetorical flourishes is to develop a clear conception of the meaning of democratic ideas, both in their historical development and their more modern applications.

Defining the task, however, by no means solves a host of problems involved in approaching democratic ideas, particularly as we try to compare them with other ideologies. Initially, while Marxism and fascism are phenomena of the nineteenth and twentieth centuries, the notion of some sort of "rule of the people" (the Greek meaning of the word *democracy*) was well known in ancient Greece. Can we legitimately compare a tradition which is centuries old with idea systems that had their origins in relatively modern times? Even if we can, does that mean that the only valid presentation of democratic thought would involve a lengthy discussion of the history of democratic ideas? Furthermore, in direct contrast to the other two idea systems herein discussed, it is very difficult to reach a consensus on an authoritative interpreter of democratic ideas. Even fascism, while it is difficult to see as a rigidly formed ideology, had its Mussolini. This is simply not the case with democracy. Granted, there were individuals who contributed more than others to the development of democratic ideas, but there was no founding father and any attempt to find an authoritative text equivalent to *Das Kapital* seems hopeless. A final complication is that the three idea systems under discussion seem at first glance to be addressing different problems and their conceptual frameworks appear to differ greatly in scope. Marxism, for example, can be viewed as an economic doctrine which believes that the solution to certain economic problems will provide political remedies; the state, after all, will wither away under pure communism. On the other hand, fascism might be viewed as primarily a political doctrine, insofar as the state is its major analytical category and any economic reforms it advocates are all in the name of building a greater nation or race. In the same fashion, many people tend to view democracy largely as a process for making decisions rather than as an attempt at a comprehensive political philosophy. That is, democratic theory sets forth certain minimal grounds for making decisions (voting, majority rule, etc.) but has little to say about the specific content of those decisions. Viewed in this manner, democracy is primarily a political decision-making process which may be used to achieve different ends. This makes it sensible to speak of "democratic capitalism" or "democratic socialism" as legitimate manifestations of democratic theory even though the economic doctrines of two such regimes would be very different. If democratic theory were nothing but a process for making decisions, then it might be possible to combine varying aspects of the three ideologies under discussion to produce some sort of synthesis. In many respects, the work of the early Marxian revisionists such as Bernstein can be seen as an attempt to institute Marxian economic goals through the use of a democratic decision-making process. Such a view of democracy as a decision-making process with the ends of the regime to be dependent solely upon the wishes of the populace at any time is superficially quite appealing in that it could lead to a diminution of conflict between the ideologies. However, to view democracy as *process only* is to ignore the fact that the democratic tradition evolved a rather clear conception of the nature of man, his motivation and his aspirations, and that conception is significantly different from either Marxism or fascism. This is but a complicated way of saying that democratic theory is a decision-making process which is based upon certain philosophical presuppositions and those presuppositions in many respects prescribe the type of decisions that can be made. Simply, democracy is philosophy as well as process.

The above musings about the problems inherent in comparing ideologies and in treating democratic theory are not intended to point to solutions, but to alert the reader to the complexity of the situation and to acknowledge the arbitrary nature of many of the choices which must be made in presenting democratic thought. We begin with the assumption that democratic thought can be viewed as an attempt at a comprehensive philosophy of man and that it can be treated in much the same fashion as Marxism or fascism. Further, in the absence of an authoritative interpreter, we shall examine democratic theory primarily in the context of the American attempt to implement a modified form of that philosophy. In doing so we are ignoring many other manifestations of democratic thought as well as arbitrarily dismissing fascist or communist claims to be truly democratic regimes. We shall concentrate, finally, on the intellectual tradition generally described as British liberalism, viewing it as the authoritative modern philosophical base from which the more practical American experiment in modified democracy evolved. Hopefully then, the problems generated by the American experiment will lead us to a better understanding of the complexity of modern democratic practice as well as affording a theoretical perspective of present day controversies in democratic philosophy.

The Legacy of British Liberalism

The term "British liberalism" is generally used to refer to an intellectual tradition which arose during the late seventeenth and eighteenth centuries, normally including thinkers such as John Locke, John Stuart Mill, Adam Smith, and David Hume. In many ways the term is quite inappropriate, for some thinkers whose ideas are habitually associated with the tradition were not English (Jean-Jacques Rousseau) or particularly "liberal," at least in the common meaning of the word (Thomas Hobbes). Further, the term cannot be thought of as connoting a cohesive school of thinking with all members elaborating on a certain body of well-defined dogma. David Hume, for example, while most commentators would regard him as a genuine member of the tradition, specifically disavowed several of the key concepts in the thought of John Locke. Much the same could be said for John Stuart Mill. Still, it is appropriate to speak of a "tradition" in that all of these thinkers were concerned with similar problems and their solutions to those problems tended to fall into a particular pattern of thinking. While it is perhaps too strong to contend that all of them succeeded in producing a comprehensive philosophy of man, they did evolve a series of themes which form the basis of modern democratic thought. With these caveats in mind let us explore some of those ideas.

As in any philosophical endeavor the liberals attempted to take a new look at man and his nature, a look unencumbered by the social and political institutions of their particular day. In much the same fashion as a Karl Marx describing the evolution of man from primitive communism to pure communism, or of a Mussolini asserting that man was by nature a social animal, they tried to envision man in his natural state. In general they attempted this feat using an intellectual device called the "state of nature." State of nature theories tried to use the human mind to view man unencumbered by habit patterns, innocent of politics, acting in ways which were basic to his very nature. Although some thinkers who used this intellectual device to describe natural man had a tendency to talk as though this state existed in human history somewhere back before civilization, this was not an attempt at a theory of history but simply a method of discovering how man would appear in his most basic condition. In any case, what did the British liberals see to be the qualities basic to human nature?

One feature of human existence under such conditions which stood out most graphically was man's individuality. He was viewed primarily as an atomic unit, rather sufficient unto himself, and interacting with other individuals primarily in pursuit of his own selfish interests. True, there were differing degrees of this *individualism* expressed by the assorted members of the liberal school. Where Thomas Hobbes saw man as a completely self-contained entity contacting other people only when he desired similar things, John Locke saw a minimal amount of connection between people because they were all subject to the constraints of the natural law of God. Despite these differences, the liberal tradition can only be characterized by its emphasis on radical individualism; man exists, prior to the establishment of society, as a self-contained individual. Immediately we can see a great difference between British liberalism and the other two ideologies we have discussed. To the fascist, man in his natural condition is human insofar as he is a member of the group or the race. His interaction with that group defines in large part his very existence. To a Marxist, natural man is gregarious, a member of a community governed by shared values; his major difficulties are economic. In British liberalism the individual is supreme. Further, man possesses certain rights, generally called natural rights, which are granted to him by the very nature of his humanity. These rights are not dependent for their existence upon their recognition by a state, or by any other human institution, but are inherent in the nature of man. To some members of the liberal tradition, men possessed the right to acquire anything they wanted, even a right to another person's body. Such unlimited, God-granted rights were, however, constrained by the fact that all other individuals possessed them. Despite differences in physical and mental ability all human beings were similarily endowed with these natural rights, leading to a position of relative equality. Men were equal to the extent that they all possessed the right to a great many things. Granted, I have the right to attempt to take away property which you have acquired, but you have a corresponding right to defend that property from any attack. Thus, we may say that the British liberal tradition viewed men in the state of nature as relative equals, whether that equality derived from a common parenthood in God or from the ability of one individual to deprive any other of his rights. Thomas Hobbes, perhaps the most individualistic of all the liberals, saw men as equal if only in the sense that anyone possessed the ability to deprive another of his life. However weak a man might be, he could always band together with others to deprive the strong man of his existence. Implicit in this notion of equality is the fact that all men possess the freedom necessary to secure their natural rights. While at times that freedom may be constrained by the presence of other men or by certain natural laws of God, in general, man is endowed with the freedom to secure the objects he desires.

Here then is a brief sketch of the attributes of man in his natural condition: he is free to pursue his ends; relatively equal; he is possessed of rights which are not subject to the authority of any other human being; and, above all, he is an individual, dependent only upon God for his existence. Of particular note in the liberal picture of natural man is what modern social theorists would call the lack of shared values. There is no natural human community which sets up standards of behavior for the individuals in it, indeed, a community or society is conspicuous by its absence. Even John Locke, whose view of the natural state is somewhat less individualistic than other liberals, felt that men shared merely a common community through their creator, and were governed by natural laws which were difficult to apply to particular cases. This lack of shared values is underscored if we look more carefully at the individual in the state of nature and, in particular, at the forces which motivate his behavior.

Man is motivated largely by a selfish desire to acquire things. He is interested primarily in satisfying his desires, in fulfilling the needs which his emotions dictate. Throughout the liberal tradition there is an emphasis on the emotional basis of human motivation, and a consequent depreciation of human rationality as a major force in governing behavior. Men are dominated by their own selfish interests and human reason serves the function of instructing them to secure those desires most efficiently. This orientation is nicely summed up in David Hume's view of reason as a "scout" for the more basic human passions. Obviously the most prevalent way these passions find their expression is through the acquisition of objects from the environment, and all of the liberals were most concerned with the notion of private property. Given what we know of the relative equality of men combined with the freedom they possess, it follows that the liberals thought that natural man had a right to acquire property for his own selfish interests. Indeed, it is probably correct to assert that British liberalism as a whole was preoccupied with man as an economic being. The mere mention of Adam Smith's name among their number indicates that. Inventing the labor theory of value which we previously encountered in Marxian thought, the liberals argued that, when a man mixed his labor with an object in the environment, that thing became an extension of himself and therefore could be legitimately owned by him. Indeed, there is much in liberalism which viewed property as man's natural expression of his potential and an indication of his personal creativity. Perhaps Karl Marx and Adam Smith are not so far apart after all. Given all of this, is it appropriate to speak of natural right to the unlimited acquisition of property in the state of nature? While some of the liberal thinkers came close to this position, the norm is better represented by John Locke who felt that man possessed a natural right to only that property which he and his family could comfortably use, thereby providing for the basic wants of all. Before this picture of man in his natural state becomes too idyllic—man is, after all, free, equal, self-sufficient—let us move to a discussion of the conflict that inevitably arises in such a state.

Conflict arises because the selfish interests of men lead them to desire the same objects and there are simply no rules of the game to determine whose interest in a thing is more legitimate. Insofar as every man had a natural right to acquire anything, it was inevitable that their desires would lead them to concentrate on similar objects, producing disagreement as to legitimate ownership. As long as an unlimited right existed, men could not feel secure in their possessions or, for that matter, in their own continued existence. It is this conflict in the state of nature which leads men to use their reason to discover ways by which their selfish interests may be better served and which leads them out of the natural state. There was, however, considerable disagreement among liberals as to the nature and extent of the conflict in the natural human condition and that disagreement had important consequences for the type of agreements men made in leaving the state of nature. In many respects, their perception of the extent of conflict in the natural state led individual thinkers to different notions of the need for society and government. Because of this we must refer to the thought of two individuals who represent the extremes of the tradition—Thomas Hobbes and John Locke.

Hobbes and Locke

Persons knowledgeable in the history of political thought must by now be thoroughly alarmed at someone calling Thomas Hobbes a liberal. By reputation at least, Hobbes is commonly seen as an advocate of an extremely powerful state. He is, perhaps, the first political theorist of totalitarianism. There is no need for us to delve into the details of Hobbes's philosophy or to attempt to resolve controversies concerning his liberality. It is sufficient to say that Hobbes's advocacy of a powerful state arose from his perception of the degree of conflict present in the state of nature, and, as such, he represents the extreme wing of the liberal tradition. His description of that natural human condition has become all too famous:

> In such condition, there is no place for industry, because the fruit thereof is uncertain: and consequently no culture of the earth; no navigation nor use of the commodities that may be imported by sea; no commodious building; no instruments of moving and removing such things as require much force; no knowledge of the face of the earth; no account of time; no arts; no letters; no society; and, which is worst of all, continual fear, and danger of violent death; and the life of man, solitary, poor, nasty, brutish, and short.[1]

Hobbes pictured man as dominated by a constant fear for his very existence. Insofar as men had a natural right to everything, including the right to kill others, no man could feel safe, and consequently all of the

---

[1]Thomas Hobbes, *Leviathan, Parts I and II*, ed., with an intro. by Herbert W. Schneider (New York: The Liberal Arts Press, Inc., 1958), p. 107.

other amenities which make human life tolerable are abandoned. Certainly the Hobbesian view of the natural human condition is far from idyllic. Yet man is not doomed to live out his life under such conditions for he is capable of using certain of his faculties to improve upon his natural condition and thus produce a situation which is at least tolerable. The obverse side of the fear which dominates all men in the state of nature is a natural desire for self-preservation. All men have the basic right of preserving themselves from attack by others and all similarly desire to continue to live. Given this common human emotion, it will be possible for men to use their rational capacities (remember, reason is a means to achieve desired things) to create an artificial entity which will guarantee at least the minimal goal of self-preservation. Their reason tells them that they can, by common agreement, give up certain of their natural rights, in order to achieve the basic goal of self-preservation. This process, called a *social contract,* was for Hobbes the beginning of society and government.

The chaotic condition of the natural state is such that man is willing to relinquish a great deal of his natural freedom in order to secure some semblance of peace. Hobbes sees men coming together and consenting to give up all of their natural rights except the most basic one of self-preservation. They then create a political agreement and transfer these rights to a person called the sovereign, who is charged with insuring the self-preservation of all members of the community. At least in theory, this sovereign has no obligations to his subjects other than insuring that peace is attained, and he may use almost any measure to accomplish that end. Small wonder that Hobbes is commonly viewed as the father of modern totalitarianism. His sovereign is empowered to issue any sort of command that will further peace in the community and his subjects have consented to obey those commands however greatly they might constrain their freedom. There is one and only one ground for revolution in the Leviathan, as Hobbes called his state; if the sovereign is not capable of insuring the self-preservation of the members of the community, they are obliged to withdraw their consent. Even here there are qualifications concerning the right of rebellion. Men are, for example, obligated to give up their lives in defense of the state as long as the sovereign remains in clear command. While it is reasonably certain from his writings that Hobbes did not expect his sovereign to develop a truly totalitarian state in the sense that he would try to control all facets of men's lives, it is also rather clear that Hobbes has given him the power to do so.

It may seem that we are now a long way from the basic premises of democratic theory—surely it would be difficult to characterize the Hobbesian Leviathan as "democratic" or for that matter as "liberal." Still, many of the central concepts of democratic thought are present in the Hobbesian view of man and the origin of the state. The innate individualism, radical freedom, natural rights, relative equality, and emotion-based motivation are all part of natural man. Furthermore, we see society and government formed as a creative act of human intelligence and as institutions designed to serve the selfish interests of individuals. We may also speak of government by the consent of the governed despite its potential scope, as well as an absolute right to resist arbitrary authority even though the grounds of such resistance are greatly limited. What is significant, however, is that Hobbes has shown us a dark side of the liberal tradition. Man, although naturally free, independent, and equal, is forced to establish institutions which greatly limit his behavior in the name of self-preservation. The prospect of a return to the state of nature is so menacing that men are willing to subject themselves to tremendous limitations in the name of order. Finally, the Hobbesian view of man as dominated by passion, always attempting to maximize his own self-interest, even if it is at the expense of other men's rights, is an early indication of one of the major problems in democratic theory. We shall meet this problem later in the form of the conflict between majority rule and minority rights as well as in a discussion of democratic elitism. However, the nominal liberalism of Thomas Hobbes provides the clearest picture of the capacity of free men to tyrannize over their fellow men and the resulting consequences for political associations. After a discussion of the Hobbesian state, the conception of politics advanced by John Locke seems liberal indeed, granting initial credence to his fame as the father of modern democratic thought. From similar assumptions, John Locke derived a conception of society and government which was quite different from Hobbes.

The Lockean view of the state of nature contains many of the same elements we have seen in Hobbes, but there are also some important differences. Men are seen as distinctly individual, free, equal, and possessed of God-granted natural rights. As creations of God, however, they are all subject to His natural laws, and as such there is some sort of shared value agreement which was absent from the Hobbesian state of nature. Indeed, Locke felt that there were moral imperatives present in the natural state so that men were obliged to respect the rights of others, including, as we have mentioned, their mutual right to acquire sufficient property to sustain themselves. In a sense, one can legitimately speak of a type of primitive community present in the state of nature—a community of mankind with God as the sovereign. Despite this overlay of shared value agreement, men are still primarily interested in maximizing their selfish interests and such a situation inevitably leads to conflict. The major reason such conflict exists is that men are unable to live wholly in accordance with the natural law. The difficulty is that while God's law is knowable by all men, the passionate elements in their makeup make it difficult to apply the general natural law to specific cases. Hence, what is necessary is a human judge, a person or institution capable of applying the natural law to specific instances. What Locke is saying is that the self-interested motivation of human beings makes them poor judges where their own interests are involved and what is needed is a disinterested third party who will adjudicate disputes. It should be obvious that the Lockean perception of conflict in the natural state is quite different from that of Thomas Hobbes. Where Hobbes saw the human condition as intolerable, John Locke saw it as merely inconvenient, a situation which men could improve through the use of their rational capacities. This is a most important distinction in that men do not feel a Hobbesian compulsion to abandon the state of nature, hence they are willing to give up far less of their natural freedom to a political or social institution. Feeling that they can improve upon their situation, they do, however, band together to form a social contract whereby all members of the community agree to relinquish some freedom so that they may live more conveniently. Where Hobbes had man relinquishing all of his natural rights save self-preservation, Lockean man withholds from the contract his natural rights to life, liberty and property. These rights, as subsequent discussion will show, provide a very broad area for individual action which is not subject to the control of state or society. Before exploring that theme, however, we must closely examine the nature of the contracting process which Locke described, for it introduces several other important elements of the liberal tradition.

Locke spoke not merely of one social contract in the tradition of Hobbes, but of two agreements, one appropriately called a contract and the other more of a trustee relationship. The initial contract was called the *contract of society,* whereby men unanimously agreed to relinquish the total freedom of the state of nature and to establish a community, withholding as individuals, however, the aforementioned three rights. The society as an entity then proceeds to the establishment of the disinterested third party, absent from the state of nature. This is the *origin of government.* The type of agreement here is, however, substantially different from the earlier contract of society. Initially, it is not properly called a contract, for the two parties to the agreement (i.e. society and government) are not equals, each possessing certain rights. The government possesses no rights whatsoever, thereby making the agreement process simply one of society's imposing obligations upon the government. The designation of a trustee relationship is frequently used to describe this situation since, in a trust arrangement, the manager of the trust must operate solely in the interest of a client (in this case the society) and possesses no legal rights in the relationship. To speak of governmental rights in the Lockean political philosophy is simply incorrect. Government has no rights, but simply incurs obligations. In addition to this, the agreement to constitute a government is not made by unanimous decision, but by a majority of individuals in the society. It is given certain powers to perform limited duties, such as providing for defense of the community and contributing to the general welfare. The extent of the powers granted government is a subject of some controversy among students of Locke and it will become a major concern of our future discussion. For the moment, however, the important fact is that the society which by majority rule establishes a government may also remove it by a negative majority vote. Further, if a government is overthrown in this fashion there is no Hobbesian-like fear of a return to a chaotic state of nature, for the contract of society remains intact, only the majority-initiated government is replaced.

The Lockean notion of a dual agreement which occurs in the process of leaving the state of nature introduced another important element of the liberal tradition. In the Hobbesian state there was a one-to-one relationship between the political system (sovereign) and the individual member of the state. While Hobbesian man did retain the right of self-preservation as an individual, there was no intermediary body to act as a mitigating force or as a check on state power. In the Lockean system there is a three-tiered relationship: the individual possesses certain rights which remain with him as an individual; he is also a member of a cohesive entity called the society; he is subject to the reasonable regulations promulgated by the governmental structure. He is at one and the same time a private person, a possible member of a societal majority, and the subject of a limited government. With such a scheme, Locke provides for a clear differentiation between the general and the particular or, better, between *public* life and *private*. There are two spheres of human existence which are not subject to political action: the area encompassed by individual rights and those areas which the majority decides are not appropriate subjects for governmental policymaking. As we shall see in the subsequent discussion, the exact delineation of these areas of appropriate governmental and societal concern is one of the most crucial problems of the entire democratic tradition. For present purposes however, the Lockean distinction between public and private spheres provides another direct contrast with Marxism and fascism. In both of the latter ideologies, all individual action is seen as the appropriate concern of the state. Under fascism, the individual achieves the fulfillment of his life by contributing to national greatness, thus making all of his actions the direct concern of the state. Under the transfer culture of modern Marxism, the individual is viewed as a builder of socialism and all of his activities are public matters. Even in Marx's vision of a pure communist society where political structures have withered away, the notion of a private life removed from the scrutiny of society would be impossible. This is but another way of emphasizing the limited nature of the role of government in British liberalism. Governments are instituted by the consent of the subjects and are given certain tasks to perform; if they do not fulfill that charge, or attempt to enhance their powers, they should be abolished.

Some Initial Problems

Before leaving the political thought of John Locke we must point out several other aspects of liberalism that are expressed in his writings. This is best accomplished through a discussion of the three natural rights that individuals withhold from the contracting procedure. The words life, liberty, and property are almost as well known as the later formulation by Thomas Jefferson of "life, liberty, and the pursuit of happiness." Indeed, it is in the area of natural rights that the linkage between British liberalism and the American founding fathers is most obvious. The word "life" is Lockean shorthand for the right of self-preservation we have encountered in Hobbes's thought. With very few qualifications, again largely in the area of common defense, the individual has an absolute right to continued bodily existence, irrespective of what governments or societal majorities might wish. Although there are some difficulties with it, this seems to be a reasonably straightforward guarantee to the individual; with respect to liberty and property, however, the going gets rougher. We have already noted that Locke was no advocate of unrestrained accumulation of property, at least in the state of nature. Man was entitled to as much property as he and his family could profitably use. However, Locke also says that, during the contracting process, men agree to permit the accumulation of nonspoilable goods such as pretty rocks or scarce metals and to use them as media of exchange. In effect, men agreed to accept a rule which would indeed permit the unrestrained accumulation of objects from the environment. Yet, even after the contract, it is obvious to Locke that there must be certain restraints placed upon selfish accumulation. For example, what happens if the public interest (common good) dictates that a highway be built through my property? How do we go about balancing the general public interest in commerce and transportation with my right to own the land? Can the government, acting in its capacity as agent of the societal majority, simply dictate that my land is to be taken away for public purposes? If so, what is to stop the same government, again with the support of a majority, of depriving me of my right to self-preservation? Clearly Locke does not want that, but he provides nothing in the way of a general rule which would prevent it. A similar situation obtains when we speak of another manifestation of the natural right of property. Locke maintained that men not only had property in physical objects, but in their personal thoughts and publicly expressed opinions. Here is another extremely important part of the liberal legacy—in effect, a natural right to freedom of speech and press, perhaps even a right to privacy. Again the same questions arise. Are there no circumstances when the majority, acting through its duly constituted government may deprive me of speech? What about seditious speech? What if my speech has the effect of depriving others of their right to free speech? Similar problems occur when we speak of the natural right to liberty. After all, one of the major reasons for leaving the state of nature was the inconvenience caused by the complete freedom with which men maximized their desires. Is this total liberty to remain? If men's actions have to be constrained to avoid constant conflict, in what ways shall this be done, and who shall make the decisions? Are we to leave these matters to majority wish, and if so, what are the consequences for individual liberty?

To expect answers to such questions from John Locke, couched as they are in a more modern framework, is probably asking too much. It is asking too much because all of them require, in different ways, a resolution of the central problem of the entire democratic tradition— how are the rights of individuals (or minorities) to be weighed against the desires of majorities? Although the phrase is somewhat hackneyed, the basic question of democratic government remains that of majority rule versus minority rights. In the subsequent discussion we shall attempt to point out the various solutions to this question which have been advanced during the course of the American experiment in democratic practice. Before attempting that, however, some summary remarks are in order.

In concentrating on the thought of Thomas Hobbes and John Locke we have obviously ignored other important members of the British liberal tradition. John Stuart Mill, for example, is far more eloquent on the subject of individual liberty than is Locke. Adam Smith provides a more incisive picture of man as economic animal than does Hobbes, and David Hume has no peer in discussing the effect of human passions. Still, Locke and Hobbes provide us with most of the basic presuppositions of modern democratic theory as well as pointing to a great many problems which will trouble their successors. There is little doubt as to the effect of British liberalism on the development of an American democratic tradition, for the writings of its major representatives were read and digested by most of the founding fathers, and it is to their efforts we must now turn.

BIBLIOGRAPHY

Barker, Sir Ernest, ed. *Social Contract.* New York: Oxford University Press, 1960. A collection of essays by Locke, Hume, and Rousseau. Particularly noteworthy is Barker's introductory essay which provides rigorous categories for distinguishing between types of social contract theories.

Gough, John. *The Social Contract.* Oxford: Oxford University Press, 1936. A classic study of the notion of contract and the appropriate limits of governmental power.

O'Conner, D. J. *John Locke.* Baltimore: Penguin Books, 1952.

Peters, Richard. *Hobbes.* Baltimore: Penguin Books, 1956.

Rejai M. *Democracy: The Contemporary Theories.* New York: Atherton Press, 1967. A good collection of essays organized around the themes of definitions of democracy and preconditions for a democratic state. Both historical and contemporary materials are included.

Sartori, Giovanni. *Democratic Theory.* New York: Frederick A. Praeger, 1965. This is a difficult book to categorize, for it involves logical analysis of democracy as a concept, historical discussion of attempts at implementation, as well as a presentation of more modern problems of democratic thought.

Wolin, Sheldon. *Politics and Vision: Continuity and Innovation in Western Thought.* Boston: Little, Brown, 1960. In general, a superb interpretive textbook in the history of political thought. In particular, his chapter on "the decline of the political" provides brilliant insights into British liberalism.

Original Works

Harrison, Wilfrid, ed. *Sources in British Political Thought, 1593-1900.* New York: The Free Press, 1965.

Hobbes, Thomas. *Leviathan. Parts I and II.* Edited with introduction by Herbert W. Schneider. New York: Bobbs-Merrill, 1958.

Locke, John. *Of Civil Government.* Introduction by Russell Kirk. Chicago: Henry Regnery, 1955.

Chapter 9

DEMOCRACY
IN
AMERICA

"Give all power to the few and they will oppress the many, give all power to the many and they will oppress the few." These words sum up the central dilemma of the democratic tradition. Once one accepts as given the notion that all people ought to have a voice in their governance, the task becomes one of devising a process of decision making which will translate the legitimate wishes of popular majorities into public policy. As we have seen in British liberalism, however, the difficulty lies in attempting to define the word "legitimate." In addition to that problem there is the historical fact that prior democratic forms of government seemed inherently unstable, quickly degenerating into either mob rule or dictatorship. The task then was one of developing a stable political system in which the inherent rights of individuals and minorities were protected, and which, at the same time, was capable of responding to the expressed wishes of majorities of its citizens. The examination of these questions as they were debated and resolved in their American context will occupy us for the greater part of this chapter. Before addressing ourselves to them, however, we must briefly examine the political and social context of the America of the late 1700s, largely as a means of discussing some of the presuppositions of a democratic society. Much as in the case of Marx's alienated industrial proletariat, democratic theory presupposes the existence of certain conditions and the presence or absence of those conditions can greatly effect the success of the ensuing government.

The equalitarian premise of British liberalism was very much part of the intellectual tradition in the young colonies. The removal of overt distinctions between classes (titles, etc.) and the influence of British libertarian rhetoric had produced a situation where political equality was taken to be the basic presupposition of all government. One need not delve too deeply into American history to recall that this notion of political equality was more often honored in rhetoric than in practice— all were created equal except black slaves, women, nonproperty holders, and so on. Nevertheless, the acceptance of the concept of political equality as an ideal, if nothing else, is an important presupposition for any regime which deems itself democratic. A more important condition which existed in the colonies was a tradition of participation in politics. The reasons for the existence of such a tradition were many, but the significant fact was that many citizens had indeed participated in government and, more importantly, felt they ought to participate in making decisions which affected their lives. While government was viewed with a good deal of suspicion by many people, it was not thought of as the preserve of some ruling class, elected or hereditary. Again, it is too easy to generalize from the active political participation that characterized the propertied classes in places like Virginia—we simply do not know the extent to which a common laborer, for example, participated in political decision making. However, in the minds of the men who were to have the greatest influence on the making of the American political system, the concept of active participation in public affairs was a basic value. Similarly, the notion that the ideas of another person ought to be tolerated even though they were deemed wrong, was a major value at least in intellectual circles. Again, much of the practice in the colonies did not live up to this ideal as evidenced in assorted witch trials and a good deal of religious persecution. Still, the value existed and was to become incorporated in the Constitution. One might go on to speak of other factors that made the climate conducive to some sort of democratic regime. A large land space, relatively homogeneous English tradition, a country removed from the immediate presence of major military powers—all of these things contributed to produce an environment which made experimentation with democratic government possible. One of the scholarly fads of recent years has been an attempt to draw up a list of preconditions necessary for the establishment of a stable democratic government. Thus we are told that there must be a rather well-developed industrial economy, widespread literacy, a homogeneous culture, toleration of political opposition and so on. Whether the construction of such lists is helpful in predicting the possibility of a viable democratic regime is a subject which need not concern us here. What is important from an ideological perspective is that the values held by the founding fathers of the American political system in general conformed to those of the democratic liberal tradition. There is no doubt that the imperfect application of those values had important, even horrifying, consequences for individuals—if one, for example, happened to be black. Perhaps it is better to look at the values embodied in the various American political documents as ideals to be achieved rather than statements of reality; as such the entire American political tradition can be seen as an attempt to achieve them. Whatever the case, let us return to the major subject under discussion; that is, how to construct a government wherein no one group is capable of oppressing another.

A Democratic Spectrum

The use of the word "democratic" has been rather vague and equivocal thus far in our presentation. It will continue to be so for the excellent reason that the word can legitimately be used to describe an entire spectrum of governmental forms. Perhaps the closest we can come to an initial operational definition of democracy is a political philosophy which advocates popular sovereignty and at the same time insists on a sphere of individual rights which are not subject to popular will. Such a definition of course provides a great deal of room for differing types of democratic regimes and perhaps accounts for most of the difficulty we have in deciding whether a particular government is appropriately called democratic. If a government, for example, were so concerned with the protection of individual rights that it refused to acquiesce to the will of a large majority of its citizens on a rather trivial matter, could we call it democratic? On the other hand, if it were determined to translate majority preferences into public policy on every occasion, irrespective of the effect of those policies on individual rights, would it be a democratic regime? Here again we meet the crucial question of defining the relationship between majority rule and individual rights. Unfortunately there is no simple answer to the question. Perhaps we can best see the complexity of the problem by speaking of a spectrum of positions on the matter—on the one end of the spectrum individuals who advocate close to pure majority rule, on the other, those who are willing to sacrifice many majority wishes in the name of preserving individual freedom. Having defined the extremes of the spectrum we will then be in the position of discussing at length the American attempt (herein called the Madisonian system) to provide a middle ground.

One of the favorite rhetorical devices of teachers of political philosophy is to declare that no serious student of democratic government has ever advocated pure, unconstrained majority rule. Amidst shocked cries from students who have been brought up to believe in the sanctity of majorities he then goes on to point out the obvious. If fifty plus percent of the population were given absolute power, what would prohibit them from grossly discriminating against the rest of the citizenry? Indeed, what would prevent that majority from decreeing that all members of the minority leave the state or even be killed. Minimally, majorities, however great their power, must provide for the continued existence of minorities. In addition, a democratic spokesman would declare that the minority at any one moment must be free to attempt to convince others of the validity of its position—that is, it must have the opportunity to become a majority at a future date. Having disposed of the "straw man" of pure majoritarianism does not, unfortunately, greatly help the situation for we still do not know what precise limitations are to be placed upon popular majorities. A person standing at the majoritarian extreme of our democratic spectrum would declare that majorities should be given wide latitude in decision-making power, subject only to minimal constraints. While majoritarian democrats are aware of the potentially tyrannical behavior of individuals and therefore agree that there must be some limitation, their central concern is the rapid translation of popular will into public policy. In general, they are simply more trustful of popular majorities, and declare that the denial of popular will in the name of protecting individual rights is really succumbing to a tyranny of the minority. If minorities are capable of frustrating majority wishes how, they ask, can we speak of popular sovereignty? Some students of John Locke claim to find a good deal of majoritarianism in his writings, and it is probably fair to assert that most of the democratic thought of the twentieth century has stressed majoritarianism. We shall, however, reserve further discussion of this end of the democratic spectrum until the next chapter; for the moment let us examine the individualistic position.

The individualistic position should by now be fairly obvious. It is in general distrustful of the decision-making power of majorities and consequently has a rather negative view of government as a whole. If we recall the distinction between public and private spheres of action made by British liberalism, this end of the democratic spectrum would advocate a very large private area with the public sector providing only for minimal common needs. Again with reference to British liberalism, the individualists' position is close to that of an anarchic state of nature, i.e., man needs government, but for extremely limited purposes. While the individualist tradition is distrustful of all types of authority, in its American manifestation it generally assumed the stance of opposition to majority power. As indicated by our earlier presentation of Lockean thought, it is quite possible to read highly individualistic overtones in his thought—man after all moves from his natural state of freedom only for individual convenience. This puts John Locke in the interesting position of being a champion of both ends of the democratic spectrum, perhaps accounting for much of his fame. At any rate, the individualistic or minoritarian tradition achieved its greatest appeal in the eighteenth and nineteenth centuries in the United States, and some would contend it is being resurrected in the mid-twentieth. Again these are subjects for the next chapter. Perhaps it should be noted here that there is no necessary theoretical conflict between the majoritarian and individualistic positions on this democratic spectrum. In theory, it would be quite possible to have largely majoritarian rule where the majority of citizens had a firm commitment to individualistic values. While majorities might possess the power to tyrannize over minorities, custom, habit, and the prevailing cultural values could, in theory, insure that they never used that power. To the individualist, generally distrustful of his fellow man and of his government, such a theoretical guarantee would simply not be sufficient. Having defined in general terms a spectrum of democratic thought, let us now examine in detail one attempt to find a middle road between the extremes of majoritarianism and individualism. While it was but one attempt it was a most important one, for James Madison's solution to the problems of democratic government provided the theoretical rationale for the American Constitution.

The American Environment

The American Declaration of Independence of 1776 provided an eloquent statement of the ideals and aspirations of a democratic society. The now familiar themes of equality, freedom, government by consent, and the right of resistance to arbitrary authority, formed the ideological framework for the American revolution. Such a statement of ideals, however lofty, did not provide a solution to the type of problems in democratic theory of which we have been speaking, nor did it establish a workable framework of government. Operating under the almost *ad hoc* rules of the Articles of Confederation for almost a decade, the young nation had reached a point where few persons were satisfied with the governance of the country, and committed democrats began to despair of the possibility of having an enduring democracy in America. The constitutional convention of 1787 provided an opportunity to reconstruct the government along more viable lines and a group of bold men made sure that that opportunity did not pass. The convention has become many things to many people: to the patriot it is the birthplace of the American form of democracy; to the student of political coalitions it is a fascinating study in political bargaining; to the person interested in political ideas it provides a forum for the discussion and resolution of enduring problems in democratic theory. We cannot delve into all of the personalities present nor discuss the ideas they presented—one must tread lightly in the preserve of American historians. If we are forced to find a figure who approximated an authoritative interpreter of the principles embodied in the Constitution there is little doubt that James Madison must be the choice. The Madisonian conception of the nature of the American system as articulated at the convention and later formalized in the *Federalist* papers provides the closest thing to an authoritative interpretation that we possess. Following numerous writers on American political thought, our presentation will largely be confined to Madison's interpretation, particularly as it is developed in *Federalist X*. Before moving to that detailed presentation, however, let us refer again to the major theme of majority and minority compatibility and note some of the effects on popular thinking wrought by the Articles of Confederation.

The American Revolution was fought in the name of resistance to arbitrary authority and in defense of the traditional rights of Englishmen. Naturally the symbol of that capricious authority became the English monarchy. Whether that was a correct assessment of the situation or not is unimportant in this context, but it did produce a widespread distrust of a powerful head of state. This fear of monarchy was, of course, reflected in the postwar Articles of Confederation which provided for little effective national leadership, much less a powerful head of state. In the rhetoric of democratic theory, the prime fear was tyranny by one individual or by a minority. The resulting political arrangements reflected that apprehension. Experience with the Articles of Confederation however, convinced many of the men who gathered at Philadelphia that the prime threat to American democracy lay not in a tyrannical individual or minority but in the capricious moods of majorities. This distrust of uneducated, mob-like majorities fits in nicely with the aristocratic attitudes of many of the founding fathers. It did, however, provide some balance to the question of controlling unwarranted authority. The central problem of American democracy then became, at least in Madison's eyes, the establishment of a popularly based government which would avoid the excess of tyranny whether imposed by a minority or a majority. It was to this problem that he addressed himself in *Federalist X,* justifiably the most famous analytical writing to emerge from the constitutional period.

The *Federalist* papers were written by John Jay, Alexander Hamilton and James Madison as individual newspaper pieces designed to convince the people of the state of New York to support the recently completed constitution. While their major purpose was persuasion, the papers also provided a defense of the philosophical presuppositions and institutional framework provided for in that document. In particular, Madison's tenth paper addressed itself directly to the classic democratic problem of tyranny, and claimed to have found a ". . . Republican remedy for the diseases most incident to Republican Government."[1]

The Madisonian System

Madison begins his discussion by presupposing the desirability of some form of popular government. There is little in the way of systematic analysis of other possible governmental types. It is simply asserted that a government which denied popular sovereignty would be imcompatible with the character of the American people. Indeed, there seemed to be almost universal agreement that some sort of popular government was what was needed, but the problem lay in devising one which would avoid the difficulties of past democratic regimes. An analysis of all past experiments with democratic governments indicated that they were constantly subject to instability. The most common cause of this instability was a majority of the citizens who, for whatever reason, attempted to impose their will upon the rest of the society and in the process deprived them of their natural rights. Simply stated, prior democratic forms had a marked tendency to degenerate into mob rule. Sensing its inability to govern, the mob would then elevate a single person to assume dictatorial powers in the name of the people, and that particular democratic experiment was finished. The cycle of majority tyranny leading to dictatorial rule and the consequent loss of freedom was all too familiar to students of history. Some even contended that it was impossible to create a stable and enduring democratic government. This tendency of a group of citizens, whether a majority or a minority of the whole, to seize power and deprive other citizens of their natural rights, was the cardinal difficulty with democracies. A solution would have to be found before the system could work. One must stop and record a distinctly Hobbesian note in Madison's analysis of human nature. Human passions are such that, in the absence of constraints, people will naturally seek dominance over their fellow man. Any political philosopher or constitution-maker must take this into account or his efforts will be for naught. This made the constitution-makers' task even more difficult in that democratic governments were most succeptable to this disease that Madison called *faction*. Democracies, to a greater extent than any other governmental

---

[1] Jacob E. Cook, ed., *The Federalist* (New York: The World Publishing Company, 1961), p. 65.

form, permitted the individual liberty which led to the development of faction. Liberty was the air that spread the fire of faction, but to remove that air would be to deny the basic premise of democratic government. Popular sovereignty would mean little if there was no liberty to form and articulate opinions. One cannot, then, solve the problem of factions by removing the liberty that permits them to exist for, as Madison says, the cure would be worse than the disease.[2] Madison advances and rejects one other possible cure for the causes of faction in democracies. Factions would not exist if it were not for the diversity of human interests which forces men into competition for dominance. In theory, then, we could remove the cause of faction by insuring that all the citizens have similar opinions. If everyone agreed on things there would be no need for any group to attempt to dominate another. Madison gives this cure short shrift, simply declaring that diverse interests are a necessary part of human nature and it would be impossible to give everyone the same opinions. Again we must stop and note that Madison has raised a very important point and, while his answer is consistent with his own philosophical premises, more modern democratic theorists will later pay a great deal of attention to the possibility of "giving everyone the same opinions." In an age where control of information and the use of propaganda are everyday realities, the possibility of controlling the opinions of an entire society is not so easily dismissed. Indeed, we have seen that the other two ideologies discussed attempt to do precisely that. Consistent with the individualistic premises of his liberal heritage, however, Madison rejected the possibility, and despaired of finding a cure for the causes of faction.

If the causes of faction are latent in human nature, the only other possible solution to the problems factions generate is to attempt to control their evil effects. While human nature cannot be substantially changed, it might be possible to devise a set of institutions which would militate against the tyrannical tendencies of men. It is in his proposed system of control of faction that the greatness of the Madisonian solution is to be found. Initially, he dismissed in a rather cavalier fashion the dangers of a minority faction. They present no difficulty because their evil designs can be controlled by the principle of majority rule. If a minority of citizens band together to seek to deprive others of their natural rights, the vast majority of citizens will realize the threat and deny them access to power. One can call this a summary treatment of the problem for it presupposes initially that the majority of citizens will recognize a threat when presented and further it assumes that access to political decision-making organs is the only means by which one group

---

[2]*Ibid.*, p. 58.

can oppress another. In the ensuing discussion of theories of democratic elitism, we shall encounter the question of minority faction presented in a much more graphic manner. However, for Madison, the ability of the majority to control the minority through the ballot box was a sufficient control over a factional minority. Disposing of that, he then addressed himself to the classical problem of democratic theory, majority tyranny. It is obvious that the control of the vote which blocked minorities will have no effect here, for majorities can elect their leaders to positions of power. This being the case, Madison must rely on devices other than the standard democratic control of political majorities; his solutions fall into three general categories. First there is a reliance on a particular type of political and economic environment; second, the introduction of a concept of representation; third, the development of a series of institutions which will make it difficult for a tyrannical majority to assume political power. Let us take up each of these aspects of the Madisonian solution in order.

It was commonplace in classical theory that the democratic form of government was best suited to small states. In that the translation of popular preferences into public policy was one of the major goals of that type of regime, it was understandably thought that the most accurate presentation of the people's views would occur if each citizen gave voice to his own thought. This type of direct democracy, while guaranteeing that the people's views were accurately portrayed, necessarily limited the size of the state. While notions of including some scheme whereby certain persons were elected to represent the views of other citizens had been advanced, the conventional wisdom held that democracies or republics should be small, the ideal being a modern variation of the Greek city-state. As we shall discuss briefly, Madison's idea of a democratic republic involved such a scheme of representation as one of its essential elements, but his real break with the tradition came with his advocacy of a very large state. Turning the classical position around, Madison argued that one of the major causes of instability in prior republics was that their small size made it very easy for a tyrannical majority to form and gain control of the government. In the close quarters of a small state it was very easy for human passions to become embroiled at a moment's notice and for the wrath of the majority to be unleashed upon innocent citizens. If the physical area of the state were much larger and its population more numerous, the formation of a majority faction would be a far more difficult enterprise. While the majority in one area of the state might be engulfed by a factional impulse, the spread of the views might well be contained by the sheer size of the country. Furthermore, given what he knew about the diversity of human passions, Madison argued that a large number of citizens would tend to produce a whole series of small interest groups, thereby making it very difficult to form a majority which was bent on depriving others of their rights. The diversity of human interests would at worst lead to the formation of numerous minority factions which could then be controlled through majority voting rules. Rather than attempt to prevent the formation of these self-interested groups, governments ought to encourage them, for the effect of many interests was to insure that no one group could gain sufficient power to be tyrannical. The existence of a multiplicity of factions would have the effect of achieving a balance, thereby mitigating against the possibility of a majority faction.

Here, then, is the Madisonian notion of an *extended republic*. We must stop and note both how well the argument flows from his premises as well as the ingenuity of the solution. Man is selfish and power-seeking by nature, and those drives have historically led to the downfall of regimes based upon popular sovereignty. Instead of attempting to change men so that they behave in a more benign fashion (an improbable task at best), let us take these selfish motives and use them to produce a situation where they cancel out each other; the private selfish vices will produce public selfless virtue. This is a clear statement of the idea which is later to be known as the theory of balance and pluralism. Because of the inability of any one group to dominate, there will be plural centers of power within the society and these will tend to balance each other to produce a society which is both stable and enduring. Further, Madison accomplished this feat without removing the freedom which permits factions to form, thus insuring that individuals will at least have the opportunity to pursue their own selfish interests. Finally, with an eye toward future discussion, it should be noted that Madison thought the major source of faction was man's desire for economic goods. It was well known that competition for scarce resources was one of the major sorts of conflict in any state, or as Karl Marx was to say some fifty years later, the state was designed primarily to protect economic privilege. Recognizing the economic basis of most factions, Madison proposed to control their evil effects by encouraging the formation of a great number of them and putting them in competition with one another. We have, then, in the political realm, the equivalent of some form of economic *laissez-faire*, whereby multiplicity and competition lead to equilibrium and insure that no one group gains ascendancy. Indeed, the entire system is designed to avoid the political equivalent of monopoly in much the same way as classical economic theory sought to accomplish the same end in the economic arena. As a preliminary remark then, we should note that the Madisonian political system seems to be most compatible with some form of *laissez-faire* capitalist economy where the state plays the role of umpire to competing factions. We shall explore the relationship between democratic political forms and varying economic systems at a later point in the discussion; for the moment let us move on to the concept of representation, the second device that Madison proposed for controlling majorities.

Up to this point we have been using the words "democratic" and "republican" as synonyms to describe a generally defined popular government. It must now be noted that Madison distinguished between the terms, calling his proposed regime a republic and contrasting it with democratic regimes. To his mind a republic differed from democratic forms in that it was larger physically and numerically, and it included a scheme of representation. This distinction has largely been lost in modern times where we tend to think of all democracies as at least potentially large states possessing some scheme of representation. The modern term "representative democracy" is very close to the Madisonian republic. However, Madison's proposed system of representation was designed to serve functions other than the mere reflection of popular opinion; he saw it as an additional curb on potentially tyrannical majorities. In many respects the word "representative" contains built-in ambiguity. Common language as well as philosophical tradition employs it with two rather different meanings. On the one hand, a representative can be viewed as a person whose task is to discover the preferences of those whom he represents on a particular matter and cast his vote in accordance with the wishes of a majority of his constituents. In this meaning the representative is seen as the accurate reflector of his constituency, simply a device to collect, synthesize, and report opinions. Modern technology might well be capable of replacing this type of representative with a computer programmed to record and transmit majority preferences. The other meaning of the word has the representative standing, as it were, in the place of his constituents and making decisions which he deems are in the best interests of those whom he represents, as well as the total community. Here the representative is seen as the *agent* of his constituents, exercising his judgment to the best of his ability as each of them presumably would do in a situation of direct democracy. In this meaning of the word, it is quite possible that the representative will act contrary to the opinions of a majority of his constituents; he might feel he has more information, possesses a broader vantage point, or simply knows better. These are two rather different notions of what it means to be a representative and presumably any conception of representative democracy will vary depending on the meaning given to the initial term. The most common resolution of this difficulty is to use the word with both meanings; in effect, assigning two separate, and perhaps contradictory, roles to the legislator. Where the representative is normally the transmitter of majority opinion, at times we expect him to assume the role of statesman and ignore his constituents' wishes if he believes them to be wrong. It is in performance of this role that people can write about "profiles in courage" whereby a representative is politically defeated as the result of his principled stand. In the Madisonian scheme, the legislative role is seen in this dual fashion, but, most importantly, the representative in his statesman role is seen as providing a check against majority tyranny. Madison is rather explicit about the matter:

> The effect of the first difference [representation] is, on the one hand to refine and enlarge the public views, by passing them through the medium of a chosen body of citizens, whose wisdom may best discern the true interest of their country, and whose patriotism and love of justice, will be least likely to sacrifice it to temporary or partial considerations.[3]

Clearly, there will be times when the Madisonian legislator will be expected to ignore the temporary or partial considerations of his constituents, thereby denying the supremacy of popular will. One of the reasons for the complexity of the process of elections described in the Constitution as well as the staggered terms of office and length of term is to provide for some distance between the representative and his constituents. Perhaps given sufficient time to think the matter over, his constituents will realize that his act in frustrating popular will was the best course of action after all. Still, the representative must eventually submit himself for reelection and too many such acts of courage will surely lessen his chances. The Madisonian concept of representation is often called an antidemocratic device, and in a sense that is correct. If we use a more majoritarian definition of democracy there is little doubt that this legislative role is designed on occasion to frustrate majority will. Still, Madison could argue that it is but a temporary check on majorities and ultimately consistent with the principles of popular sovereignty, for the constituents have the last word at election time. It is rather difficult to speak of the Madisonian conception of the legislator *in vacuo* for it is part and parcel of the elaborate framework of institutions that were devised to provide additional safeguards against tyranny. Insofar as this third general category of mechanical or legal checks involves the entire structure of the United States Constitution, our discussion must, of necessity, be limited, but we can hardly ignore the political framework that was to make the whole system function correctly.

We have seen that the effect of Madison's first defense against tyranny (hereinafter called the *size principle*) was to produce a society in which varied interest groups were free to pursue their designs while insuring

---

[3]*Ibid.,* p. 62.

that no one group could achieve sufficient dominance to become tyrannical. The framework of legal rules and governmental institutions advanced in the Constitution was designed to implement the size principle by providing access to major interests while assuring that there were appropriate checks on all the groups concerned. In a sense the entire Constitution, with its elaborate system of checks, powers, and balances is but a political reflection of the size principle discussed earlier. Presupposing a multiplicity of interests we must now give them access to political power so that they may press their claims effectively, and, correspondingly, have sufficient power so that they may block potentially tyrannical actions by other groups. The initial device designed to accomplish this was the constitutional document itself which was to be the supreme law of the land and which would prescribe the powers and limits granted to government as a whole. The Supreme Court was to become the ultimate arbiter of claims regarding the powers and limitations set forth in the document. This firmly established the principle of limited government as well as insured a legalistic framework of operation. It has often been said that every matter in the United States eventually becomes a court case and this is precisely what was intended, firmly established legal remedies for the routinization of conflict. The other two major institutions of the federal government were specifically designed to give representation to large interest groups within the country. The President, although he was to be "above faction," was also viewed as particularly responsive to the propertied classes, and his power of veto provided a means to check the excesses of the legislative branch. This is readily apparent if we recall the method of election of a President as it was originally detailed in the Constitution, wherein he was chosen by a group of electors who were acting as representatives of their respective states. The division of the legislative branch into an upper and a lower chamber each with similar but not identical powers gave access to other interest groups. Representation in the Senate was by states, thereby insuring that the interests of large populous states would not overshadow those of the smaller ones. Granted, the existence of relatively independent states would have dictated some sort of federal arrangement in any case, but if we assume with Madison that certain types of interests can be geographically defined (i.e. by state boundaries), the Senate affords them an important voice. The House of Representatives served as the voice of the people and, through the requirement of frequent elections, was presumably closest to the everyday wishes of the population. The House of Representatives was the most majoritarian institution in the entire Madisonian scheme and was designed to provide representation for more populous urban areas. These three major institutions, combined with the bicameral division of the legislature, are separate, each with unique powers, but they are also interconnected through the necessity of gaining the acquiescence of other branches before public policy can be formed. In certain instances, of course, it is possible for the will of one branch to dominate over another—as in the case of overriding a presidential veto—but the general principle is nicely summed up by the old phrase of "check and balance."

In a similar fashion the practice of staggering elections and terms of service was seen as another check against potentially factional majorities. While members of the most populous house are elected every two years and presumably reflect rapid changes in public opinion, assumption of control in the Senate and the presidency takes a minimum of four years. Once again, it would take four years for a majority bent on tyranny to assume control of sufficient power to put their designs into effect. If we include the Supreme Court—whose members are to serve, with good behavior, for life—as a check on tyranny, presumably a majority could be frustrated for as long as it took a certain number of old men to die. It must be emphasized, however, that these are only structural limitations on majority power; in the real world a Supreme Court which did not somewhat follow the election returns would undoubtedly endanger the legitimacy of the institution. Similarly, in a system which is to some extent based on the self-interest of representatives being reelected, a senator would be foolish to ignore completely a powerful shift in popular will among his constituents, even though he was not up for immediate reelection. It is probably impossible to achieve an absolute veto over legislation strongly desired by a majority over a long period of time without sacrificing the idea of popular sovereignty. Minimally, what Madison was trying to achieve with institutional checks and balances and these other mechanical devices was *delay*, a period of time in which members of a majority faction might rethink their actions and change their behavior. In this context we should note the emergence of a slightly more optimistic side to the Madisonian view of human nature. Earlier it was stated that his assumptions concerning the essential selfishness of human beings were more in line with Hobbes's thoughts on the matter than they were with John Locke's more benign view of man. While this remains true, Madison was sophisticated enough to see that there were different types of selfish interests, some more disruptive for political systems than others. He was particularly impressed with how rapidly some popular passion could infect a majority and result in some precipitous action which further reflection would have led even selfish men to avoid. We know that Madison was much impressed with the political writing of David Hume (much of *Federalist X* is borrowed from Hume's work) and that a major category of Humean thought was a distinction between calm and violent passion.

While both of these types of passion were based upon individual self-interest, the former were more volatile and temporary while the latter looked to long-range selfish concerns. The violent passion of men might tell them to try to take away the natural rights of members of the community for some offense against popular opinion, but their calm passion would warn that on some future occasion they too might be subject to the wrath of some new irate majority. Note that both of these passions are based upon selfish interest, but they would lead to quite different kinds of behavior. If institutional checks and balances could produce a delay in which tempers were allowed to cool, long range self-interest, or as Madison called it, "enlightened self-interest," might prevail. One of the reasons for the preoccupation of many of the founding fathers with processes of education was an attempt to insure that citizens would adopt this long-range view of their interests. While Madison paid perhaps too little attention to such matters of habit and education in the *Federalist*, one of the later obsessions of the leadership of the country was the production of a well-educated citizenry. Some commentators argue that if Madison had been more concerned with developing democratic habit patterns in the populace and with insuring the existence of a liberal value structure, he need not have been so concerned with institutional checks on majority tyranny.[4] Whatever the case, the institutional checks were at least in part intended to encourage the ascendency of enlightened self-interest.

"In the extent and proper structure of the Union, therefore, we behold a Republican remedy for the diseases most incident to Republican Government."[5] These words, from the concluding paragraph of *Federalist X*, are Madisonian shorthand for summarizing the entire endeavor of the founding fathers as well as their claim to fame. We have attempted to describe the "extent and proper structure" remedies of the Madisonian republic using the threefold distinction of *size, representation*, and *mechanical checks*; let us now briefly look at his claim to have found a "republican remedy." Madison desired a government based upon the principle of popular sovereignty which avoided the tyrannical excesses of past forms of popular government. Further, in permitting individuals the liberty to acquire property, form interest groups, and press demands on government, the system had to be capable of accommodating the constantly changing desires of men, while avoiding the excesses of instability. To form a stable and enduring republic, he felt it would be necessary to compromise the basic principle of popular sovereignty to the extent necessary to insure that men did not abuse each

---

[4]See the discussion in Robert A. Dahl, *A Preface to Democratic Theory* (Chicago: The University of Chicago Press, 1956), pp. 17-21.

[5]Cook, *The Federalist*, p. 65.

other's rights. The question that remains is, on the one hand, whether the constraints he instituted were sufficient to prevent tyranny and, on the other hand, whether they so constrained majority will as to violate the basic principle of popular sovereignty. Much of our discussion in the ensuing chapter will address itself to these questions as we examine the attempts of more modern democratic theorists to wrestle with these problems. Some preliminary comments on the Madisonian project, however, seem in order here.

Reactions to Madisonianism

Many individuals, particularly after the constitutional system had been in operation for a period of time, felt that Madison's efforts to check majority faction had not been successful. He had, it was argued, made no provision whatsoever for the development of the political party system which emerged early in the history of the republic. That being the case, even if one granted that his system controlled the development of *natural* majority factions, it did not stop the formation of the *artificial* majority factions produced by political parties. Parties were capable of forging temporary alliances between quite disparate minority factions for the purpose of securing control of the political structure, whereupon they went about achieving their minoritarian goals at the expense of the rights of others. Although this type of faction was not the natural majority type that Madison so feared, it was equally capable of tyrannical action. This general position was most eloquently advanced by John C. Calhoun, the major spokesman for Southern interests in pre-Civil War days. In the name of further defense of individual and states' rights, Calhoun argued for an extension of the control mechanisms on majorities, largely by giving any major interest group (states, sections) veto power over any legislation which affected it.[6] Such a position would have further diminished the power of the political system and greatly expended the sphere of private action. Whatever the details of Calhoun's proposals, he is an excellent representative of those who believed that Madison correctly identified the major problem of majority faction but that his control devices were only partially effective and would have to be supplemented.

On the other side of the coin, many individuals, some of whom we shall meet in the next chapter, asserted that Madison had been so preoccupied with the potential of majority tyranny that he produced a system which so constrained majorities that it made a mockery of the

---

[6]John C. Calhoun, *A Disquisition on Government*, ed. with intro., C. Gordon Post (New York: The Liberal Arts Press, Inc., 1953).

principle of popular sovereignty. From this perspective, the sociological and political checks against majorities made it very easy for a small group of men to frustrate legitimate majority desires, thereby producing a government by minority. Minimally, the minority in control of the government at any particular time could deny legitimate popular claims, but it also could produce the opposite of Madison's great fear—that is, tyranny by the minority. Finally, in somewhat of an extension of the above argument, there are those who contend that Madison achieved precisely what he intended. From this vantage point, Madison was a Virginia aristocrat, terrified of the possibility of majority power over the propertied interests of his class, yet sufficiently sophisticated to realize that some form of popular government was inevitable in America. As such, he devised an ingenious system which gave some power to popular majorities, sufficient to permit them to "blow off steam" and to believe they were actually governing, while making it virtually impossible for them to achieve enough control to initiate basic change in the capitalist economic system. This economically based analysis views the Madisonian system as a type of sophisticated conspiracy to perpetuate control by propertied and moneyed classes by buying off the people with some minor democratic concessions.[7]

Needless to say, we are as yet in no position to evaluate these varying interpretations of the Madisonian enterprise. The types of questions raised here do, however, comprise a loose conceptual framework for the debate concerning the nature and success of the American democratic experiment, a debate which continues to this day. The existence of that debate is in itself, however, somewhat of a testimony to the success of Madison and the founding fathers in that the system they devised still exists, if only in broad outline. Few would argue with the proposition that the political system they devised has been capable of supporting change and enduring for a long period of time. Many, however, will argue with the statement that the remedies which produced stability were republican or that the system has produced a truly democratic society.

BIBLIOGRAPHY

Arieli, Yehoshua. *Individualism and Nationalism in American Ideology.* Baltimore, Md.: Penguin Books, 1966. A wide-ranging study of the

---

[7]Charles A. Beard was the most famous advocate of this general view. See Charles A. Beard, *An Economic Interpretation of the Constitution of the United States* (New York: The Macmillan Company, 1961).

tension between the poles of the individual and the nation in the American experience.

Boorstin, Daniel J. *The Genius of American Politics.* Chicago: The University of Chicago Press, 1953. A good statement of the thesis that the American political experiment owes its success to a lack of reliance on rigid philosophical premises, and an emphasis on pragmatic adaptation to changing circumstances.

Dahl, Robert A. *A Preface to Democratic Theory.* Chicago: University of Chicago Press, 1963. Considered by some to be the best short introduction to the subject.

Eidelberg, Paul. *The Philosophy of the American Constitution.* New York: The Free Press, 1968. Subtitled "a reinterpretation of the intentions of the founding fathers," Eidelberg's work is valuable for its analysis of the purposes particular institutions were designed to accomplish.

Main, Jackson Turner. *The Anti-Federalists: Critics of the Constitution.* Chicago: Quadrangle Books, 1961. The antifederalists side of the debate over the Constitution. These debates bring into sharp focus many of the enduring problems of democratic thought.

Riemer, Neal. *The Democratic Experiment.* Vol. 1. Princeton, New Jersey: D. Van Nostrand Company, Inc., 1967.

Tocqueville, Alexis de. *Democracy in America.* New York: Random House, 1954. Tocqueville's classic study of the formative stages of American democracy, including a rather early warning of the dangers inherent in excessive majoritarianism.

Original Works

Calhoun, John C. *A Disquisition on Goverment.* Edited by C. Gordon Post. Indianapolis: Bobbs-Merrill, 1953.

Cooke, Jacob E., ed. *The Federalist.* New York: World Publishing Company, 1961.

Madison, James. *Notes of Debates in the Federal Convention of 1787 Reported by James Madison.* Edited by Adrienne Koch. New York: W. W. Norton, 1958.

Solberg, Winton U., ed. *The Federal Convention and the Formation of the American States.* New York: Liberal Arts Press, 1958.

Chapter 10

DEMOCRACY
IN
THE
TWENTIETH
CENTURY

Many students of American history view the Constitution of 1787 and the political philosophy it embodied as a conservative reaction to the majoritarian democratic ideals expressed in the Declaration of Independence. Where the Declaration recognized equality, freedom, and the supremacy of popular will as the ultimate goals of government, Madison's system compromised on equality, attempted to restrict freedom through competition, and placed severe checks on the power of popular majorities—all in the pursuit of stability. One need not agree with such an assessment of the motivation of the founding fathers to recognize that the overall pattern of development of the American political system since 1787 has been toward *increasing majoritarianism*. We have already noted that the early development of a political party system provided focal points for groups interested in attaining power, and to a certain extent mitigated the balance which Madison thought would be achieved through a multitude of diverse factions. While American political parties remain rather weak in contrast to their highly disciplined European counterparts, the existence of a two party system did make it possible for majorities to gain control of the government and implement their wishes. In addition, the gradual extension of the franchise throughout the nineteenth and early twentieth centuries inevitably moved the system toward great majoritarianism. As individuals who lacked property, blacks, and women entered the political arena as full-fledged members, their demands on the political system would have to be taken into account, if not fully satisfied. However imperfect the

American political system of the mid-twentieth century might be, it functions in a far more majoritarian fashion than its eighteenth-century ancestor. Structural changes such as the popular election of senators and the evolution of the role of the presidency gave greater power to the people at the expense of states and propertied interests. The extent of that evolution toward majoritarianism and some reactions to that process comprise the subject matter of this final chapter on democracy. To some extent we must delve into American political history to explain the ideological changes which accompanied the evolution of the institutions after 1787. To avoid extensive historical discussion, however, let us concentrate on the changes in the presidency as a sort of case study.

It has been noted that the presidency was to some extent designed to insure that the man who occupied the office was above politics. As such, the election of a president was left to an Electoral College of presumably distinguished men appointed by the states, who would gather and choose the best man for the office. George Washington as the first man to hold the office was somewhat successful in retaining the image of nonpartisanship, but the advent of the party system made this an impossible task. Further, despite the rhetoric of a nonpartisan leader, the method of election of the president insured that, to a certain extent at least, he would be the representative of minority interests. Insofar as the members of the Electoral College were appointed by the legislatures of the varying states, and those legislatures were dominated by men of property it is appropriate to view this office as a further check against majorities. The next one hundred and fifty years in the history of the institution are marked by a sporadic but continual movement toward majority control. The first major change is commonly seen as occurring with the election of Andrew Jackson in 1828 as a self-styled "man of the people." While the nature and extent of Jacksonian democracy is still a matter of some controversy, there is little doubt that the representation of the office as being responsive to popular wishes marked a significant change from the intention of most of the founding fathers. Once begun, the pattern of greater and greater influence of popular majorities on the presidency becomes the dominant theme in the development of American democracy. The facts of expanding presidential leadership in response to popular wishes and societal needs are familiar even to persons with only a superficial knowledge of American history: Abraham Lincoln's assumption of near-dictatorial power as Commander-in-Chief during the Civil War; Theodore Roosevelt's active leadership in foreign and domestic affairs; Woodrow Wilson's role as an international force in the First World War; Franklin D. Roosevelt's aggressive behavior on the economic and military fronts. One could go on and on, but these examples make it clear that the American presidency in the twentieth century, largely as a result of foreign and domestic crises, became the prime focus of popular opinion, and as such became increasingly responsive to the wishes of popular majorities. The changes in this one institution reflect in a graphic manner an alteration in the concept of the entire governmental enterprise in America and parallel a changing view of the nature of democratic government itself. Largely through the expanded scope of presidential action, the traditional liberal value of limited government gradually was eroded.

Public Versus Private

Recall that the entire American experiment with democratic government was initiated in a period of profound fear of the power of states. Drawing on the ideas of classical British liberalism, the founding fathers produced a system which was intended to insure that the individual possessed a large sphere of action which was not subject to the rules established by the political system. To use the standard terminology, speech, religion, assembly, movement, and economic activity were areas largely removed from governmental interference. It was this emphasis on the essential privacy of individual action which made the American experiment consistent with the highly individualistic ideals of the liberal tradition. The system also, however, was predicated upon the assumption that individuals and groups would press their demands upon the government in an attempt to produce policies which maximized their private interests. In a real sense there was a built-in conflict between the liberal emphasis on highly limited government and the realization that groups would attempt to use the system for their own aggrandizement. The Madisonian solution of an extended republic with built-in checks and balances and a system of representation was in part intended to insure that there would be no governmental action unless there was a broad consensus on a particular matter. In his pursuit of protection from the dangers of majority and minority tyranny, Madison produced a political system which reinforced the liberal ideal of limited government by making it quite difficult for majorities to form on any issue. If the multiplicity of interest groups and the checks and balances performed their function of balancing competing interests, there would be little in the way of a mandate for action of any sort on the part of the political system. That being the case, the scope of government would not only be limited by law, but also by the absence of a widespread call for action of any type. It was in this way that the Madisonian system reinforced the inherent individualism of the tradition, for it tried to insure a large private sphere of interaction. The gradual evolution of the presidency toward majoritarianism combined with the other democratic changes mentioned earlier, in many respects undermined the check and balance functions of the system. While there is currently a good deal of disagreement as to the extent of majoritarianism in America, as will be obvious from the ensuing discussion of democratic elitism, let us for the moment accept the statement that changes in institutions as well as advances in communications made it easier for cohesive majorities to form and insured that government would be more responsive to them. If that was the case, what were the consequences for the traditional liberal conception of government? Two of the immediate and far-ranging consequences were that the sphere of private action dear to classical liberalism was inevitably diminished and the entire question of the extent of legitimate majority action arose once again.

In order to discuss the shrinking area of private action in a system with growing majoritarian tendencies, we must recall several points made as early as the introduction to this book. There it was stated that all governments, irrespective of their ideological goals, had to satisfy certain minimal demands which arose from their population if they were to avoid instability and revolution. No series of demands sought by large numbers of citizens could be ignored by any political system for a long period of time without risking that extreme instability. In the transfer culture of communism as well as in fascism, concerted attempts were made to control the types of demands advanced by the citizenry. Thus, in both of those types of regimes there was extensive use of propaganda and censorship in an effort to mold popular opinion and give the leadership elements as wide as possible latitude to pursue their goals. If the types of demands advanced to the political system could be limited at their source, one of the major types of societal instability could be avoided. In democratic governments, however, this type of control of opinions cannot be attempted, for one of the basic presuppositions of democratic philosophy is that individuals must be free to develop and pursue their interests. This is the same problem in a somewhat different form that Madison raised when he discussed and dismissed the possibility of limiting factions by giving all members of the population the same opinions. If the liberty which permits the development of myriad demands on government cannot be abridged, we must then be prepared for a constant clamoring among groups in the society who wish to secure the passage of legislation beneficial to their interests. Realizing this, Madison erected the types of checking devices discussed in the previous chapter. Since the growing majoritarianism of the American system meant a more rapid translation of popular wishes into public policy, it was probably inevitable that government would expand its scope of action so as to be able to respond to those demands. Indeed, if it did not respond to them, it would be constantly risking instability. Faced with such a situation, one would naturally expect governmental legislation to satisfy the demands of significant portions of the population whenever they arose. Thus, whenever the informal and customary control mechanisms of the private sector seemed insufficient to solve problems or to contain conflict, a demand was inevitably pressed on the political system to solve the problem through political rules, i.e., to pass laws. As soon as this occurred, the government had, in effect, turned a matter formerly private in nature into a subject of public policy. To clarify this process, let us refer in a somewhat superficial way to the depression crisis in 1929.

Although the American government had been involved in the economic sector to a considerable extent prior to the depression, the myth that the free enterprise system contained a self-control mechanism through supply and demand was still very much part of the conventional wisdom. Ever since John Locke had declared that property was something inherent in the individual and subject to only minimal regulation by government, the notion of a free-market economy was something of a liberal dogma. Faced with the crisis of the depression and the apparent inability of the informal market mechanisms to solve that crisis, the political system was immediately bombarded with demands that it step in and legislate the depression out of existence. It could not help but respond to those demands if it valued the continued existence of not only a particular government but the entire form of government. Note that we are not discussing whether governmental actions during the depression solved that particular economic crisis, but only saying that the political system had little choice but to take some sort of action. One can duplicate this example in many other areas. A decline in the cohesiveness of the family structure leads to demands that the government support the children of unstable or broken families; a decline in the status of religious institutions as keepers of the public morals leads to demands that laws be passed prohibiting deviant behavior or controlling the types of books people are allowed to read. All of these actions have the effect of greatly increasing the scope of public action and reducing the area which was formerly private. Again we must insert a caveat to the effect that the transference of a particular subject matter from the private to the public sphere does not necessarily mean that the freedom of the individual to do as he wants is greatly lessened. The informal control mechanisms of religious institutions can be just as restrictive of individual action as any formal law, and local committees to ban books can keep them off the shelves as effectively as any governmental edict. What is important here is that we are chronicling a distinct change in the conception of the appropriate role and function of political institutions. The highly limited government of classical liberalism is a thing of the past. The emergence of something that we shall call positive liberalism lends a quite different character to twentieth-century democratic thought.

Positive Liberalism

The development of the idea that government ought to play a more positive role in the lives of its citizens advanced only gradually in the United States. If one wanted to attach a date to its emergence, one could point to the latter part of the nineteenth century when the political system became actively involved in the protection and control of the economy, or to the expansion of functions that occurred during the First World War, or to the aforementioned depression. The date one might choose is somewhat immaterial. From the point of view of democratic theory the significant fact is that the one hundred years between 1850 and 1950 marked a profound change in the processes of American democratic government. While the core values of classical liberalism remained relatively intact, certain of their number were given greater emphasis while others moved to a lower position in the value hierarchy. We have already noted that the trend toward majoritarianism had a profound effect on the classical liberal conception of limited government. Instead of viewing the political system as an umpire, balancing the competing claims of private interest groups, the positive liberalism of the twentieth century saw government as an active force in producing a better life for its citizens. The impartial third party of Lockean theory is replaced by the welfare state. Perhaps the most important value change which occurred in the evolution from classical to positive liberalism was in the status of the individual. We began our discussion of the entire democratic tradition by emphasizing that the idea of the free, relatively isolated individual, was the one concept shared by all of the fathers of democratic thought. While that value is retained by positive liberalism, its force is considerably diminished. Inevitably, as government began to expand its sphere of activity, it generated rules which necessarily constrained the freedom of individual action. To use a rather crude example, the freedom of the unscrupulous businessman to advertise a product falsely is reduced to the extent that he is required to be at least somewhat truthful in his claims for his products. The old notion of *caveat emptor* (let the buyer beware) is replaced by the legal responsibility of the producer not to sell unsafe products. Note that there is no need to attach any sort of moral judgment to these changes in values; we are attempting simply to describe an evolution in the conception of the individual in democratic thought. One may heartily approve of governmental legislation to prohibit shoddy business practices or he may feel such action is interferring with his individual rights; the fact is that freedom to act is being constrained. It should also be noted that governmental legislation to limit individual action is very much a part of classical democratic thought. Man, after all, limits himself merely by becoming a member of a society. The controversy arises regarding the appropriate scope of legislation by political systems which call themselves democratic.

Paralleling the reduction in importance of the unconstrained individual in positive liberalism is the rise in importance of the old democratic value of equality. Indeed, some commentators see a necessary interrelationship between the values of liberty and equality or note a tension between these two cardinal values of the tradition.[1] Minimally one can assert that equality was the most ill defined and limited of the values of classical liberalism. Recall that Thomas Hobbes saw men as equal in only the negative sense that they all possessed the ability to kill one another. Even Thomas Jefferson, after declaring men equal in the eyes of God, went on to approve a governmental system which denied men equality on the basis of their skin color. The major question involving the interrelationship between the values of liberty and equality however, arose in the economic area. Beginning around the turn of the century, people began asking how one could be free if he did not have the means to exercise that freedom. To use a slightly more modern example, a man in the city of Chicago possesses a theoretical freedom to leave that city for any other place in the world. That theoretical freedom does not, however, put the money in his pocket that will permit him to exercise it. Isn't a person similarly situated, who possesses the means to exercise his abstract right of free movement, actually more free than one who does not? Stated in a slightly more complex way, people were beginning to see that economic inequalities conferred greater power to some men and that the abstract values of liberty and equality meant little without the ability to fulfill them. Similarly, the theoretical equality between black and white is little more than meaningless rhetoric if the black man is systematically denied the opportunity to achieve equality in fact. To return to our initial point however, governmental legislation which is designed to achieve at least some degree of economic equality, or laws

---

[1]Peter Bachrach, among others, gives an excellent short account of this problem. Peter Bachrach, *The Theory of Democratic Elitism: A Critique* (Boston: Little, Brown and Company, 1967), pp. 26-46.

which attempt to insure that blacks will be treated equally in fact as well as theory will undoubtedly constrain the freedom of other members of the community. This is precisely what is meant by the tension between freedom and equality. When my ability to discriminate on the basis of race, religion, or sex is abridged through the action of government, my personal liberty is limited. While all right-thinking men would applaud such legislation on the grounds that such discrimination deprives others of their rights, from the classical liberal point of view, it does reduce individual freedom. The response from positive liberalism would simply be that the classical value of freedom is meaningless without relative equality. The hallmark, then, of the positive liberalism of the twentieth century is the attempt to use the political system to insure greater degrees of equality in a democratic society. How successful those attempts have been is a subject for later discussion. Having introduced the positive liberal position that government ought to try to achieve greater degrees of equality in society, we are now in an excellent position to discuss twentieth-century attempts to marry modified Marxian economic doctrines with democratic decision-making processes—attempts which produce the phenomenon known as democratic socialism.

Democratic Socialism

In concentrating on the American variation of the development of democratic theory and practice we have avoided discussion of the implementation of democratic doctrines elsewhere in the world. The early American combination of democratic political forms and capitalist economics produced a situation whereby economic considerations were, in theory at least, not matters of governmental concern. It was mentioned earlier that the highly individualistic political ideals of classical British liberalism seemed to blend quite nicely with a capitalist economic system. The classical liberal notion of a large sphere of human activity removed from the power of government was quite compatible with *laissez-faire* economic theories, perhaps even required the latter. With the rise of what we have been calling positive liberalism in twentieth-century America the situation begins to change. Insofar as the achievement of some societal equality is now seen as an appropriate activity of government, economic matters inevitably became subjects of greater public concern. One need not enter into the rather misstated debate as to whether the United States has become increasingly socialistic over the years to recognize that there is no theoretical incompatibility between positive liberalism and economic socialism. Once one recognizes that a major goal of the political system is to insure relative equality in the society there is nothing, in theory, to prevent it from establishing rules which try to insure complete economic equality. Obviously such a situation has not occurred in the United States. However one chooses to view such things as graduated income tax and welfare programs, they were not instituted with an eye toward achieving economic equality and certainly have not served that function. In the assorted regimes which have emerged in Europe during the past half-century under the banner of democratic socialism, however, the concern with achieving greater economic equality has been more overt. Whether they have been more successful in that endeavor is a subject best left to politicians and historians.

In pursuit of the ideal of economic equality, democratic socialism involves using the political system as a device for insuring certain minimal services for all members of the society and as a means to effect some redistribution of wealth. Normally, this takes the form of providing many services to all citizens with the funds for such activities coming from general revenues. The type of "cradle to grave" services found in Great Britian and Scandinavian countries are indicative of the effort to provide common protections for all members of the society. In addition to such welfare state benefits, national control of major industries such as transportation, coal and steel production are common ventures of democratic socialist regimes. Finally, government is seen as an agent which consciously acts to provide for the redistribution of wealth within the country through measures such as high inheritance levies and sharply graduated income taxes. It should be emphasized that in almost all socialist regimes such policies to equalize wealth go just so far. That is, to speak of complete equalization of wealth in countries such as Britian or Sweden is simply not correct. In practice, democratic socialist regimes have attempted to modify some of the extremes which result from more unregulated capitalist economic systems, rather than attempting full equalization. Indeed, many self-avowed social democratic parties in Europe have in recent years become far less dogmatic about their economic policies, contenting themselves when in power with minor alterations in the existing economic system. Some comparison with socialism of the Soviet variety as well as with national-socialism seems inevitable in this context.

On a theoretical level the economic policies of these three doctrines seem quite similar; in particular, all are adamant in asserting the principle of control of the economy by the government. The extent of governmental control in each of these idea systems varies a great deal. In the Soviet Union all sectors of the economy are nationalized and, despite the many difficulties they have encountered in pursuing it, their goal remains economic equalization. As we have seen, the socialism of Mussolini's Italy was content for most of its existence with leaving the greater portion of the economy under the control of the private sector, with government acting as a force to prevent disabling class antagonism. In contrast to fascism, democratic socialist regimes retain the class-based nature of their movement, although their attempts at economic change fall far short of the sweeping socialization schemes of the USSR. Given such a set of similarities in economic matters, the major differences between Marxian socialism and fascism on the one hand and democratic socialism on the other lie in the political and social areas. The socialism of democratic socialism is a set of economic policies which are instituted because they are desired by a majority of the people in the country. One of the reasons for the relative lack of dogmatism in socialist economic policies is that such regimes are avowedly responding to the changing wishes of the people. As such they are probably inevitably more flexible in their policies and would find it difficult to impose some grandiose five-year program of the Soviet variety even if they desired it. The most obvious and significant difference between these regimes lies in the fact that democratic socialism in practice retains all of the core values of the classical liberal tradition. Although it is true that positive action by the political system to solve a host of societal ills reduces the scope of individual liberty, or, if one prefers, makes that liberty greater because more people are capable of exercising it, modern democratic socialism refuses to renounce democratic core values in the name of pursuing some far-off societal utopia. Thus, the traditional guarantees of free speech, religion, assembly, procedures of due process of law, etc., are retained by these governments. Most importantly, particularly in contrast to fascism and Marxism, political parties which are antisocialist are allowed to form and can remove the existing party from office if their policies lose favor with the public. Such an alteration in governments from socialist to nonsocialist can produce some interesting shifts in public policy as witnessed by the cycles of nationalization and denationalization in the British steel industry, but this is obviously necessary if democratic-socialist parties base their rule on popular support. Both European democratic socialism and the positive liberalism in the United States are indications of a further alteration in the democratic theory of the twentieth century. We have already spoken of the growing majoritarian trend in the United States political system but the underlying value transformation that led to that change—increasing trust in the goodness and liberality of the average man—must be explored further if we are to understand some of the current difficulties which beset democratic theory.

Mass Democracy and the Revolt from Positive Liberalism

We have already spoken of the widespread acceptance of democratic ideals which characterized the first half of the twentieth century. Even the totalitarian regimes in Moscow, Rome, and Berlin felt it necessary to call not only their ultimate goals but their everyday practices democratic. In the United States it was generally felt that the ills which beset the country were only temporary and existed largely as a result of insufficient democratization. The recurring movements of populism, progressivism, and the new deal surely expressed at least one common theme— popular control through popular government was the prime solution to human ills. Indeed, the United States was seen as somehow morally superior to other governments, destined to lead them in experimentation with the only desirable form of modern government. Thus we have the drive early in the century to "make the world safe for democracy," and later numerous interventions throughout the world to insure the "self-determination" of all nations. Current historical interpretations of such events vary widely in ascribing the motivation for such activities, but from the ideological perspective one thing seems sure—there was a significant alteration in the concept of the average man's capacity for self-government. The eighteenth-century fear of popular majorities and its view of human nature as entirely self-interested are replaced by a confidence in the basic rationality of man and a corresponding decline in the fear of tyranny by the people. In such a climate, small wonder that the Madisonian checks against majority tyranny seemed rather anachronistic and the system in need of reform. In the United States much of this benign view of democratic man arose as a result of the success of the American economy and as a result of widespread popular education. Public education, it was contended, would teach even the most selfish man to act in terms of his enlightened self-interest, while the widespread acceptance of democratic values would mitigate any remaining tyrannical tendencies. Furthermore, since most of the conflict that arose between individuals was based upon scarcity (even Madison saw economic need as the prime source of faction), the economic success of the United States, and later the Western world as a whole, would inevitably reduce the level of conflict. Simply, an educated man with a full stomach would not be so inclined to join a movement dedicated to eradicating some group of his fellow men. It is easy to overemphasize the general optimism concerning democratic regimes which existed in both scholarly and popular circles during this period. After all, such optimism had to depreciate the importance of a major economic depression and two world wars, to say nothing of racism, poverty, and hunger. Still, taking a long-range perspective, the first half of the twentieth century was the age of the consensus historian who emphasized the essential harmony of American life, and the student of politics who proclaimed a gradual end to ideological conflict.

Despite this optimistic view of the potential of democratization to improve the human lot, there were some storm clouds on the horizon which would eventually seriously darken the picture of a benign and trustworthy average man. While the antidemocratic phenomena of the Russian Revolution and its Soviet aftermath could be explained by the fact that Russia had no prior experience with democracy or by the police-state control by the party, the mass movements of fascism were a different story. Here was a regime, dedicated to the eradication of democracy and the subordination of the individual to the state, which undoubtedly enjoyed a great deal of mass support. In the face of economic crisis and rapid societal change human nature seemed, once again, to be showing its darker side. Further, many intellectuals viewed with great alarm the tendency of mass groups within countries such as the United States to adopt highly undemocratic actions in the name of defending democracy. The perennial conflict with the Soviet Union produced the communist "witch hunts" of the McCarthy era which purported to save democracy by taking away the rights of those who questioned any aspect of the American political system. The picture of the enlightened democratic man was beginning to pale a bit. Even while some persons were proclaiming the end of ideological conflict, investigations into the attitudes held by the average American were beginning to show that he had scant regard for the traditional democratic liberal values. Members of the working class, thought by some to be the front-line troops in the battle for increasing democratization, were found to hold highly authoritarian attitudes, willing to sacrifice traditional freedoms in the face of even minor crisis situations. All of these things and many others contributed to produce a picture of democratic man which was markedly different from the optimism of the earlier period. It was now recognized that the rational individual of the optimistic period was highly susceptible to the irrational appeals of demagogic leaders and that significant numbers in the population were willing to join mass movements with very little provocation. The preoccupation with the rational man of majoritarian democracy gave way to a fear of the "true believer" potential in human beings. With the partial shattering of the image of man produced in the benign period came a cry for a more realistic appraisal of modern democratic government. Their confidence in the potential of democratization as a total solution to all men's ills shaken, students of democratic theory began to look more closely at the actual progress that had been made by the United States in achieving its stated goals of freedom, justice, and equality. Some whose ultimate faith

in democratic society remained unshaken by these discoveries asked why
so many of the ideals of the society remained unfulfilled and proposed
varying solutions to achieve them. Others, despairing of the possibility of
true democracy or fearing its consequences in a mass society sought
other means to insure that liberal values and culture resisted the threat
of mass man. In a somewhat curious marriage both of these groups of
people can be described as theorists of *democratic elitism.*

Democratic Elitism

We should note initially that while elitist analysis of modern democratic
society is directed primarily toward the United States, it has implications
for any democratic regime as well as for democratic theory as a whole.
It begins by attempting to assess realistically what the basic value of rule
by the people really means in a complex modern society. Relying on the
arguments presented by past thinkers such as Gaetano Mosca and
Roberto Michels as well as modern organizational theory, they assert
that popular rule means very little indeed. It can be demonstrated
conclusively that any large-scale organization, including government, is,
of necessity, organized in a hierarchical fashion. That is, there are
certain persons, who, by the nature of the tasks they perform, possess
far more power than others. Any organization can thus be divided into
two groups of people—the elite who make all of the basic decisions and
the mass which follows them. The reasons for such a bifurcation are
many and varied. Obviously every member of a group, be it a government or a fraternal organization, cannot be expected to know all of the
details involved in running the organization. In the case of political
systems, persons who are nominally citizens of the state are primarily
concerned with earning a living for themselves and fulfilling their individual interests. To expect the average person to be a full-time partici-
pant in the political process at the same time is simply absurd. The
complexity of modern society thus demands that we adopt a specialization of labor whereby some persons become experts in running organizations and fulfill that task on a full-time basis. We have seen that
classical democratic theory confronted a similar problem and solved it
by introducing the concept of representation, so that democratic governments might exist in large states. To the elitist, however, such a solution
really raises more problems than it solves, particularly in complex
modern societies. A representative is, they contend, by the very nature
of his position cut off from those whom he purportedly represents. He
possesses far more information than his average constituent, pursues his
task as a professional politician, in all probability has a broader perspec-

tive than any of those he represents; in short, his concerns and position are quite different. One would not, after all, expect the chairman of the board of General Motors to submit a questionnaire to all of the stock-holders of the company asking them how many cars they should build that year and then proceed to act on their recommendation. The average stockholder simply could not make an informed judgment on such a matter unless he were willing to spend a considerable portion of his life studying the market for automobiles, that is, unless he were willing to become an expert. To return to political concerns, there is an even more pervasive phenomenon which colors the types of decisions which can be made. The representative's (and here we use the word to refer to any elected decision maker) position makes it possible for him to influence greatly even the types of questions which are submitted to the popula-tion. By posing two alternatives as the only possible courses of action in any situation, he can effectively preclude discussion of a third alternative which might be more desirable from the people's point of view. In effect, he can set formidable limits on the types of governmental action that can even be considered.

This, then, is the cornerstone of the elitist position. The complexity and need for expertise in modern societies insures that popular represen-tatives are divorced from their constituents and are capable of making and to a certain extent must make decisions independent of popular wishes. We must note that as yet there is no moral judgment attached to such a position. From his realistic perspective, the elitist simply asserts that, like it or not, this is the way it is, a fact of modern society.

Confronted with such an argument, the defender of classical dem-ocratic theory might admit that it is necessary to have this situation when the process of running government is such a complicated business. He would, however, probably go on to assert that it really doesn't matter, for the representative's constituents can remove him if they desire when he comes up for reelection. If a person acting in the name of the people fails in their eyes to perform his tasks correctly they can simply vote him out of office. This is, in effect, the old Madisonian argument for the appropriate means of controlling minority tyranny. Expanding on the type of reasoning used earlier, the elitist would respond that periodic elections provide no real popular control, for the choices to replace a bad representative are greatly limited. The existing elite controls the access to the political system, thereby insuring that only candidates who possess elite values are offered as choices to the electorate. This is accomplished through the political party structure, through the necessity of having great amounts of money to wage a successful campaign, and through a series of legal rules and customs. Further, even if a "common man" surmounted all of these obstacles and was elected to office he would have little power, for within the governmental institutions themselves there are additional control devices as exemplified by seniority and committee systems in Congress. These as well are dominated by the elite. Under such circumstances the only choice available to a voter at election time is between competing elite groups who possess basically the same values, which precludes the possibility of any real change in governmental policy. If this is the way it is, what does the phrase "government by the people" mean? Before attempting to respond to that question, we must record a further extension of the elitist argument which makes the phrase "popular government" even more inapplicable to modern American society.

Up to now we have avoided mention of any particular individual advancing the elitist position preferring to refer to a vaguely defined group of democratic elitists. The major reason for this is that it is a most diverse tradition and sufficiently current to make it difficult to single out leading representatives. There is one man, however, C. Wright Mills, whose name is most closely associated with this position, and whose analysis of modern American democracy provides a further extension of the basic elitist position. Accepting as fact the statement that complex organizations are of necessity hierarchical in structure and that a clear distinction must be made between elite and mass, Mills went on to argue that economic factors in the United States had produced a two-class society wherein even the *government* was powerless to effect any basic changes in policy. Let us ignore for the moment the prior argument that elected representatives are by virtue of their positions divorced from the people and assume that they actually do reflect popular desires. What real power does the average representative or senator possess? Very little if any, Mills contended, particularly regarding the basic matters such as war and peace or significant changes in the economic structure. The elected representative is at best in a middle-range power position, for the great decision-making capability lies in the hands of an economically based *power elite* which is largely outside the control of the political system. Membership in this group is defined by birth and wealth, although it is possible for a member of the nonelite to become part of it by adopting the values of that group. Elite members go to the same schools, belong to the same social clubs, intermarry and in general share similar values. While there may be minor disagreements between members of the elite over the everyday matters of public policy they share a firm commitment to preserving the existing value and class structure. Franklin D. Roosevelt is frequently cited by scholars ascribing to this position as indicative of the overall cohesiveness of the power elite. Elected to the presidency in a period of severe economic crisis and equipped with a mandate for massive social and economic change,

Roosevelt succeeded with a series of patchwork measures (and a war) in avoiding any fundamental change in the nature of American society. In much the same fashion, President Eisenhower drew rather unexpected applause from power elite theorists when he cautioned against the government becoming a captive of a "military-industrial complex" which sought to use the political system for its own selfish ends.

The sum of the power elitist argument then is that the government is largely controlled by a small group of men who owe their power to their economic and social position in the society. If this be the case, there can be no true change in the system, for the members of the elite group will simply not permit any decline in their status. Government, and consequently the representatives of the people, are reduced to making relatively unimportant decisions which, in the end, can only serve to perpetuate the existence of the status quo. We must note that there are distinctly Marxian overtones to this type of analysis in that it sees the economic variable as crucial in determining people's actions and it relies heavily on a two-class analysis. Further, it might also be termed Marxian in that it views government, in effect, as the tool of a capitalist class which seeks to use the political system to perpetuate and extend class power. Whatever one chooses to term the Millsian type of analysis, from the theoretical perspective its import lies in the fact that it makes explicit a reevaluation of the concept of power in democratic systems.

Traditional democratic theory presupposed that by providing people with equal voting power one could keep the limited functions of government consistent with popular desires. In attempting to divorce political matters from the economic realm and by viewing the political system as an umpire between competing factions, classical liberalism and the Madisonian implementation of it paid insufficient attention to the power that money confers. From the power elitist perspective, the American political system has always involved tyranny by a *minority* which derives its power from its economic position. The attempts to implement greater economic equality through the institution of positive liberalism provided, the elitist asserts, nothing more than sops to the people and perpetuated a class-based capitalist economic system. Viewing the American political system as a device for perpetuating minority interests, the elitist thus calls for revolution in the system in the name of producing a true democracy. The only way the minority control of the system can be checked is through giving greater decision-making power to the people. Similarly, the only way the norm of equality which positive liberalism purported to be trying to achieve can actually be fulfilled is through increasing democratization of both political and economic decision making. This form of democratic elitism ends up in the position rather similar to that of the optimistic democrats that we presented as dominating the first half of the twentieth century. There is here an implicit faith in the basic common sense of the average man, and that any problems with the American democratic experiment can be solved through increasing democratization.

Before moving to a brief discussion of the other form of elitist reaction to positive liberalism, we must point out some of the possible difficulties in the democratic elitist position discussed thus far. Initially, critics have contended that the elitists have been able by no means to demonstrate the existence of a distinct class of people who constitute the power elite. Indeed, even if one is able to show great similarity in background among major political and economic decision makers, does this mean that they automatically share similar values? Further, the elitist must be able to prove that there is no fundamental difference between competing elite groups, and this, so critics contend, has yet to be accomplished. If varying elite groups change their policies in an attempt to win popular support, then the elitist charge that the voter has no real choice during elections is refuted. Other critics have contended that it can be demonstrated that numerous individuals of nonelite origins have risen to elite status with their values essentially intact, and have been able to effect serious change in public policy. Finally, critics contend there is a distressful lack of precision in the elitist argument. We are told that some ill-defined elite group constantly uses government for its own purposes at the expense of popular wishes, and that they agree on fundamental matters. What is meant by fundamental? If it means nothing more than retention of the essentials of the existing economic system then the elite is probably rather accurately reflecting public opinion. These and similar matters are the stuff of current controversy among students of American democracy, so it would be both presumptuous and foolhardy to attempt to resolve them here. Let us then follow a safer path and move to a discussion of the second form of elitist reaction to the prevalent positive liberalism of the twentieth century.

Earlier we established the existence of a distrust of modern mass democracy, largely because of the propensity of the common man to join mass movements and to hold antidemocratic values. The elitists discussed thus far are really not part of that reaction and in a sense are appropriately seen as an extension of the democratic optimism prevalent earlier in the century. It is in this sense that they are called *democratic* elitists. Another even more loosely defined group of individuals who merit the term "elitist" deserve brief mention if only because they form somewhat of a modern equivalent of the old Madisonian position.

Impressed (perhaps depressed is the better word) by the apparent potential of modern democratic man for irrational action, and distrustful of the masses' ability to support traditional democratic values in the face of crisis, these thinkers advocate elitist control of the society in the name of preserving democracy. If that seems a bit paradoxical, it only serves to show again the many uses of the word democratic.

This position, frequently called *normative democratic elitism,* believes in effect that the mass must be protected from itself. It notes that research into the values held by members of modern democratic states shows that it is the well-educated and generally affluent minority which has the highest respect for traditional democratic values. The average man is far more prone to adopt authoritarian solutions to problems, is quick to attempt to silence dissent, and in general finds it difficult to live with individual deviation from normal behavior. There is a tendency in majoritarian democracies to attempt to standardize all forms of conduct and to punish any deviation from those norms. As the sphere of governmental activity expands, we have found that it establishes rules of behavior in areas which were formerly part of the private sphere of activity. In a majoritarian democracy what this means is that the wishes of a majority of the people gradually become the accepted standards of conduct for the entire society. What bothers the elitist is that these mass tastes seem inevitably to reflect the wishes of the lowest common denominator of individuals in the society. What develops is a *mass culture* composed of television programs designed to appeal to the greatest possible number of people, news programs which simplify complex events to make them understandable, architectural styles designed for broad appeal, and fads in clothing styles which reflect the changing desires of the masses. One can go on and on. While this phenomenon of mass culture is not in and of itself a bad thing for democracies, the elitist sees it as inevitably discouraging individual deviation from the established norms. Thus the individual who does not conform is far less successful than one who does, but the society loses the type of creative energy which seems to be generated most often by nonconformists. Put in terms of political values, mass democracy seems bent on destroying the individuality which is the core idea in democratic theory. In a way we are back to the points made earlier about the tension between liberty and equality. In pursuit of equalitarian goals, majoritarian democracies tend to standardize everything, creating a society with a homogenized culture which stamps out individual liberty.

It should be apparent why one can call this elitist position somewhat equivalent to the old Madisonian stance. While the basic value of popular sovereignty is not denied, the elitist recognizes that the masses under the banner of majority rule will tend toward excessive use of their power, thereby depriving others of their liberty to act as they choose. Here then is a more modern equivalent to the Madisonian tyranny of the majority where communications advances make it quite possible to give everyone the same opinions. Far from being unhappy with the fact that modern society necessitates some type of distinction between elite leadership and mass following, the normative elitist sees the leadership group as a prime bulwark against the excesses of majorities. If the people did indeed rule as the classical tradition tells us they ought, the liberal individualistic values of the tradition would soon be lost. There is some question whether this view can legitimately be called democratic in that it explicitly relies on elite control of the masses. If one insists on a majoritarian definition of democracy, it obviously cannot be so called. If, however, one defines democracy in more individualistic terms while retaining an overall commitment to popular sovereignty, normative elitism is probably as democratic as the Madisonian variety. The elitist, while recognizing the desirability of ultimate control by the people, is very happy that complex modern organizations insure that educated liberal elites control much of the day-to-day activity of the state.

Hopefully the reader can now see that we have come almost full circle in our discussion of democracy. The normative elitist's fear of excessive majority control leading to conformity and authoritarianism is quite similar to the Madisonian concern with majority tyranny. In the same vein the gradual democratization and pursuit of the goal of equality which are the dominant themes of positive liberalism are expressive of the majoritarian side of the democratic spectrum that was present in the British liberal tradition. In describing this spectrum of democratic thought as it became embodied in the American political tradition, we have tried to show the full range of possibilities in types of democratic governments. However, despite this flexibility in defining specific governmental forms we have also emphasized that there remains a core of values which make it appropriate to speak of democratic philosophy. There is no doubt that the arrangement of those core values can undergo a good deal of change; in one period the value of individual freedom is in ascendancy, in another equality predominates. But there are limits to this flexibility, and any country which denies the individual liberty to dissent from existing policy in the name of producing a more perfect democracy or denies its citizens equality on racial, class or ethnic grounds has violated those limits. Perhaps that is the only possible summary remark one can make regarding democratic theory; a set of values and a decision-making process which permits a good deal of flexibility in response to popular demands, but which establishes clear limitations on the type of demands that can be raised.

BIBLIOGRAPHY

Bachrach, Peter. *The Theory of Democratic Elitism: A Critique.* Boston: Little, Brown and Company, 1967. Probably the best short introduction to theories of democratic elitism. In addition, Bachrach points to numerous problems in those theories and gives indications of possible solutions.

Commager, Henry Steele. *The American Mind.* New Haven: Yale University Press, 1959. Another broad gauge study of American intellectual history.

Kariel, Henry S., ed. *Frontiers of Democratic Theory.* New York: Random House, 1970. An excellent collection of articles centering around the contemporary debates between classical democratic theorists, new "democratic realists," and the challenges which have been raised to this modern democratic analysis. Probably the best way of approaching democratic theory today.

Kariel, Henry S. *The Decline of American Pluralism.* Stanford, Calif.: Stanford University Press, 1967.

Lowi, Theodore J. *The End of Liberalism: Ideology, Policy, and the Crisis of Public Authority.* New York: W. W. Norton & Company, Inc., 1969. An excellent book which is at one and the same time a study of the origins and practice of democratic liberalism (our term has been "positive" liberalism) and a polemic which attempts to find solutions to modern crises of liberalism.

Radice, Giles. *Democratic Socialism.* New York: Frederick A. Praeger, 1966. A good short introduction to democratic socialism.

Riemer, Neal. *The Revival of Democratic Theory.* New York: Appleton-Century Crofts, 1962. An interesting discussion of the problems and future potential of democratic theory.

White, Morton. *Social Thought in America: The Revolt Against Formalism.* Boston: Beacon Press, 1957. A thought-provoking study of American intellectual development in the early twentieth century. While it does not directly address itself to political concerns, it is excellent for understanding the general temper of the times.

Original Works

Domhoff, G. William. *Who Rules America?* Englewood Cliffs, N.J.: Prentice-Hall, 1967.

_____. *The Higher Circles: The Governing Class in America.* New York: Random House, 1970.

Girvetz, Harry K., ed. *Democracy and Elitism.* New York: Charles Scribner's Sons, 1967.

Mills, C. Wright. *The Power Elite.* New York: Oxford University Press, 1959.

Chapter 11

SOME
CONCLUDING
COMMENTS

An almost iron-clad rule of both political philosophers and editors of books says that one must avoid commentary on current events. The philosopher would abstain from such comments on the grounds that it is difficult to achieve a proper perspective of events when one is caught up in them. Time, after all, gives perspective, if not objectivity. Editors, on the other hand, dislike discussions of the contemporary scene for it dates a book, making a new edition necessary after a short period of time. At the risk of violating the rules of both of these respected professions, it seems impossible to conclude any study of modern ideologies without at least some thoughts on a decade which is already being referred to as the "turbulent 1960s."

One of the questions left unanswered in the introduction to this work asked about the relationship between idea systems and political action. There it was asserted that although no causal relationship between ideologies and political acts could be proven, common sense seemed to indicate that they were indeed connected. The debate over the question of ideology and action has greatly intensified in recent years, in proportion to the wave of political activism which has swept throughout the world. Student radicals who profess to be practicing some form of reformed Marxism are dismissed by others as products of overly permissive parents. The ideas they espouse, their elders say, are merely a smoke screen for an infantile desire for action and self-satisfaction. In other words, the *ideas* they advance are not important. Some self-styled revolutionaries seem to confirm that type of analysis by declaring that the *struggle* to achieve their goals is as important if not more important than the achievement itself. Despite such claims, emanating from participants and critics alike, it seems safe to assert that few periods in recent history have witnessed a greater concern with political ideas and their implementation. Youthful groups in the United States cry out that the traditional democratic values of freedom, equality, and self-determination have been used as camouflage to disguise a society that is racist, imperialist, and elitist. Students in the streets of Prague or Paris condemn their respective governments on grounds that are surprisingly similar. The cry of "power to the people" rings out in countries throughout the world. The ideological battles of the cold war, with the "free world" and "fraternal socialist states" in constant competition for converts, seem to pale in an era in which the United States and the Soviet Union are deemed equally guilty of imperialism and racism. Indeed, some might contend that the more traditional idea systems discussed in this book are dated to the extent that they have little to say about the current world. In spite of such feelings, this is not the place to attempt to systematically relate the revolutionary slogans of modern revolutionaries to the idea systems we have discussed. Such a project would require another book. Rather, in support of the contention that these three ideologies form the theoretical base for many of the criticisms being leveled at modern societies, let us simply indicate a few areas where a knowledge of these more basic idea systems can help in understanding contemporary affairs.

The United States and the Soviet Union stand today as the major representatives of two of the idea systems we have studied. We noted earlier that communism and democracy, as bodies of ideas, can be separated from the attempts of various states to put those ideas into practice. However, in modern times the prime charge against both the U.S. and the USSR is that they continue to talk as though they have achieved a democratic and socialist society respectively, while in fact they are a long way from realizing those goal cultures. Indeed, some would contend that each is so far from the fulfillment of its ideal that the best solution is to completely scrap the existing society and start all over again. Whether we call it a performance gap or studied hypocrisy, each of these states is accused of denying its own set of ideals. The Soviet Union, while declaring itself to be a democratic socialist society, systematically represses dissent and refuses to acknowledge legitimate claims of its citizens. As the self-acknowledged leader of the socialist world it has seen fit to intervene in the internal affairs of fraternal socialist countries who stray from the prescribed path to socialism as envisioned by Moscow. It is condemned from within its own ideological camp by Mao Tse-tung for subverting the goals of the revolution through the development of a new bureaucratic class structure which makes a mockery of the socialist norm of equality, and surely prohibits the development of a communist society. Similarly, to its critics the United States in making the world safe for democracy has foisted upon a considerable portion of the world an economic system which serves only to fill the pockets of a small group of capitalists. Proclaiming itself a free and equal society, it has denied black people a place in its economic system and developed a body of customs and laws which insures that they can be neither free nor equal. It is, in short, both imperialist and racist. From within its own camp, democratic elitists accuse it of having a rigid class structure which benefits the few at the expense of the many, precluding once again the possibility of achieving the espoused ideals of democracy.

This is not the place to attempt to judge the validity of the critiques of the two most powerful nations in the world. We can, however, with knowledge of the ideal societies of democracy and communism, recognize the imperfections of both of the existing political systems. Further, we can note the similarity of the type of criticism directed at both of them. Minimally, critics are asserting that there is a large gap between the ideals of the society and its everyday practices; a performance gap which cannot be glossed over with nice-sounding rhetoric. Even more interesting is the fact that the substance of the criticisms of both the U.S. and the USSR are in many respects identical. We have already alluded to the fact that the ideal societies of classical democratic theory and classical Marxism, in spite of some real differences, contain many similar goals. Both Karl Marx and James Madison could agree that one of the prime goals of their societies was the removal of the arbitrary control one man might have over another. The democrat concentrates on limiting the power that one group, be it minority or majority, is able to achieve over other groups in the society. Thus, classical democratic theory concerned itself with developing political institutions and creating an environment in which the power of any single group to tyrannize over another was greatly limited. While realizing the legitimacy of claims advanced by individuals and groups, it was primarily concerned with the tendency of man to try to dominate his fellow creatures. In a similar fashion, classical Marxism described the dialectical process imbedded in nature which would eventually lead man to a society in which all were equal, and in which the state, as the prime instrument of coercion, would wither away. The shared value agreement of a pure communist society, combined with the plentitude provided by a sophisticated economic system, would insure that no one man would be able to arbitrarily control the actions of another. Granted, Marxists saw the prime source of such control in economics, the function of a necessarily oppressive class system. Classical democrats, while surely not ignorant of the effect of economic factors in human affairs (remember, again, that economic factors were for Madison the principal source of faction), tended to concentrate on the development of political institutions which would mitigate the "evil" effects of such competition. In spite of these real differences in analysis, to say nothing of their prescriptions for the immediate future, one can argue that these supposedly antithetical idea systems share a common belief in the freedom and equality of each individual. In both cases this belief translates into a concern that no individual or group of individuals be allowed to impose their views on others in the society.

Even our brief look into the complexities of the idea systems encountered in this book ought to make the reader wary of the type of superficial comparison engaged in above. Despite their similar cries for freedom and equality, the student should now know that the freedom a dedicated Marxist longs for would be much different from that of a democrat. Still, we are trying to describe a reaction to existing authority which seems to be central in modern times, and are not attempting a specific comparison of the goal cultures of communism and democracy. With that in mind, isn't there a real similarity between the protester who damns the power elite in the United States and one who condemns the rigid bureaucratic class in the Soviet Union? Don't demands for decentralization and democratization evoke the same images as the cry of "power to the people"? Aren't the critics of new class revisionism in the Soviet Union and the power elite theorists in the United States reacting to similar phenomena? In the eyes of their critics, both of these societies which profess to be liberating the individual have succeeded in developing structures which increasingly *limit* individual freedom of action. The ideals which they profess to be fulfilling don't seem to match the everyday actions of the state; the grand ideals of freedom and equality translate into daily oppression and inequality. The way one perceives such charges depends, at least in the United States, on one's position on an increasingly complex spectrum of political ideology, and no attempt can be made here to evaluate them. From the point of view of the student of ideas, the identification of a bureaucracy, class, or state structure as the major obstacle to the achievement of each societies' ideals is interesting. In this light let us turn for a few insights to the third system of ideas we have examined.

The Nation-State: A Reaction

Mussolini long ago predicted that the twentieth century would be the age of the nation-state, and surely we must agree that he was at least partially correct.[1] The reasons for the centrality of the nation in recent thought are no doubt many; one could begin a list by noting that complex economic systems seem to require centralization and direction, or that the conflict in international affairs dictates a high degree of national solidarity and unity of purpose. At any rate, the modern nation-state, whether it calls itself democratic or socialistic, has dominated political action and discourse for the first half of this century. From the perspective of the two ideologies we have discussed, this fact must be viewed as a rather curious phenomenon, in that both classical Marxism and classical democratic theory can, to a large extent, be described as *antistatist* ideologies. However different their conceptions of an ideal society might be, it has been shown that they were at one in their opposition to the arbitrary control of one individual over another. Granted, Marx was more specific in his condemnation, declaring the state to be a necessarily oppressive device of a ruling class, but the inherent individualism and distrust of political institutions present in classical liberalism place it in much the same position. If, as Mussolini predicted, the individualism of the nineteenth century was to be replaced by the collectivism of the twentieth, how are we to explain the presence of the nineteenth century ideologies of Marxism and democracy in the mid-twentieth?[2] Furthermore, how are we to view the two most powerful *states* in the world espousing idea systems which in large part condemn the notion of state power? Perhaps in attempting to wrestle with such questions we can gain additional perspective on the contemporary political scene.

The earlier statement regarding the antistatism present in the traditional formulations of Marxism and democracy may seem to some too strong. After all, classical liberal theory believed the state to be essential for a truly human existence, and Marx and Engels, even in their most utopian moments, saw the necessity for some sort of organization (nonoppressive, of course) to provide for the overall direction of the society. We are dealing then, with a question of emphasis. Yet when one talks about current complaints against the two major powers, that is precisely the point. Critics contend that there has been far too much emphasis placed on centralization, too much hierarchy, too little power left to the people; in short, too much statism. If we are correct in identifying the resistance to authority arbitrarily imposed as one of the central themes of modern rebellion, then it seems proper to see such criticism as a reaction to the notion of a powerful state. Here, then, is an aspect of fascist ideology that seems directly applicable to current debates. In the eyes of many of their critics, both the Soviet Union and the United

---

[1]Benito Mussolini, "The Political and Social Doctrine of Fascism," trans. Jane Soames, in Somerville and Santoni, *Social and Political Philosophy,* p. 440.
[2]*Ibid.*

States have forfeited their ideological heritage and have adopted much of the coloration of fascism. In spite of their professed ideological goals, both countries have overemphasized the notion of the state to the extent that it has become an end in itself. Analysis of the statements of young radicals in the United States shows little indication of a love for Soviet society in spite of the fact that their critiques owe a large debt to classical Marxist analysis. To their minds, the leadership elements in the Soviet Union are as guilty of leading their countries down the road to fascism as those in the United States. The role models for young revolutionaries throughout the world are people such as Mao, Fidel Castro, and Che Guevara, while the leaders of the U.S. and the USSR are viewed as cold bureaucrats, callously manipulating the ideals of their societies to maintain the status quo.

What are we to make of such criticisms? Have the two most powerful idea systems of the twentieth century succumbed to a type of fascist practice which destroys the idealism that made them so successful? In keeping with the spirit, and, hopefully, the practice of this work, no attempt can be made to evaluate such judgments. The reader, however, should now be in a better position to judge whether the cries of "fascism" are justified, and to react to the charge that the ideals of communism and democracy have been lost through the glorification of the nation-state. Minimally, the often heard comment that fascism as an ideology was confined to two states existing during a particular historical period should be immediately rendered suspect. Furthermore, our understanding of that phenomenon ought to make some sense of the cries of "left-fascism" that are directed against the youthful critics themselves. To the extent that they overemphasize the notion of struggle as being valuable in and of itself, or value commitment for commitment's sake, they are adopting one of the central values of the fascist tradition; that is, that the act and the dedicated struggle are more important than the achievement or the goal. Here, finally, we have an excellent example of how a knowledge of the theoretical foundations as found in these three idea systems can help one make some sense of the contemporary political scene. On the one hand, we have the foes of the U.S. and the USSR condemning those countries as fascist; on the other, the established authorities damning those same critics for adopting fascist tactics, or even ideals. An understanding of the phenomenon of fascism permits one to observe that both groups may be, to some extent, correct. In overemphasizing the idea of the nation-state and in castigating critics for being unpatriotic, establishment leaders are conforming to a vital part of the fascist tradition. However, it is also true that when critics emphasize action at the expense of thought, commitment to ill-defined goals, or for that matter are extremely intolerant of the ideas of others, they, too, have adopted a fascist stance. Whether the adoption of some of the values of fascism qualifies either group for the general label "fascist" is a judgment which can only be left to the reader.

In conclusion, let us turn to one final speculation concerning contemporary ideas which is directly related to what we have been calling the reaction to statism. Coupled with a general aversion to authority arbitrarily imposed which we have noted, there appears to be a resurgence of an ill-defined individualism in modern times. Many political commentators have noted this fact, and have added the observation that this individualism, particularly in the United States, seems to transcend some traditional ideological cleavages. For example, there is at least some similarity in the frustration of the conservative who threatens to solve the problems of overcentralized government by throwing the briefcases of Washington bureaucrats into the Potomac, and the radical who insists that the common man have a major voice in decisions which affect his life. There is a good deal of evidence to indicate that the individual, rather than the collectivity, is becoming the reference point for political discourse on both the right and the left of the political spectrum. Can this vaguely defined individual focus be seen as part of a general reaction to the idea of a powerful nation-state? In many ways it can. In the United States, in particular, people seem to be saying that the positive liberalism of the twentieth century, in pursuing the democratic goal of equality, has produced a situation where centralized control has resulted in a great loss of individual freedom. We have discussed this tension between the norms of freedom and equality at an earlier point, but for present purposes it has a rather different import. What commentators seem to be saying is that the democratic ideals of freedom and equality remain quite valid, but the vehicle chosen to implement them has gotten out of control. In America, of course, that vehicle has been the federal government. It is in this context that it is appropriate to speak of the presence of a goal and transfer culture existing even within the rather ill-defined confines of democratic theory. Under positive liberalism the state evolved into a societal device to realize the values of the democratic goal culture. Those critics who now proclaim the downfall of liberalism—and they are many—are declaring that the state, at best, has proved inadequate for the task and, at worst, has become an end in itself. State power, ostensibly a device to insure the implementation of the goals of democracy, has, in many ways, precluded the possibility of those goals being achieved. If we can revert to the terminology used earlier, the transfer culture of the state has submerged the goal culture of the entire society.

Similar criticisms have been directed toward the Soviet Union, with perhaps a more telling effect. In the Marxist tradition, the concepts of party and state are seen explicitly as temporary devices which will be used to provide the prerequisites for a truly communist society. In the Soviet Union, however, the state and party apparatus shows no signs of withering away, and the longed-for classless society seems mired in a bureaucratic swamp. Once again, the transfer culture of state and party, designed by Lenin to achieve pure communism, seems to have subverted that very goal. Here, then, from a somewhat more ideological perspective, is another way of looking at some of our contemporary problems. We point to no solutions, nor do we attempt to evaluate the validity of the critiques, but only note that a knowledge of the underlying ideology can help one in understanding.

The highly speculative nature of these final comments is only intended to encourage the reader to view contemporary affairs at least to some degree from the perspective of the three idea systems we have studied. Simply put, the student's knowledge of his own world and its ideals and aspirations is incomplete without an understanding of the theoretical underpinnings which condition them. In so many ways, "communism, fascism, and democracy" provide that theoretical base.

INDEX

Absolute Idea, 27, 28
Absolutism, 46
Action, 9, 44, 121, 179
Adventurism, 44, 66, 94, 102
Agitation, 44, 50, 71
Alienation, 3, 25, 49
Anti-Bolshevism, 99, 101
Anti-intellectualism, 101, 102, 107
Antirevolutionary, 87
Anti-Semitism, 13, 18, 105, 113, 115, 117, 118
Antithesis, 26, 84
Anti-Zionism, 105
Articles of Confederation, 143, 144
Aryan, 114, 115, 116, 117, 119, 120, 121, 122

Balance and pluralism, theory of, 148
Bayreuth Circle, 114, 115
Bernstein, Eduard, 42, 43, 94, 126
Bloody Sunday, 48
Bolsheviks, 13, 19, 41, 51, 61, 68, 100, 119
Bourgeoisie, 12, 32, 37, 50, 54, 57, 81

Brainwashing, 82
Brest-Litovsk, Treaty of, 53

Cadres, 79
Capital:
  constant, 37, 56
  variable, 37
Capitalism, 6, 21, 24, 86
Castro, Fidel, 88, 184
Catharsis, 12, 120
Censorship, 66, 69, 70, 160
Centerists, 42 (*see also* Orthodox Marxism)
Central Committee, 63
Centralism, democratic, 51
Chamberlain, Houston Stewart, 115, 118
Change, 8, 11, 88, 96
  qualitative, 83
Chauvinism, Great Russian, 63, 66
Checks and balances, 152, 153, 159, 160
Chiang Kai-Shek, 67
Civil Society, 26, 27, 28, 29
Class, 97, 99, 106, 113, 140, 155, 175, 182

antagonism, 99
bourgeois, 57
conflict, 83, 86
stratification, 87
structure, 55, 171, 181
system, 7
warfare, 94
Class-consciousness, 37, 44, 45, 49,
    50, 79, 81, 97
Classical Marxism, 46, 53, 57, 83,
    94, 95, 181, 183, 184
Coexistence, peaceful, 72, 73, 86
Collectivity, 98, 99, 185
Collectivization, 55, 64
Comintern, 67, 79
Communism, pure, 57, 65, 68, 128,
    135, 186
Communist Manifesto, 18, 20
Communist Party, 46, 49-52, 53, 65,
    67, 69, 84
  Chinese, 78, 84
Community, 31, 32, 129, 133
Competition, 35
Consciousness, human, 95
Consensus, 126, 159, 168
Constitution, American, 140, 143,
    144, 150, 151, 157
Coup d'etat, 13, 50
Cuba, 57
Cultural Revolution, 87
Culture, 11, 13, 32, 77, 109, 111,
    117, 140, 169
  goal, *see* Goal culture
  mass, 174
  Nazi, 120-21

Das Kapital, 19, 20, 33, 126
Decentralization, 71, 182
Decision making, 6, 126, 127, 142,
    146, 164, 173
Determinism, 111
Declaration of Independence, 143,
    157
Deradicalization, 73
De-Stalinization, 69, 71, 73, 84
Dialectical materialism, 20, 28, 58,
    82

Dictatorship:
  People's Democratic, 81
  of the proletariat, 53, 61, 125

Eckhart, Dietrich, 115
Elitism, 93, 95, 96, 101-4, 107, 119,
    133, 147, 160, 169-75
Emotionalism, 103, 107, 119
Engels, Friedrich, 18, 19, 21, 38, 41,
    42, 44, 88, 183
Environment, 7, 8, 9, 22, 28, 31, 32,
    33, 38, 82, 95, 96, 110, 111,
    130, 140
Equality, 119, 129, 130, 133, 143,
    157, 163, 164, 165, 168, 180,
    181, 185
Equilibrium, 148
Evaluation, 89

Faction, 145, 146, 151, 152, 154,
    160, 167, 182
Family, 26, 28
Federalist papers, 144, 152, 153
Feuerbach, Ludwig, 27-28
First World War, 55, 94, 96-97, 120,
    154, 162
Freedom, 31, 38, 119, 129, 130, 132,
    133, 134, 137, 141, 143, 145,
    157, 161, 163, 164, 168, 175,
    180, 185

Goal culture, 8, 9, 10, 43, 51, 52,
    121, 122, 180, 182, 185
Goals, 12, 13, 53, 54, 86, 88, 99,
    101, 102, 106, 147, 154, 160,
    166, 167, 168, 174, 180
  national, 101-4
  policy, 45
  socialist, 43, 45
God, 28, 78, 98, 128, 129, 133, 134,
    163
Guerrilla warfare, 79, 80

Hegel, G. W. F., 22, 25, 26, 27, 31,
    112
Hegelianism, 18, 25, 102
Hero, cult of the, 85

Hitler, 2, 6, 10, 12, 13, 67, 92, 93, 102, 103, 105, 107, 109, 113-22
Hobbes, Thomas, 128, 129, 131-36, 137, 152, 163
Hume, David, 127, 128, 130, 137, 152
Hungary, 71, 72

Idea systems, 13, 179
Idealism, 95, 184
Imperialism, 46, 55-58, 73, 77, 79, 80, 83, 180
Individualism, 11, 128, 159, 183, 185
Industrial Revolution, 9, 20
Industrialization, 50, 65, 82, 116-17
Intelligentsia, 45, 46
Interaction, 8, 24, 31, 82, 84, 111, 129
Internationalism, 57, 88, 89, 94

Jews, 10, 13, 104-5, 117, 118, 119, 122

Khrushchev, 69, 70, 71, 73

Labor, 22, 23, 24, 29, 31, 32, 33
  necessary, 35, 36
  specialization of, 169
  surplus, 35
Labor camps, 65, 66
Labor theory of value, 20, 33, 34, 130
Laissez-faire, 148, 164
Leadership, 79, 92, 101-4, 107, 116, 119, 153, 175, 184
Lenin, 2, 5, 13, 20, 39, 43, 44, 45, 46-49, 61, 63, 64, 77, 94, 97, 100, 186
Locke, John, 126, 128, 129, 131-36, 137, 142, 152, 161, 162
Luxemburg, Rosa, 43, 49, 97

Madison, James, 2, 143, 144, 145, 146, 147, 148, 149, 150, 151, 152, 153, 154, 155, 160, 167, 181, 182

Madisonian system, 141, 145-55, 159, 174
Majoritarianism, 142, 157, 158, 160, 162, 168
Majority rule, 98, 133, 135, 145, 146
  versus minority rights, 137, 141
Marxism:
  of the center, *see* Orthodox Marxism
  classical, *see* Classical Marxism
  of the left, 43
  of the right, *see* Revisionism
Masses, 51, 95, 96, 103, 119, 171, 174
Mein Kampf, 2, 109, 118, 119
Mensheviks, 62
Mill, John Stuart, 127, 128, 137
Mills, C. Wright, 171, 172
Motivation, 127, 130, 133, 134
Mussolini, 3, 13, 89, 92-97, 102, 103, 109, 119, 126, 128, 182, 183
Myth, 96, 98, 104, 109

Nation-state, 1, 2, 6, 26, 53, 65, 66, 68, 73, 87, 88, 91, 93, 96-101, 105, 106, 116, 182-86
Nationalism, 57, 66, 81, 94, 96, 99, 105
Natural rights, 98, 129, 130, 132, 133, 145
New Economic Policy (N.E.P.), 54-55, 81
Nietzsche, Friedrich, 96

October Manifesto, 48, 50
Organic metaphor, 97, 100, 103, 119
Origin of government, 134
Orthodox Marxism, 42, 44

Pantheism, 110-11
Passions, 137, 145, 147, 153
Plato, 3, 8
Poland, 71
Politbureau, 64
Private property, 28, 38, 129, 130, 134, 136, 161

Proletariat, 44, 45, 49, 50, 51, 52, 53, 55, 57, 65, 79, 80, 81, 96, 125, 139
dictatorship of, 53, 61, 125
Propaganda, 54, 65, 104, 106, 120, 146, 160
Public policy, 98, 142, 147, 166, 171, 173

Racism, 93, 105, 113, 115, 117, 118, 122, 180
Rationality, 112, 130, 134, 167
Reason, 130, 132
Revisionism, 42, 86, 182
Revisionists, 19, 43, 45, 56, 94, 126
Revolution, 41, 42, 44, 46, 55, 56, 64, 80, 94
American, 144
Bolshevik, 52, 55, 62, 67
bourgeois, 50
Chinese, 85
democratic, 71
Industrial, 9, 20
permanent, 50, 83
proletarian, 45, 50, 71
Russian, 51, 52, 71, 79, 168
superstructural, 52
violent, 43
world-wide, 58, 66
Russification, 63, 65

Second Party Congress, 47, 62
Second World War, 72, 91, 102, 122
Secret police, 65, 69, 106
Self-consciousness, 22, 23, 31
Self-determination, 167, 180
Self-interest, 133, 152, 153
Self-preservation, 132, 133, 134, 135, 136
Smith, Adam, 33, 127, 130, 137
Social contract, 132, 134
Socialism:
radical, 94
realization of, 43
Solidarity, 45, 96, 117, 183
Stalin, 20, 62-74, 77, 100, 121
Status, 12, 24

Status quo, 56, 73, 87, 172, 184
Substructure, 30, 33, 43, 50
Super profit, 56, 58
Superstructure, 30, 43, 50
Supply and demand, 33, 34
Supreme Court, 151, 152
Synthesis, 26, 27, 83, 116, 126

Thesis, 26
Third Reich, 115, 120, 122
Third world, 56, 73
Tito, Joseph Broz, 67, 70, 71
Totalitarianism, 61, 121, 131, 132, 167
Transfer culture, 46, 52, 53, 55, 57, 58, 61, 65, 135, 160, 185, 186
Trotsky, Leon, 49, 50, 63, 64, 66
Twentieth Party Congress, 69, 71, 72, 84
Tyranny, 142, 144, 145, 150, 155, 159, 167, 170, 172, 175
majority, 147, 150, 175

Underdeveloped countries, 56, 57, 58, 79, 80, 86, 88

Volk, 105, 109, 110, 111, 119, 122
Volkish spirit, 110-11
Voluntarism, 95, 96, 101

War, 54, 63, 64, 68, 73, 122, 172
capitalist, 94
nuclear, 86
Wars of national liberation, 57, 58, 73
Wealth, 11, 30
Welfare state, 162, 165
Will:
human, 95, 96
national, 102
popular, 141, 142, 150, 152, 157
World War I, *see* First World War
World War II, *see* Second World War

Yugoslavia, 70, 71